Language, Culture and Identity

Advances in Sociolinguistics

Series Editor: Professor Sally Johnson, University of Leeds
Since the emergence of sociolinguistics as a new field of enquiry in the late 1960s, research into the relationship between language and society has advanced almost beyond recognition. In particular, the past decade has witnessed the considerable influence of theories drawn from outside of sociolinguistics itself. Thus rather than see language as a mere reflection of society, recent work has been increasingly inspired by ideas drawn from social, cultural and political theory that have emphasized the constitutive role played by language/discourse in all areas of social life. The Advances in Sociolinguistics series seeks to provide a snapshot of the current diversity of the field of sociolinguistics and the blurring of the boundaries between sociolinguistics and other domains of study concerned with the role of language in society.

Language, Culture and Identity

An Ethnolinguistic Perspective

Philip Riley

continuum

Continuum
The Tower Building
11 York Road
London SE1 7NX

80 Maiden Lane
Suite 704
New York NY 10038

British Library Cataloguing-in-Publication Data
A catalogue record for this book is available from the British Library.

ISBN: 978–08264–86288
      978–08264–86295

Library of Congress Cataloging-in-Publication Data
A catalog record for this book is available from the Library of Congress.

Typeset by Data Standards Ltd, Frome, Somerset, UK.
Printed and bound in Great Britain by Athenaeum Press Ltd., Gateshead, Tyne & Wear

For Marianne
Sine qua non

Contents

Acknowledgements

The text of this book includes passages from a number of articles I have published over the past twenty years. I am grateful to the editors of the publications in question for permission to use them here:

(1987a) 'Who do you think you're talking to? Negotiation, perception and categorisation processes in exolinguistic discourse', in V. Bickley (ed.), *Languages in Education in a Bilingual or Multilingual Setting*. Hong Kong: Institute of Language in Education, pp. 118–33.

(1987b) 'Social identity and intercultural communication', *Levende Talen*, 443, 488–93.

(1991) 'Having a good gossip: sociocultural dimensions of language use', in Roger Bowers and C. Brumfit, *Applied Linguistics and Language Teaching*. Basingstoke: Macmillan, pp. 53–64.

(1992) 'What's your background? The culture and identity of the bilingual child, in C. Brumfit, J. Moon and R. Tongue (eds), *Teaching English to Children*. London: Collins.

(1996) 'Developmental linguistics and the competence/performance distinction', in G. Brown, K. Malmkjaer and J. Williams, *Performance and Competence in Second Language Acquisition*. Cambridge: Cambridge University Press, pp. 114–35

(1999) 'On the social construction of "the learner"', in S. Cotterall and D. Crabbe, *Learner Autonomy in Language Learning: Defining the Field and Effecting Change*. Bayreuth Contributions to Glottodidactics vol. 8. Frankfurt am Main: Peter Lang.

(2000) 'Je vous ai compris. Aspects ethnolinguistiques de la compréhension', in J. Pécheur (ed.), *Une didactique des langues pour demain*, No. Spécial *Le Français dans le Monde*. Paris: CLE International, pp. 79–95.

(2001) '« Allô je parle à qui? » Salutations, communion phatique et négociation d'identités sociales', in F. Carton (ed.), *Oral: variabilité et apprentissages*, No. Spécial *Le Français dans le Monde*. Paris: CLE International, pp. 87–96.

(2002) 'Epistemic communities: the social knowledge system, discourse and identity', in G. Cortese and P. Riley, *Domain-specific English: Textual Practices across Communities and Classrooms*. Bern: Peter Lang, pp. 41–64.

(2003a) 'Self-access as access to Self: cultural variation in notions of self and personhood', in D. Palfreyman and R. C. Smith (eds), *Learner Autonomy Across Cultures: Language Education Perspectives.* Basingstoke: Palgrave Macmillan, pp. 92–109.

(2003b) 'Le "linguisme" – multi-, poly-, pluri-? Points de repères terminologiques et sociolinguistiques, in F. Carton and P. Riley (eds) *Vers une competence plunlurgue, Le Français dans le Monde* No. Spécial, pp. 8–17.

(2004) 'Multilingual identities: "Non, je ne regrette rien"', *The European English Messenger*' XIII, 1, pp. 11–17.

(2005) 'Ethos and the communicative virtues in exolinguistic service encounters', in G. Cortese and A. Duszak (eds), *Identity, Community, Discourse: English in Intercultural Settings*. Bern: Peter Lang, pp. 167–82

(2006) 'Self-expression and the negotiation of identity in a foreign language', *International Journal of Applied Linguistics*, 16.3, 295–318.

I also owe thanks to: Jenny Lovel of Continuum for suggesting this book in the first place and then having the patience to wait for it; Katja Riley for her invaluable help and expertise with computers and Marianne Riley for literally taking over as my right hand and typing large sections of the manuscript.

1 Introduction

Some years ago, I went on a short working visit to Hong Kong, and since it was to be my last visit to that marvellous place for the foreseeable future, I took my wife and our fifteen-year-old daughter, Katja, for a fortnight's holiday before work started. We had been there three or four days when I noticed that Katja wasn't her usual cheerful self. So I asked if anything was wrong.

'Well, yes,' said Katja. 'We are behaving like tourists.'

'But Katja, love, we *are* tourists!'

She brushed this objection off, though, so I asked what sort of thing she was thinking of.

'Well, we for example only go to restaurants where there are other Europeans and the menu is in English. I want to see the authentic China, and go in restaurants where there are no tourists.'

I resisted the temptation to point out that if she was there, there would be a tourist, and just said,

'Oh, right, well I'll see what we can do.'

So the next time we wanted to eat, we found a little popular restaurant, just off the Jade Market, where we were the only tourists. In such restaurants, there are no menus: instead, the walls are covered with notices. In Chinese.

'Right, Katja', I said. 'It's your turn to order.'

She got the point, and said to the waiter, 'Three of those, please,' pointing at random to one of the notices over our table.

Off went the waiter, and we sat back and watched the dishes being provided to other diners. Snake soup. Piles of goose tongues. Pork with black mushrooms. As the minutes ticked away, our excitement grew. What would we get?

At last, the waiter returned and, with something of a flourish, presented us with three plates of sausage, bacon and eggs.

To this day, we still don't know if that is what we really had ordered, or whether the waiter had just decided for us that we were the sort of people who wanted bacon and eggs. Whatever the case may be, it was a real learning experience for Katja (and one which, I have to say, she took very well indeed, laughing till the tears came). She learnt that our identity is not just something we can decide on ourselves. Because it is at least partly social, our identity is decided on – 'constructed' – by other people. And if they are in a position of relative power, like the waiter, they can take decisions for us, and even if those decisions are for our own good, there is a risk that we may not approve of them.

This, then, is the topic of this book: identity and the ways it relates to language and communicative behaviour.

I am fully aware of the sheer hubris involved in someone who is not a professional philosopher addressing the problem of identity. Even if I had been in any doubt about it, the following quotation from Hume would have served as a salutary warning:

> Upon a more strict review of the section concerning personal identity, I find myself involved in such a labyrinth that, I must confess, I neither know how to correct my former opinions, nor how to render them consistent. (*Treatise of Human Nature* (1739/ 2000), Bk. 1, Appendix)

So I shall have to ask those of a philosophical turn of mind to be indulgent with me. My only excuse for daring to tackle identity is – 'because it's there': as social scientists, linguists, language teachers, it forces itself on our attention, whether we like it or not, because each of us is surrounded by others who are constantly telling us *who we are*. It is the *forms of telling* and the kinds of *us* and *we* they construct which is the focus of this book.

Inevitably, in a book on identity, the author's own background, experience and motivations insist on calling attention to themselves, sometimes at the expense of academic decorum. I have allowed myself to take liberties with the conventions of scientific discourse by introducing personal examples and anecdotes, and understand that this may jar on some readers' sensibilities, in which case I apologize. But adopting a tone of Olympian objectivity would in many ways contradict some of the ideas about identity (and, in particular, ethos) developed here, and there are times when only a personal example will do, either because it is the only example available, or because it represents the very source of the idea being expounded.

For those of a forensic cast of mind, eager to prove that I am simply trying to reach a better understanding of my own identity, I can only reply: well, yes, to some extent, just like everybody else. And I am perfectly happy to provide the following circumstantial evidence: my paternal grandparents were Irish, my maternal grandparents Italian. My wife is a Swedish-speaking Finn and we have spent most of the past thirty years living and working in France. Our three children were born in three different countries – Finland, Malta and France. Our eldest daughter has married a Frenchman and they live in Brussels. Our son has just married a Portuguese girl ... I know from experience that this information often elicits concerned inquiries about my identity, and that my firm denials regarding schizophrenia, anomie and cultural and linguistic confusion are greeted at best with scepticism and at worst as proof that deep down in my psyche I have something pretty murky to hide. And yet, if really pushed, I would say that much more important to my sense of personal identity than these national and linguistic labels are the facts that I was the first member of my family to go to university, that I am a lapsed Catholic and Chelsea supporter, and that I once was Corporal in charge of the squad which won the Coldstream Guards' Drill Shield. But that's another story.

1.1 Theoretical and historical background

In this book, I have called on two rather different intellectual traditions: *the sociology of knowledge* and *ethnolinguistics*.

1.1.1 The sociology of knowledge[1]

The sociology of knowledge examines the social factors which condition what passes for knowledge in a given society, the relationships between social structures and thought, its main areas being the maintenance of social reality and the social knowledge system. As one might expect, it has a long, rich and complicated pedigree. Bacon, More, Vico and Montesquieu are just some of the thinkers cited as precursors. Unquestionably, though, the most important source of formative concepts was the German hermeneutic and phenomenological tradition, as it was absorbed into the social sciences in the late nineteenth and early twentieth centuries by a long line of thinkers including historians and philosophers (Dilthey[2], Scheler, Hegel, Husserl) and sociologists (Marx, Durkheim, Simmel), its terms and its agenda being largely set in the great metatheoretical debate as to the feasibility and nature of social science as it evolved from *Methodenstreit* to *Werturteilsstreit* to *Wissenschaftsstreit*, that is, from methodological questions involved in the investigation of social facts, to the critical evaluation of standpoints and the possibility of objectivity, to the role of science. They have since been joined by practitioners of a wider range of the social sciences, including anthropologists, linguists, literary critics, economists and social psychologists. The discipline was given its name and its first synthetic and systematic expression by Karl Mannheim (1936).

Thinkers as different as Husserl and Marx focused on questions concerning the social and historical factors which condition knowledge. Aware that knowledge, like truth, varies according to which side of the Pyrenees one finds oneself on, they aimed at describing the forms which that variation can take and at identifying the social factors which influenced them. In framing these questions, they set the agenda for philosophers and social scientists for generations to come. How, for example, can 'history' be anything more than an arbitrary list of 'events' if we do not understand the values, motivations and modes of thought of the participants in those events? How can we explain anything, rather than simply recording it? How can we come to know the past, and others, and the pasts of others? Is a 'social science' possible, or a contradiction in terms? If it is possible, what would be the appropriate paradigm of investigation?

The overarching theme of this meta-discipline is the relationship between social structures and thought, and the ways in which both scientific and everyday knowledge is socially conditioned.

Schematically, the basic concepts and objectives of the fledgling discipline in its present form were established by three men: Karl Mannheim (1893–1947), Alfred Schütz (1899–1959) and Norbert Elias (1897–1990). All three were forced into exile by the Nazi régime in the 1930s. Mannheim and Elias went to teach in England, Elias later moving to an exceptionally long and productive 'retirement' in Amsterdam. Schütz went to the USA, where he worked as both an international lawyer and as a teacher.

It was very largely through their publications and teaching that the sociology of knowledge and the whole intellectual tradition that had produced it became known – or at least available – in Britain and the USA. However, although they were members of a common tradition, each of the three had areas of special interest.

As mentioned above, it was in the work of Karl Mannheim that the sociology of knowledge found its first really systematic expression:

> The sociology of knowledge ... seeks to analyse the relationship between knowledge and existence ... (and) to trace the forms which this relationship has taken in the intellectual development of mankind ... it hopes to develop a theory concerning the significance of the non-theoretical conditioning factors in knowledge. (Mannheim 1936, p. 237)

Mannheim's main field was *theoretical* knowledge, that is, formalized bodies of knowledge such as those which are usually described as 'specialized', 'abstract' or 'scientific'. However, instead of asking 'Is this theory true?', the sociologist of knowledge asks why it is or was true for those people in that context. The object of scrutiny is no longer the constitutive elements of a theory – the ideas, hypotheses and evidence on which its internal logic is based – but the social contingencies, the 'unscientific' influences, such as the interests of particular classes or groups which shape their and their society's world-view. Why should certain theories or modes of thought be preferred as explanations rather than others? Different political, educational, religious and economic theories determine the ways of thought regarded as 'true' in different contexts: exactly what makes us believe what we believe when we think we are being 'realistic' or 'logical' about such matters?

For Schütz, the principal area of investigation was *commonsense* knowledge, what 'everybody knows' in a given group or society. This shared knowledge provides the basis of social reality, the beliefs and values, the social objects and institutions which inform our daily lives and behaviour, as well as the practical reasoning processes we employ continually to 'make sense' of specific real-life situations. The import- ance of Schütz's influence can quickly be gauged by citing some of his students and their work: Peter Berger and Thomas Luckman *The Social Construction of Reality* (1966 – their title is in fact a word-for-word translation of one of Schütz's own), Aaron Cicourel *Cognitive Sociology* (1973) and Harold Garfinkel *Studies in Ethnomethodology* (1967). Indeed, Schütz provided the ethnomethodological movement of the 1960s and 1970s with almost everything but its name. On the one hand, he was a brilliant mediator of the German hermeneutic tradition (with a particular debt to Simmel); on the other, he made available to his American students a set of intellectual and methodological tools for the description and analysis of interactive discourse, which he saw as the primary mechanism for stocking, maintaining and distributing com- monsense knowledge.

If they are to understand 'what's going on', both analysts (such as sociologists) and actual participants need to know in their different ways something about the historical and social processes through which knowledge is established and communicated from individual to individual, from group to group and from generation to generation. Such knowledge is essential if they are to make valid judgements about the meaning and appropriateness of behaviour, their own or others'. This was the topic of Norbert Elias's *The Civilising Process: The History of Manners* (1939, English translation 1978). By examining the devel- opment of 'normal behaviour' such as table manners, and by analysing the discourse used to teach and describe it, Elias was able to identify not only the norms in question, but to draw conclusions about changes in the processes through which the social self is constructed and perceived. Strangely, though, it was to be over twenty years before similar, multi-level studies of what Michel Foucault (1966) was to call 'the archaeology of knowledge' began to appear. Goffman's *The Presentation of Self in Everyday Life* (1959) is a monument to this approach.

As we have seen, then, the field of the sociology of knowledge embraces the whole range of a society's intellectual output, including its belief systems and ideologies, its collective representations, its theories and discourses and its culture, as well as the social structures and practices which vehiculate them. Whereas classical epistemology and the history of ideas both deal with ideas and knowledge as if they were immanent, independent of social influences, vacuum-packed, the sociology of knowledge focuses on the social construction of consciousness and reality. Knowledge cannot be dissociated from knowers, and they are subject to pressures and influences which are certainly not limited to purely theoretical considerations.

An important aim of the sociologists of knowledge is to describe and analyse *the social knowledge system* (although few of them use that expression; see, however, Holzner and Marx 1979; Habermas 1981; Riley 1996): from this perspective, society is seen as a set of functions and structures for the management of knowledge, including knowledge creation, organization, distribution, storage, legitimization and utilization.

The principal mechanism of both the social knowledge system and group praxis is discourse. *Discourse analysis* therefore involves the investigation of the relationships between discourse and the social knowledge system on the one hand, and discourse and communicative practices on the other. The first of these tasks has been addressed by historians and social theorists interested in the conditions of production of ideologies (Marx and Engels 1968 and *passim*; Durkheim 1912; Foucault 1966; Althusser 1971; Billig 1981; Fairclough 1992; Potter and Wetherell 1995). The second has been undertaken by analysts originally inspired and trained by Schütz after his removal to the United States. Their field of research is now generally known as *ethnomethodology* (Garfinkel 1967; Leiter 1980; Benson and Hughes 1983).

This process of construction can be approached in two ways, 'top-down' and 'bottom-up'. The top-down approach is one that takes as its starting-point the social structures and conditions in which knowledge and discourse is produced. We owe this line of thought to Marx more than to any other writer:

> It is not the consciousness of men that determines their existence: their social existence determines their consciousness. (in Feuer 1959, p. 43)

Forms of thought are generated by socio-economic structures. This social determinism has become one of the commonplaces of post-modernist philosophy, as encapsulated in Louis Althusser's dictum 'Ideologies interpellate individuals', and in Foucault's theory that the identity and nature of the modern individual is a recent invention and bound to change or even disappear. The bottom-up approach takes as its starting-point the dyad, two individuals engaged in communication, constructing intersubjective reality together in interaction.

It is important to note that two very different approaches to 'discourse' are being referred to here: in the first, top-down one, discourse is the linguistic manifestation of ideology – 'meaning in the service of power'. In the second, bottom-up approach, usually referred to as 'discourse analysis' or 'conversation analysis', discourse is seen as language in use, 'situated language'. (Coulthard (1977/1985) is a very accessible introduction to the field.) Ideally, one would like to see an integrated approach, one in which specific forms of interaction could be shown to be instantiations of ideologies, whilst at the same time taking into account in a non-determinist way the participants' awareness of themselves as agents enacting identities. That is, we would have a theory of identity that was at one and the same time an account of the ways in which identities are shaped in discursive practices and a theory of self-expression, of the knowing subject.

This implies rethinking identity in terms of the relationship between discursive practices and individuals or 'subject-persons'. Two major thinkers, Michel Foucault and Louis Althusser, addressed this issue from the top-down perspective and it is to them that we owe much of our modern understanding of the ways in which social discourses shape identity. Inevitably, they collided head-on with those coming in the opposite direction, in particular the psychoanalytic movement as represented by Lacan. Where Foucault and Althusser reduced every-thing to discourse and were essentially anti-psychoanalysis, Lacan reduced everything to the Oedipal drama, trivializing the role of the social. This contradiction – social determinism versus solipsistic narcissism – has marked identity studies ever since and forms a formidable obstacle to any attempt to study or produce an integrated account of the relationships between social and psychological reality. Interestingly, neither side seems to have paid attention to empirical work in either discourse analysis of the bottom-up kind (Lacan was dismissive of linguistics, and for Foucault psychoanalysis was just another ideology, a discourse of power relations) or in social (i.e. top-down) psychology. Their very different theoretical positions disquali-fied both men from examining the question as to why certain individuals occupy particular subject positions rather than others.

1.1.2 Ethnolinguistics[3]

A different approach to the same problem has been adopted by ethnolinguists or anthropological linguists working within the contrastive paradigm exported from Germany to the USA by Boas (Duranti 1997; Foley 1997). Particularly relevant to this book is the study of communicative practices baptized *the ethnography of communication* by Dell Hymes (Hymes 1964; Calame-Griaule 1965; Gumperz and Hymes 1972; Farb 1974; Saville-Troike 2002; Scollon and Scollon 1995; Hanks 1996). Despite very considerable differences in terminology and methodology, as the presence of the root *ethnos* ('a people', or more generally 'group') shows, these two approaches share an interest in the identifying relationship between a group and its communicative practices. Ethnolinguistics has variously been approached as the study of a group's experience of life as it is organized and expressed through the group's language tools and as a science whose aim is to examine the relationships between a language on the one hand and society and culture on the other. (Alvarez-Pereyre (1981), is an anthology of articles aiming to define and delimit the discipline at a time when it was struggling for recognition.)

Given these ambitions, it is not surprising to find that problems of demarcation and terminology are rife in this field, and there has been much heart-searching by sociolinguists as to whether ethnolinguistics can be said to exist as an autonomous discipline, rather than being a patchwork of interdisciplines or simply the juxtaposition of the terms 'ethnology' and 'linguistics'.

These problems are not unimportant, but they will not be pursued here, nor will I be trying to distinguish ethnolinguistics from 'anthropological linguistics' or 'linguistic anthropology': like Alessandro Duranti I believe that the terms are very nearly synonymous, though they do have distinct genealogies. I have no difficulty with his definition of 'linguistic anthropology' as 'the study of language as a cultural resource and speaking as a cultural practice' (1997, p. 3), as the thrust of this book is not to define the field, but to study the linguistic and communicative aspects of the social knowledge system.

In very general terms indeed, modern ethnolinguistics can be regarded as the mongrel but legitimate successor to the nineteenth-century traditions in philology, dialectology and anthropology. When Johann Gottfried von Herder (1744–1803) published his *Abhandlung über den Ursprung der Sprache* (*Treatise on the Origin of Speech*) in 1772, he challenged the generally-accepted 'Aristotelian' thesis that thought precedes language. For Herder, the two are inseparable, since language is at one and the same time the tool, the contents and the form of human thought, and every act of knowledge is only possible through the medium of language. This interdependence means that the modes of thought and the culture of a people can only be studied and analysed in and through their language.

Herder's influence on nineteenth-century German thought was profound and widespread. Goethe, the Schlegel brothers and the Grimm brothers followed his lead on poetics and aesthetic theory, Wilhelm von Humboldt his philosophy of language, and Dilthey his epistemology. His ideas fell on fertile ground, since they seemed to provide clear support for many of the claims and attitudes of European nationalism, especially German nationalism. Herder helped formulate the discourse of the political independence of linguistic groups, a characteristically Romantic perspective which still underpins most popular discussion of notions such as 'culture' or 'nation'. His influence on European linguistic scholarship was considerable, but nowhere more so than in Germany itself, the centre of philological study throughout the nineteenth century. Jakob Grimm, for example, thought that the linguistic phenomena described by his 'law' represented an assertion of independence by the ancestors of modern Germans. Wilhelm von Humboldt, even as he stressed the role and importance of creativity in the individual's language use, spoke of *Weltansicht*, the characteristic property with which any given language is imbued, so that the use of a single word implies the whole of the language and the world it describes. Each language describes the world quite literally *in its own terms* forming a unique mode of thought and expression, by definition only accessible to 'native speakers', those born into the community in question. Wilhelm Wundt and Heymann Steintal founded the study of *Völkerpsychologie*, ethnopsychology, which concentrates on the relationships between 'linguistic psychology' and 'national psychology'.

In the light of our earlier discussion of the sociology of knowledge, it is satisfactorily ironic to note that, far from being the autonomous and neutral lines of inquiry announced by their practitioners, German philology and history were the principal centres for the production of discourse justifying the ambitions of German Romantic nationalism. For as long as there was no unified nation-state, 'Germany', 'the German language' and 'the German people' could only exist and function as social realities on the basis of this discourse. It is here that the two disciplines under discussion converge: it is precisely this kind of reflexive relationship between discourse and social conditions and contingencies which is, as we saw earlier, the focal point of the sociology of knowledge. Karl Marx was making this point when he expostulated famously in *The German Ideology*:

> It has not occurred to any of these philosophers to inquire into the connection of German philosophy with German reality. (1845, p. 8)

Although a number of German academics emigrated to the USA in the late nineteenth century, it is safe to say that the most important anthropologist was Franz Boas (1858–1942). He preached and practised a data-based, fieldwork approach to the study of cultural evolution as an antidote to the sweeping theories current at the time. However, it is clear from his writings (see *Race, Language and Culture*, 1942) that he was, as one would expect, thoroughly familiar with the Herder–Humboldt tradition. As Professor of Anthropology at Columbia University from 1899 to the end of his life, he gave American anthropology its characteristically German interest in language: indeed, he established the *International Journal of American Linguistics*. He was a great influence on Edward Sapir (1884–1939) whose book *Language* (1921*)* can still be read as a magnificent introduction to anthropological linguistics. And one of Sapir's students was Benjamin Lee Whorf. The famous (some would say notorious) 'Sapir–Whorf Hypothesis', according to which:

> We dissect nature along lines laid down by our native language ... Language is not simply a reporting device for experience but a defining framework for it ... every language is a vast pattern-system, different from others, in which are culturally ordained the forms and categories by which the personality not only communicates, but also analyzes nature, notices or neglects types of relationship and phenomena, channels his reasoning, and builds the house of his consciousness. (Whorf 1956, p. 252)

far from being a cataclysmic revelation, was an attempt to formalize a set of ideas which had existed since Herder at least.

As the influence of Saussurean structuralism increased in academic departments of Linguistics, there developed a growing tendency to neglect or even despise the nineteenth-century inheritance as 'diachronic', 'mentalistic' and 'unscientific'. When Saussure proclaimed that he aimed to study 'language in itself and for itself', he did so largely because he wished to establish a discipline which would not overlap with the other social sciences, in particular anthropology. This reductionism was highly productive in that it allowed investigators to concentrate on those aspects of language which can be dissociated from the context of production: phonetics and phonology, morphology and syntax – the internal structures of the code. The price paid for this convenience was a high one, however, since the dynamic and social aspects of language – the social contexts of messages, the parameters of variation, who was speaking to whom, where, when, how and why, everything that connected language to its uses and users, *identities* and *meanings* – were rigorously excluded from consideration. This state of affairs was particularly marked in the USA, where Bloomfield's version of Saussure's doctrine was allied, again through historical contingencies, to what one is tempted to call a mindless behaviourism. With hindsight, we can see that in the name of science, a most unscientific piece of logic was followed, as extrapolations were made from pigeons picking at popcorn to human beings, that is, from a species that does not possess language to one that does. This in turn seemed to provide further justification for regarding problems of world-view as mystification.

The version of linguistics to be found in some English-language textbooks and university syllabuses, where it is presented as a form-focused discipline beginning with de Saussure and ending with Chomsky, is an ahistorical travesty. This was demonstrated by Dell Hymes in his 'reader', *Language in Culture and Society* (1964), a fine historical anthology documenting the continuity and richness of the anthropological tradition with respect to language. Hymes has also, of course, made a major personal contribution to the field, focusing on what he has called 'the ethnography of communication', the study of intercultural communication in the categorization of communicative situations and their constitutive communicative practices. His concept of 'communicative competence' – the individual group-member's capacity to adapt to the exigencies of the situation – is a necessary complement, or even challenge, to the 'linguistic competence' of Chomsky's 'ideal speaker-hearer'.

The main areas of ethnolinguistics include the relationship between language and culture, communicative practices, and cognitive models of language and thought. The ethnolinguist tries to describe and understand the role of language in shaping the ways in which members of a group relate to the world, to one another and to others. These *ways of knowing and being* are the stuff which identities are made of. Identities, that is, consist of meanings, and specific configurations of meanings can be implemented functionally as roles through the community's communicative practices.

The literature on identity is already enormous and seems to be increasing exponentially. For some twenty years I have been reading around the subject, yet I am very conscious that in fact I have consulted only a minute proportion of relevant publications. To readers who might feel that the first of the two preceding sentences is hyperbole and the second false modesty, I can only say: Google. Obviously, where appropriate I have followed academic referencing conventions and acknowledged sources. Some texts, though, can have a profound influence that goes beyond specific points to shape the reader's whole approach to a subject. I have already mentioned several of those to which I am consciously indebted in this way, but in conclusion I would like to add a small number of recent titles which I have found of especial help and interest, in the hope that readers wishing to pursue the topic will do likewise.

The first is John E. Joseph's *Language and Identity: National, Ethnic, Religious* (2004) which contains a detailed overview of linguistic approaches to identity. Unfortunately, I only read this insightful and learned work when I had almost finished preparing this book, but it was still very encouraging to find support for at least two of the important points I wished to make. These are, first, that the expression of identity should be added to the two 'traditional' major functions of language, representation and communication. I greatly benefited from the clarity of Professor Joseph's exposition of this argument and in particular from the way he relates it to the history of linguistic theory. He argues that although the expression of self and the emotions is one of the principal functions of language, it has largely been neglected by linguists as being a matter of aesthetics, falling within the field of literary criticism and the rhetoric of persuasion. This perspective, inherited from Aristotelian dualism but still massively present in contemporary code-centred linguistics, saw the emotions as related to the body rather than to the mind and, therefore, as not being amenable to or worthy of scientific investigation.

Second, Joseph argues that identity studies have always privileged the subjective dimension, the self, whereas if we wish to study language as a social phenomenon, we need to redress the balance by paying at least as much attention to the ways in which identities are ascribed and constructed by others on the basis of the culture-specific repertoire available. This reasoning corresponds precisely with the rationale of this book and its focus on ethos (identity as a process of co-construction by speakers and hearers), membershipping strategies (the linguistic realizations of that process) and culture (the knowledge on which the repertoire is based).

The second recent title is Roy Porter's sadly posthumous *Flesh in the Age of Reason: How the Enlightenment Transformed the Way We See Our Bodies and Souls* (2003).The history of ideas does not come better than this. Porter was superbly skilful in linking philosophical, theological and scientific ideas concerning identity with social events and practices. As Simon Schama says in his foreword (p. xi), Porter 'sees moments where a familiar modern preoccupation gets born and

12

circulated in the wider culture'; for example, he sees the 'change in the second half of the eighteenth century from a culture which celebrated embonpoint and fleshiness as a sign of vitality to Byron's narcissistic regime of diet and exercise, as a genuinely fateful moment: the beginning of the obsession with youthfulness (especially svelte youth) as a paradigm of beauty'. The relevance of such insights to topics such as identity and self-presentation can be confirmed by even the most cursory glance at popular magazines: my own newsagent, for example, stocks no less than three titles which are totally dedicated to slimming and many others which carry regular articles on the topic.

One of the multiple historical and intellectual strands in Porter's work follows the influence of the notion of the individual human soul on western views concerning personhood and its progressive replacement by the notion of identity in the rational humanism of the Enlightenment. As his title indicates, the focus of his study is on body–soul dualism, precisely because that is the dominant model in the western world, in both learned and popular discourse, so much so, in fact, that identity was and is often naively seen as incorporated, coextensive with the body.

My third title is Manuel Castells' *The Power of Identity* (1997) which is Volume II in his trilogy *The Information Age: Economy, Society and Culture.* In a work of great scope and massive detail, Castells sets out to analyse the relationship of identity to other social movements, including globalization, environmentalism, feminism, religious fundamentalism and nationalism. The book abounds in case-studies and narrative, but it is also extremely well-documented and is exemplary in its presentation and explanation of statistical data. His account of globalization and identity as the primary but conflicting forces of the network society is both a masterclass in the sociological determinants of personhood – the forces shaping personhoods and the changing repertoire of available identities – and in the collective and individual forms of resistance to which they give rise.

A very different sociological approach is adopted by Jean-Claude Kaufmann in his *L'Invention de soi. Une théorie de l'identité* (2004). Indeed, I personally would be tempted to class this as a work of social psychology rather than sociology, but this hesitation is due to the book's interdisciplinary strengths, as well as to its unusual perspective. This can perhaps be most succinctly summarized by quoting the title of one of Kaufmann's earlier publications: *Ego: Pour une sociologie de l'individu* (2001). If Castells' analytical approach can be roughly described as 'top-down', moving from vast social movements and forces down to small groups, Kaufmann's is 'bottom-up', largely concentrating on self-representation and on the cognitive strategies adopted by individuals as they navigate their life course through a changing institutional and social environment. His detailed historical overview and critical discussion of twentieth-century approaches to identity in sociology and social psychology and, to some extent, philosophy and anthropology, is of real value, especially as he is familiar with both 'Anglo-Saxon' and 'continental' research and writers. His own theory is an interesting amalgam of individual psychology and socio-constructionism, but its most striking aspect is his claim that there has been a very recent and very profound revolution in the overall social framework from which identities emerge, resulting from the increasingly complex and numerous identity-related choices faced by individuals. This has had the effect of heightening individuals' aware-ness of and control over the construction of their own identities, where previously this was largely a function of the state:

> Identity is an historic process, which, after a period of transition during which identities were managed by the State, only fully surfaced at the individual level as self-invention less than half a century ago as a result of the reversal of the relationship between social structures and their cognitive counterparts. Not that the latter have become any less efficient or less powerful because individuals have suddenly been mysteriously liberated from them, but simply because they became contradictory, which could only result in the individual's being obliged to reflect on them. From that point onwards, it is the individual who has to construct out of the social materials available, the ethical and cognitive framework conditioning and guiding his actions. The social construction of reality is filtered through individual identities. (Kaufmann 2004, p. 291; my translation)

This is both a bold hypothesis and a striking historical claim. Readers will rightly want to know to which individuals and in what societies it is meant to apply, and they will find, perhaps to their surprise, that Kaufmann's densely referenced text goes a long way towards justifying his conclusion. For the moment, I will limit myself to just two remarks concerning the relevance of Kaufmann's ideas to the present work. First, it is to be noted that Kaufmann treats identity as a complex and dynamic process, and not as something fixed, static and unitary. In fact, this approach is common to almost all contemporary treatments of identity, including all the other books in this selective list, but for many people (especially those who have a strong sense of their own identity, I presume) it seems to be completely counter-intuitive, a wilful denial of the facts of experience and of common sense. To which I can only reply, exactly: there is a considerable divergence between technical accounts of identity and commonsense views precisely because there is cultural diversity in commonsense views. Any theory of identity, therefore, which aims at some sort of anthropological generalizability rather than at a local ethnographic account – any account, that is, that investigates the degree of variability, the possible types of personhood, rather than what it means to be a person in the belief system of a given group – will invariably seem to contradict the specifics of identity as experienced by individuals. Second, I would like to argue that when Kaufmann speaks of 'the relationship between social structures and their cognitive counterparts' and when he affirms that 'it is the individual who has to construct out of the social materials available, the ethical and cognitive framework conditioning and guiding his actions' he is providing support for the socio-epistemological framework – the 'Social knowledge system' and 'Culture as knowledge' – which occupies the very first sections of this book.

The last of the recent books on identity which I will mention is Geneviève Vinsonneau's *L'Identité culturelle* (2002). Besides providing a clear and detailed summary of the history of identity and culture as anthropological concepts, Vinsonneau gives an exceptionally broad and interesting description of the interdisciplinary contexts in which these concepts are stimulating innovative thinking and methodology: sociology and social psychology, of course, but also social interaction, intercultural communication and intercultural psychology. Her richly illustrated examinations of the relationships between identity and topics such as political and religious ideologies, rites and rituals, territory and the body are particularly timely.

The publication of these works in a relatively short period is clearly indicative of the salience of the notion of identity in contemporary social debate and analysis. So too is the fact that they represent a convergence of interests between such a broad range of the social sciences: linguistics (Joseph), history (Porter), sociology (Castells and Kaufmann, though from very different perspectives) and anthropology and psychology (Vinsonneau).

However, I should emphasize that the current of thought which will be presented here has been contributed to over a lengthy period and by scholars with a spectacularly diverse range of disciplinary interests and backgrounds and not just by those who can be described as sociologists of knowledge or even as sociologists *tout court*. A selection of their names suffices to explain why no historian of ideas has succeeded in grouping them into a single coherent school or in finding a single convenient and appropriate label for the ideas in question: Dilthey, Scheler, Dewey, Mead, Vygotsky, Marx, Sartre – to one degree or another, the list could include all the major contributors to Western thought of the past 200 years.

Although – as one would expect in any list which includes social interactionists, psychologists, Marxists, social constructionists, phenomenologists and existentialists – thinkers such as these disagree on many important issues, they agree on two points which are fundamental to the sociology of knowledge and to the approach to culture and identity which is adopted in this book.

The first point is that the source of personal identity is social. Identities are not formed *ex nihilo*, or through some kind of parthenogenesis. They are the product of social interaction between the individuals and other members of society. Reflection on our interactive experiences – facilitated and canalized by language – enables us to become who we are, to extrapolate from the inter- to the intrapersonal. The structures of society, language and interaction are, therefore, the sources of individual identity. The communicative strategies acquired in interaction provide the discursive and cognitive basis of the individual's interior monologue. With the current vogue for Vygotsky's socio-constructionism, which has considerably influenced the approach adopted in this book, it is easy to forget that similar hypotheses were also formulated by Cooley (1902) and Mead (1934).

Second, the individual's consciousness of identities – their own and others' – is part of their overarching knowledge of social reality, their *Weltansicht*.

Although his work is far less well-known than Marx's, Max Scheler (1874–1928) deserves more attention than he is wont to receive, if only because his extreme anti-rationalist and anti-positivist views throw into relief the different aspects of the debate on social-scientific methodology (Straude 1967; Dupuy 1959; Stark 1958). Scheler studied under both Dilthey and Simmel, though he himself considered his meeting with Husserl as the crux of his intellectual life. From Husserl he derived a belief in the importance of intuition (he himself received flashes of inspiration in night-clubs and cabarets, a fact which is perhaps not unrelated to his dismissal from his post in 1910 as Professor of Ethics for 'personal immorality') and his work can be read as an imaginative attempt to apply the phenomenological approach to the sociology of knowledge, exemplified in the following quotation:

> The *essential* character of human consciousness is such that the community is in some sense implicit in every individual and that man is not only part of Society, but that Society and the social bound are an essential part of himself: that not only is the 'I' a member of the 'we', but that also the 'we' is a necessary member of the 'I'. The forms of group life in which man lives condition not only his perception of the world around him, but also affect his own self-image. (Scheler 1926, p. 57)

This is a clear echo of Simmel's statement that:

> The 'you' and 'understanding' are the same, expressed in the one case as a substance and in the other as a function, ... it is the transcendental basis for the fact that man is *zoon politikon*. (1957, p. 68)

Here, Simmel is making a philosophical point, but he is also making stipulations as to what counts as social science. His position is that the 'you' or the 'other' is recognized and understood as being endowed with a conscious mind, that the minimal unit for the analysis of social interaction is fundamental. His introduction of terms such as dyad, interaction and intersubjectivity represents a consistent and logical attempt to create a way of thinking about society that does not start with the individual. He rejects the Kantian view, one which is shared by many modern sociologists and philosophers, that we can only speak of society as our representation of it, subject to the particular modality in which our intellect orders and forms sensations, that 'society exists in the eye of the beholder', on the grounds that the elements of society, members, representations and institutions, are not simply of the world, they have a world. They are either conscious themselves, or the products of consciousness. They exist as social objects through their participation in the consciousness of others and it is the processes which make this possible, which make society possible, which are the true object of sociology.

Whilst it is obviously no surprise to see these similarities in approach between social scientists in the same linguistic and scientific tradition, it is intriguing to find a very similar point being made, but with reference to a different philosophical tradition, by Sartre in *L'Être et le néant*:

> The philosophy of the nineteenth and twentieth centuries has learnt the lesson that it is impossible to avoid solipsism if we start out by considering myself and Other as two separate substances; any union of these substances is clearly impossible. This is why an examination of modern theories shows them to be attempts to situate a fundamental and transcendental relationship with others at the level of individual self-consciousness and this relationship is constitutive of self-awareness. (1943, p. 277–8; my translation)

The main question Sartre is attending to here is that of how two 'substances', that is, embodied individuals, can communicate, and his discussion is framed within the terms and agenda developed by thinkers in the Descartes, Berkeley, Leibniz tradition. Nonetheless, the conditions for intersubjectivity and the linking of individual self-consciousness with 'others' is clearly the same issue and approach being dealt with by the other writers mentioned and quoted above: the role of knowledge of others in the constitution of personal identity. But some of Sartre's attitudes and answers would be anathema to Simmel's famous 'How is Society possible?', which in turn was an echo of Kant's 'How is Nature possible?'

It is our ability to form dyads, to enter into intersubjective couplings, which makes identity possible. Clearly, then, no account of identity which fails to take this aspect of human nature into account can be considered as even remotely adequate as it is the essential and defining characteristic 'of our species and the foundation of society'. Speaking of 'Identity and a problem in the sociology of knowledge', Thomas Berger (in Curtis and Petras 1970) argues that it is in fact the sociology of knowledge which provides the appropriate theoretical framework for a fuller and more socially adequate account of identity than more traditional philosophical and epistemological accounts, since one of its main objectives is to analyse the relationships between social reality and subjective reality. The sociology of knowledge is a sociological critique of consciousness which examines the ways in which individuals construct the 'objective', taken-for-granted reality of everyday life and the ways in which it correlates with their subjective reality. The objectivated world is subjectively plausible to successfully socialized individuals; that is, their psychological reality confirms objective reality. For example 'I' become a man and a teacher by appropriating to myself objectively observable characteristics; 'men' react like this, 'teachers' speak and behave like that. Consequently, 'I' know who and what I am.

> Identity, with its appropriate attachments of social reality, is always identity within a specific socially constructed world. Or, as seen from the viewpoint of the individual, one identifies oneself, as one is identified by others, by being located in a common world. (Berger 1970, p. 378)

The common world is common to the extent that shared knowledge, culture and language permit individuals to establish a reciprocity of perspectives or definition of the situation. As Berger continues: 'The social definition of identity takes place within an overarching definition of reality'. Failure to establish a reciprocity of perspectives can, therefore, lead to misidentification. Columbus was surrounded by 'Indians'.

In a passage of exemplary clarity, Berger emphasizes the central role of language in these processes:

> Language is both the foundation and the instrumentality of the social construction of reality. Language focalises, patterns and

objectivates human experience. Language is the principal means by which an individual is socialised to become an inhabitant of the world shared with others and also provides the means by which, in conversation with others, the common world becomes plausible to him. On this linguistic base is erected the edifice of interpretive schemes, cognitive and moral norms, value systems and, finally, theoretically-articulated 'world views' which, in their totality, form the world of 'collective representations' (as the Durkheimian school put it) of any given society. (*ibid.* p. 376)

The text which follows is organized in the following way:

Chapter Two examines the concept of culture and presents a model of social epistemology where the structures and functions of knowledge management are related through participation in social interaction to language and identity. Some of the ways in which culture-as-knowledge permeates language are discussed and illustrated, and socio-cultural competence is considered and related to wider sociolinguistic contexts such as societal bilingualism or multilingualism.

In *Chapter Three*, the notion of identity is taken for closer scrutiny. It is argued that, since knowledge is distributed differentially through various types of communicative practices according to the socio-discursive positions occupied by individuals, they are a major element in the identity formation processes. Particular attention is paid to three kinds of practice: membershipping strategies, phatic communion and rearing practices, since they are amongst some of the most important ways in which individuals achieve or have thrust upon them specific, contextually salient aspects of identities and roles.

In *Chapter Four*, it is argued that, since identities are constructed through a series of oppositions to others, 'the foreigner' is central to any account. However, the rich sociological literature inspired by Simmel's seminal essay on 'The Stranger' largely neglects the role of language. This section attempts to bridge that gap by examining specific and problematic aspects of identity, including anomie, recognition and pragmatic failure. Fundamental to the argument is a view of language variation and communicative practices as providing the resources and the coordinates for the construction of identities and self-expression.

Chapter Five looks at some of the ways in which identities are being engineered or reconfigured through globalization and verbal hygiene (call centres, intercultural training, etc.). Recent approaches to the understanding of the negotiation of identity – in particular, the neo-Aristotelian concept of ethos and the notion of communicative virtues – are presented and, finally, the nature and roles of two polar extremes in the identity formation processes, language standardization and scaffolding, are briefly discussed.

Notes

1 I know of no single-volume survey of the field: the interested reader would probably be best advised to go straight to Mannheim (1936: German version 1929) or to Berger and Luckmann (1966). Simonds (1978) is a helpful guide to Mannheim's work. Good introductions to ethnomethodology are Benson and Hughes (1983) and Leiter (1980). Frisby (1992) provides an in-depth study of the development of the discipline in the inter-war period, with particular attention to the work of Max Scheler, Georg Lukas and Karl Mannheim.
2 Dilthey's *Introduction to the Human Sciences: An Attempt to Lay a Foundation for the Study of Society and History* (1883) still provides one of the best points of entry into this tradition.
3 Hymes (1964) provides an excellent overview and selection of the literature on anthropological linguistics. Farb (1974) and Saville-Troike (2002) are good introductions to the ethnography of communication. Duranti (1997) and Foley (1997) are both richly detailed, yet in many ways complementary, academic surveys: both deal with aspects of ethnolinguistics such as kinship, cognitive models and metaphor which are not mentioned here.

2 The social knowledge system

2.1 Notes on the concept of culture

In 1952, two of the twentieth century's most eminent anthropologists, Alfred Kroeber and Clyde Kluckhohn, published a work entitled *Culture: A Critical Review of Concept and Definitions,* in which they explained and discussed some 160 approaches to the notion. As they feared, their book, far from producing a consensual clarification, did nothing to stem the torrent of new definitions during the half century which followed, and more recent examinations of the topic (Kuper 1999; Cuche 1996; Eagleton 2000) have simply strengthened their conclusions: the term is highly polysemic, not to say frustratingly ambiguous, and yet it is at the same time the defining epistemological structure of social anthropology and is essential to any understanding of the modern social sciences.

This paradox is only underlined by the fact that the term is used more and more frequently and more and more widely, not only in academic or intellectual contexts, but also in the discourse of a multiplicity of social domains, to refer to the specific characteristics of diverse social groups: sport and gastronomy, the media, politics and the arts, immigrants, the deaf, age and economic classes – indeed, it is difficult to find a group or domain to which it has *not* been applied and this all-pervasiveness is in itself a striking and important ethnographic observation (this is equally true as regards 'identity'). A second point, and one that has greatly exercised the minds of anthropologists and ethnographers, since it problematizes their position as observers of 'others', is that this Western concept often has no lexical equivalent in the 'cultures' or 'societies' they study and that their members do not concern themselves with questions concerning the nature and definition of 'culture', 'a culture' or even 'our culture'.

The etymology of the term is extremely interesting for the light it throws on intellectual history, although the processes and forms of semantic development undergone are commonplace enough: over the centuries, the use of a word with a relatively limited and concrete referent, Latin *cultura,* 'work with animals, or in the fields', is extended, first to aspects of the immediate environment – by the thirteenth century it can refer to a field or plot of cultivated land – and then figuratively to the development of a particular mental faculty by the sixteenth century. It is only in the eighteenth century, first in France, then in England and Germany, as part of the complex series of social and intellectual developments we conveniently bundle together under the heading 'The Enlightenment', that 'culture' begins to acquire some of its more figurative psychological and educational extensions. In the *Encyclopédie* (1751–1772), it appears in collocations such as 'la culture des arts et des sciences' and this is followed by a gradual extension, continuing well into the nineteenth century, to qualitative effects on the minds involved: culture as intellectual education or training.

However, the term 'culture' possesses at least two connotations which prevent us from considering it as being simply a synonym of 'education'. First, it has retained from its origins ('cultivated land') a metaphorical opposition to 'nature': it is a product of human activity and effort, the sum of knowledge which humanity has produced, accumulated, stored and transmitted throughout history. Given an elitist spin, it is this line of development which will lead, on the one hand, Matthew Arnold (1822–1888) to define culture as 'the acquainting ourselves with the best that has been known and said in the world, and thus with the history of the human spirit' and as 'the study of perfection' (1869, p. 6), an approach which in some ways has found fresh and forceful though not uncritical expression in Terry Eagleton's *The Idea of Culture* (2000). And on the other hand, it will also lead Sir Edward Burnett Tylor (1832–1917), the first holder of a Chair of Anthropology in Britain and founder of the British school, to declare that:

> Culture is that complex whole which includes knowledge, belief,
> art, law, morals, custom and any other capabilities acquired by man
> as a member of society. (1871, p. 1)

This 'anthropological sense' of culture was finally recorded in the 1933 supplement to the Oxford English Dictionary. (We will return to the question of culture-as-knowledge in Section 2.4, below.)

Second, in the context of Enlightenment thought and attitudes, 'culture' is related to notions such as 'progress' and 'reason' and to optimism concerning the future of humanity: given the benefit of education, Man is perfectible. It is at this point that 'culture' overlaps – or perhaps collides would be more appropriate, given the history of the relations between France and Germany, the two main protagonists in the ensuing debate – with 'civilization'. As Cuche explains in his masterly disentangling of this knot of related ideas, the two terms were at this point quite close, though with 'culture' being used more frequently in accounts of individual progress and 'civilization' in contexts referring to the development of groups. But a political wedge was driven between the two, as each was adopted by specific national and social groups to buttress their own ideologies and interests.

'Civilization' was used from the thirteenth century onwards to describe the gradual refinement of manners and was taken up by philosophers wishing to account for the good life in terms of the process which saves humanity from ignorance and irrationality. In Cuche's account, as well as in Norbert Elias's earlier classic *The Civilising Process* (1939), 'civilization' provided the emerging bourgeoisie with the intellectual tools they required to construct a political model which would satisfy and justify the exigencies of their ambitions, largely by providing a secular version of religion. In this mindset, optimism replaced hope, and humanity rather than the heavenly host was at the centre of the universe. In a highly schematic form, the consequences of these developments were twofold: intellectual and academic on the one hand, social and political on the other.

Intellectually, there was a crying need for what one might call a secular theology, a discipline that would respond to Alexander Pope's (1688–1744) exhortation:

> Know then thyself, presume not God to scan.
> The proper study of Mankind is Man.
> (*An Essay on Man* 1732, Epistle 2.1, p. 201)

From approximately the middle of the eighteenth century onwards, numerous candidates were put forward to occupy the vacant position of the 'science of Mankind'. In 1755 Diderot wisely suggested the plural expression 'human sciences', 'wisely' because he had seen that the vastness of the field and the bourgeoning of specialization and specialisms would characterize intellectual life for the foreseeable future. This was followed by suggestions of varying orders of generalization: in 1787 Alexandre de Chavannes (1731–1800) in his remarkably prescient *Anthropologie ou science générale de l'homme* coined the word 'ethnology', which he defined as the study of 'the history of the progress of peoples towards civilization'.

In revolutionary France, Destutt de Tracy (1754–1836) proposed in 1804 establishing a discipline devoted to the study of 'ideology', which would study both intellectual history and ideas. But the *idéologues* soon learnt the lesson that was to be driven home even further by Marxism: you question the dominant ideology at your peril. Napoleon encouraged them at first, but when they turned their attention to <u>his</u> *idéologie* he was definitely not amused. From Marx onwards, 'ideology' became a pejorative term, related to mystification, for any theory of which the speaker does not approve.

In Britain, Tylor, following Gustav Klemm, had greater success with 'anthropology', which etymologically at least fits Pope's requirements to the letter, as it means simply 'the study of mankind'. He did not coin the term, though, which had existed in English since the sixteenth century.

There are far too many claimants to the paternity of sociology as a discipline to be even listed here, but there is no doubt that the word itself was coined by Auguste Comte (1798–1857). Systematic reflections on the nature, aims and epistemology of the social sciences in general, though calling on a massive philosophical and historiographical tradition, can reasonably be attributed to Dilthey's *Introduction* (1883) which seems to contain the kernel of all subsequent socio-scientific theories, as he explores and develops a multiplicity of approaches to 'understanding life on its own terms', which he saw as the overarching aim of the *Geisteswissenschaften*.

The sociopolitical effects of the 'culture'/'civilization' debate were felt most keenly in Germany. Although the term was borrowed directly from the French, the German word *Kultur* fared far better than its Gallic progenitor. It was taken up as a discursive weapon by German bourgeois intellectuals in their struggle for ascendancy with the court aristocracy (Taylor 1941). They used it as a vehicle for a set of values, intellectual values obviously to start with, but they soon came to be identified intimately with profoundly spiritual and emotional notions such as authenticity and sincerity, particularly as regards the individual's orientation towards the nation and literary and popular cultural traditions. These values were presented in a favourable light when compared with the 'civilization' of the aristocracy, enshrining as it did a tradition of courtly values, where superficial appearance and ceremony were all and refined manners were more important than the arts or sciences. Anticipating the emergence of the German nation-state, the bourgeois intellectuals were fashioning the discursive positions from which they would formulate and issue new identity claims, at the same time presenting the aristocracy's devotion to French courtly fashion and comportment as a betrayal of German national values and identity. Unsurprisingly, the increasing polarization of their value systems was manifested in terms of their language allegiances and choices, with the aristocrats speaking more and more French and the bourgeois intellectuals more and more German.

One of the principal reasons why the notion of *Kultur* was so swiftly and successfully adopted was that it resonated with German Romantic attitudes. In 1772, Herder had spoken of *Volksgeist*, the spirit, soul or genius of a people, the art, language and knowledge which, in the absence of unifying political structures, is a source of unity. What in a Romantic perspective was seen as the German people's frustrated longing for nationhood was compensated for, Elias (*ibid.*) suggests, by a growing pride in national *Kultur*. The effects of this development were to widen even further the gap between 'culture' and 'civilization', since the former is now seen as specific to a people, whereas the latter is universal. This is a point of major importance, since it marks the moment when the idea of cultural relativity begins to take root in first German then European thought. Unlike 'civilization', which pertains to the species, 'culture' is local, the way of life and the world-view of a people, expressed in and through their language. Human beings can think because they are blessed with the gift of language, but their thoughts are necessarily expressed in and on the terms of the specific language they use, their 'mother tongue'. Germans think like Germans because they think in German.

It would be wrong, of course, to imagine that the traffic in these ideas was one-way, as the enthusiastic reception of Madame de Staël's *De l'Allemagne* (1813) so amply demonstrates. (It was not, however, an enthusiasm that Napoleon shared. He described it as 'not French', which seems to rather miss the point.) French intellectuals interested in German literature and philosophy repatriated the notion of culture/ *Kultur* with its freshly-grafted connotations of collective particularisms. Nonetheless, then and now, it is the notion of 'civilization' and its related values which predominate in French thought and attitudes. This can most clearly be seen in the still highly topical debate on the foundations and criteria of national identity. When Ernest Renan gave his landmark lecture on the question 'What is a nation?' (1887), he rejected the German (and etymologically implied) approach that it is essentially a genealogical concept – 'a community of individuals who have the same origin' – that is, a matter of birth, in favour of willingness to subscribe to a set of universal values, those of the Enlightenment and the Republic, that is, a matter of choice. As I write, in the aftermath of the Autumn 2005 riots which saw 10,000 vehicles destroyed mainly by youths of foreign descent but having French nationality, and the government, if not the Republic, rocking on its heels, a heated debate is under way between those who wish to see statistics of the ethnic origins of French citizens collected and those who feel it would be a betrayal of Republican values. Other conflicts, such as the wearing of the Muslim *foulard* or veil at school, can be seen as allomorphs of the same elementary substance. These are only some recent instances of the French state's conscious intervention in the identity formation processes by using legal discourse to define the forms of identity which will be available and by placing constraints on their modes of expression.

For the social scientist, a disturbing and relatively recent extension of the semantic coverage of 'culture' – and one that was richly illustrated in public discussion of the events just referred to – is its use as a politically correct synonym for 'race'. Whenever we hear that 'they' (Arabs and Beurs, Somalis, Gypsies, Turks, immigrants, 'bogus' asylum seekers and so on) 'don't have the same culture as us', we can be reasonably sure that it will soon be used as justification for the attribution of generalized and invariably negative characteristics to members of the groups in question. However, since the speaker makes no explicit reference to physical characteristics, he or she feels (perhaps sincerely) able to refute accusations of racism. Typically, therefore, such accusations will be anticipated by expressions such as 'I'm not a racist, but . . .'. At the risk of labouring the point, it has to be made clear that this is a logical and lexical travesty of the socio-scientific understanding (all right, understandings) of the term 'culture', since it is being used to refer to some putative innate moral, intellectual or social characteristic common to all members of the group in question. If the uses of the term 'culture' have proliferated so remarkably, it is precisely because it was developed in a theoretical framework that rejects as incorrect, inadequate or inappropriate purely biological accounts based on concepts such as 'race' or 'innateness' for describing the extraordinary diversity of most aspects of human behaviour. 'Culture', that is, represents an attempt to understand humanity in terms of how and what is learnt. As such, it is antonymically incompatible with terms deemed appropriate for the description of an individual's or group's biological inheritance.

What one might call 'old-fashioned' racism, in the sense that it calls on nineteenth-century biologically-based psychological theories, involves the systematic attribution of non-physical characteristics such as intelligence, temperament or moral integrity to persons on the basis of perceived physical differences such as skin colour, eye colour and peri-orbital musculature, the shape of the skull and of the nose, ears and lips. At the risk of seeming flippant about what has been one of the most horrendous misunderstandings of all time, it is reasonable to ask why it was differences in these locations rather than, say, left elbows that received most attention and measurement. One possible answer is that the anthropologists were unconsciously recognizing the preponderance of head and face in our recognition and identification of individuals. We are apparently capable of extraordinary feats of memory as regards the recognition of faces, able, for example, to say whether or not a photograph glimpsed briefly amongst ten thousand others has previously been seen. Nothing could be a stronger argument for the importance to us of the capacity to identify individuals with whom we have already interacted. And nothing could be a weaker argument for the existence of a correlation between the mental and cultural characteristics of groups and 'scientifically' established facial types, Malik (1996) is a sober, detailed refutation of racist theories.

The resounding failure of phrenology – to my knowledge by far the most detailed attempt to extrapolate from physical to psychological and moral characteristics (Secord 2000) – should have sufficed to demonstrate the futility of such a project. In many cases, of course, it did. Modern social anthropology was largely though not exclusively developed on the basis of observations conducted by anthropologists, psychologists and linguists aimed at testing the strength of the relationship between physical and non-physical characteristics. Their results were incontrovertible. For example, between 1908 and 1910, Boas carried out detailed skull measurements on 17,821 immigrants to the USA and was able to demonstrate statistically that within roughly a generation in the new environment sufficient variation had occurred to negate all correlations and classifications that might have been established on the basis of such data (Boas 1912). Particularly remarkable was his finding that the size and shape of immigrants' skulls was different from those of their parents, since much of contemporary racial theory was based precisely on skull shape – and on the hypothesis that it did not change from one generation to another. In other words, 'races' are not definable because they are not stable. To the extent that *communities* are stable, of course, there will be a tendency for individuals from specific groups to resemble one another: the degree of variability will depend on how 'watertight' the group is. As a result of isolation or the deliberate application of a policy of social exclusion, even some very big groups, such as the Japanese, have succeeded in maintaining high degrees of impermeability for relatively long periods, but the lesson of the work of Boas and his successors is that the resulting low degree of variability is an effect of social discontinuities rather than physical continuities. This is also why it is rubbish to claim that DNA 'proves' race to be a scientific concept. Far from establishing systematic, necessary and causal relationships between physical and non-physical characteristics, DNA acts, in Denys Cuche's expressive phrase, as 'the brushwork of history', revealing demographic movements, the waxing and waning of populations, their degrees of impermeability (and with respect to whom), and the ways in which they are reconfigured and affiliated. This is precisely why patterns of DNA correspond in interesting ways with patterns of language: they are both evidence of social, not physical, continuities, reflecting the swirl of intergroup interaction in time and space. There are no genes for specific languages, or for identities.

Unfortunately, prejudice of this kind is often impervious to logic and even to experience, and in the light of contradictory evidence is simply displaced to other domains, just as the discreditation of phrenology led in some cases not so much to a more rational approach to psychology as to an equally unscientific, if superficially more sophisticated, investigation of the relationship between IQ and 'race' (Billig 1981). In this context, it is important to remember that even if one accepts the existence of a unitary and measurable faculty of intelligence, despite serious evidence to the contrary, the work of psychologists like Herrnstein and Murray (1994) or Arthur Jensen, Richard Lynn and Hans Eysenck is totally vitiated by their inability to come up with anything like a satisfactory definition or measure of 'colour', 'black-ness' or 'whiteness' ('race', 'Asian', etc.). All their experimental and statistical ingenuity is brought to bear not on an unknown but unitary physical factor and its putative relationship with intelligence, but on what is in genetic terms a physically superficial continuum. 'Race' and 'colour' are really complex *social* phenomena with deep subjective roots. The psychologists mentioned above may be clever statisticians, but their semantics is pitiful. In their positivist frenzy to count things, they have forgotten what counts, which, to put it simply, is the way people see colour, their own and others'. It was precisely this failure to distinguish between physical and social reality which created such confusion for the administrators of the policy of apartheid in South Africa, so pointedly satirized by Tom Sharpe (1973). Observations from Central and South America and India confirm the basic point that people with the same 'objective' degree of skin colour can be categorized socially in different ways.

Skin colour, rather than being an objective, self-evident fact, is a cultural artefact, in the sense that it is subject to classifications based on criteria which are social and socio-psychological. However, that is by no means the end of the story, since social classifications are not always in a one-to-one relationship with self-classification or self-ascription, as the following example shows: in a highly instructive article entitled 'Language and negotiation of ethnic/racial identity among Dominican Americans' (2000), Benjamin Bailey shows how the self-ascriptions of Dominican Americans clash with other-ascriptions. Dominicans think of themselves as 'Dominican', 'Spanish' and 'Hispanic', not as 'black' as opposed to 'white'. They resist the phenotype-based, 'racial' categorization recognized by the majority of the US population. They speak Spanish, so they *are* Spanish, not Afro-

American (although as members of a minority, they may still identify strongly with blacks, and this is shown in their choices of forms and styles when speaking US English).

In a case study, Bailey shows how a young Dominican, Wilson, uses multiple language varieties to highlight facets of his identity according to the situation. Wilson selects Dominican Spanish, American English or Afro-American from his repertoire of varieties with great facility, demonstrating a considerable degree of control over his social identity and ethos. In Bailey's words:

> Language situationally precedes phenotypes as a criterion for racial classification and racial identities can shift across linguistically, interactionally constructed contexts. (2000, p. 582)

The particular language forms, speech acts and activities selected by Wilson serve to index social identity further, by instantiating the 'we/they' dichotomies out of which identities are constructed. For out-group members, though, the contradictory signals sent on the one hand by his colour and, on the other, by his multi-variety language proficiency can lead to ambiguity as to his identity.

Racism, the belief in the innate superiority of a particular group and, consequently, of its culture and language, provided the rationale for colonialism, a major factor in the generation of modern models of identity, as could also be seen in the French riots I mentioned earlier. The underlying assumption of superiority is often the only commonality between groups whose motivations were otherwise extremely disparate, contradictory even (merchants, missionaries, slavers, administrators), which in itself demonstrates the extraordinary power it exerts in delineating identities. By providing 'proof' of superiority, racism justifies interference as both right and duty. The most rapacious purveyor of taurine excrement of them all, Cecil Rhodes, summarized this perfectly when he spoke of 'native needs': the 'natives' need the white man, they need civilization,[1] they need Christianity, and they need education. That he was consciously adopting and manipulating this set of discursive strategies is further proof of its power. His own views are more clearly seen in less guarded comments: 'I prefer land to niggers.' 'The natives are like children. They are just emerging from barbarism.' 'One should kill as many niggers as possible.' (quoted in Adebajo 2006). Again, in his *Confession of Faith* (1877), Rhodes wrote:

> It is our duty to seize every opportunity of acquiring more territory and we should keep this one idea steadily before our eyes that more territory simply means more of the Anglo-Saxon race, more of the best, the most human, most honourable race the world possesses. (cited in Kitzan 2001, p. 88)

At least he was sincere in his racism. But if this example illustrates how ethnocentricity – of which Rhodes's racism is an extreme form – penetrates public discourse, motivating and justifying specific aspects of group behaviour, it should also serve as a warning against taking 'discourse' at face value, as if it had some kind of immanent, independent existence. To do so is to accept the highly deterministic account of 'discourse', an essentialism which accords it power without responsibility, by dissociating it from speakers and by denying their agency. Far from being the unconscious pawn of socio-historical forces, Rhodes knew what he was doing, and saying. (We will be returning to the nineteenth century and to the discursive production of identities in the section on rearing practices in Section 3.5.)

2.2 Structures and functions of the social knowledge system

Knowledge, taken in the widest possible sense, is 'what makes society possible'. To make the many into one, they have to have something in common. This common knowledge is shared and acquired in and through language, but before we look at that process of making common, which is, after all, the etymological basis of 'communication', let us briefly examine the overarching, socioepistemic framework within which it takes place: the social knowledge system (see Figure 2.1).

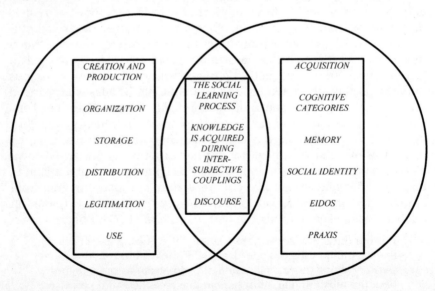

Figure 2.1 The social knowledge system

Any society can be described as a set of structures and functions for the management of knowledge, which, taken together, form *the social knowledge system* (Holzner and Marx 1979; Riley 1996, 2002). The most important of these are:

CREATION AND PRODUCTION

Society is continuously producing knowledge, both local and scientific – events and inventions, facts and fads, ideas and theories – which has to be 'epistemologized' into new domains and bodies. Access to new, or, indeed, any knowledge, both depends on and determines the individual's social identity.

ORGANIZATION

Existing knowledge – everything that 'counts as' knowledge – is organized into disciplines and domains with their own principles of relevance and objects, such as biochemistry and philately. Bodies of knowledge include scientific knowledge, but also practical knowledge, common sense, religious or revealed knowledge and magic.

STORAGE

Knowledge is stored in social institutions, such as language, codes of law, oral history, literature and mythology, and is stocked in repositories such as libraries, records offices and archives, data banks, expert systems, etc.

DISTRIBUTION

Knowledge is distributed differentially, creating epistemic communities, i.e. social figurations or groupings based on shared knowledge, with their own discursive roles and positions, which are major determinants of the forms of identity available in the community in question. Professions and occupations are the most obvious kinds of epistemic community, and almost invariably have some form of knowledge-based entry requirements, but teams and clubs, associations and gangs usually share some kind of local knowledge which unites and identifies them. They also have communicative networks and practices, including sermons, gossip, scandal, rumour, debate, publications, secrecy, etc. Reading, whether paper or screen-based, and social interaction, whether face-to-face or mediated by technology, are the principal modalities of knowledge propagation.

LEGITIMATION

Dominant discourses are established through discussion, power, interest and ideology. They are justified by authority, rationality, consensus, revelation, magic or pragmatic procedures. Non-dominant discourses may attempt to challenge or subvert such claims on their own terms, by accepting their forms of argument but rejecting their conclusions, or by denying the validity, relevance or legitimacy of the forms of argument employed. For example, two biblical scholars might agree the Bible is the Word of God, whilst coming to very different conclusions as to just what He is saying in a particular verse, whereas a third scholar might reject the very idea of revelation as being incompatible with human reason and treat the Bible as word, not Word.

USE

Knowledge is demonstrated, applied and transferred: it is implemented through technologies, skills and competencies. (Competence as both an individual capacity and as a socially recognized right to occupy a specific discursive position is discussed in Section 2.5, below.)

Such a bald list inevitably makes the topic of social epistemology seem abstract and rarified, so it is important to remember that we are discussing fundamental aspects of everyday life. Let us consider, for example, an important institutional node in the system which will certainly be familiar to all readers, the school. Now every school timetable, every syllabus, examination paper, end-of-term report and diploma is a reflexive statement about the ways in which knowledge is organized. The knowledges taught at school and the ways in which they are organized, imparted and evaluated are part of the wider social context in which the school is situated. And anyone who says 'I am a teacher of French' or 'I am a student of biology' is describing their social role and identity on the basis of a body of knowledge. Both teachers and learners will also appeal regularly to other aspects of the social knowledge system in the form of categories such as 'beginners v. advanced', 'first-formers v. sixth-formers', 'physical sciences v. social sciences', 'the arts v. Art', and so on.

2.3 The social learning process

All knowledge is conditioned by the social knowledge system and by the *communicative practices* through which it is negotiated and distributed (see Section 3.3). These forms of transmission include rearing practices (see Section 3.5) and both formal and informal

32

pedagogies and methodologies – 'How you explain', 'How you teach', 'How you bring up children', and so on.

The primary mechanism of the social knowledge system and, therefore, of the social learning process is *language*. The distribution and acquisition of knowledge takes place during dyadic or group interactions in which participants establish *intersubjectivity*, a state of shared meaning. The ability to establish intersubjectivity, to enter into social and meaningful contact with another, is a necessary condition for the formation of identity. It may well be triggered by an innate capacity to recognize others as human beings, and to attribute mental processes, attitudes and intentions to them, that is, to recognize them as persons. It is worth noting that this approach, known as 'Innate Intersubjectivity Theory' is not a product of armchair speculation: the triggering mechanisms of social recognition have been the subject of detailed empirical research by anthropologists and psychologists (Jahoda and Lewis 1988). Colin Trevarthen, one of its main proponents, has provided this summary, under the heading 'Towards a theory of innate cognition for social and cultural skills':

> In recent years, detailed examination of how normal infants respond to the adult who gives affectionate care has brought evidence for potent control behaviours in the infant that stimulate a particular diet or syllabus of supportive and instructive behaviour from caretakers ... some of the newly chartered behaviours, additional to the behaviours that make sure that the infant is adequately fed and protected from harm, or healed if sick are purely psychological in function and consequence. (1988, p. 37)

Trevarthen argues, then, that these types of behaviour, including various kinds of vocalization, eye-contact and movements, and body movements and orientation are, in the fullest sense, other-directed communicative behaviour. Moving on to those psychological consequences, he describes their functioning:

> They ensure an increasingly elaborate mental and behavioural engagement between the infant and other persons and appear to be produced by innate, self-regulatory brain systems that are, in effect, representations of primitive concepts of persons and how to communicate with them, verbally or non-verbally. In time, and by controlling relationships with persons who teach, they set the direction of development for cognitive processes of culture. (*ibid.*, p. 38)

> This theory of socio-cultural development to explain these phenomena has been called Innate Intersubjectivity Theory. It claims that infants possess an inherent readiness to link the subjective

> evaluation of experience with those other persons. It sees children starting cognitive learning in a cooperative and imitative relationship to other more experienced companions and actively contributing to the propagation of collective knowledge. (*ibid.*, pp. 37–8)

What we have here is a strongly-argued, and, it must be said, well-supported Chomsky-like view that culture is acquired on the basis of biological programming: the capacity to enter into intersubjective relationship we are born with is the foundation of our ability to form and acquire cultures. Trevarthen, that is, is extending the hypothesis of the Language Acquisition Device beyond morphosyntax and into pragmatics and interaction. One might say that he is moving from LAD to SAD (Sociolinguistic Acquisition Device). From here, he proceeds to postulate universal stages of development during the first two years.

Trevarthen is right to identify intersubjectivity as the crux of this argument. Moreover, this approach does seem to bring together in a coherent way many of the scattered observations from anthropology and set them in a communicative context which is very much what one wants of such a theory. I am thinking of such things as the role of attention-getters in child–adult discourse; imprinting for face recognition but also for cognitive triggering and stimulation; adult-initiated simulated exchanges and turn-taking. The theory is plausible, too: after all, all normal human infants do learn to communicate and in pathological cases (deafness, blindness, autism) the difficulties and dysfunctions do correspond *mutatis mutandis* to what is predictable from the theory. And, finally, the theory is supported by the rich amount of data which Trevarthen has gathered during fieldwork in north-west Africa. It is also perfectly compatible with the vast bulk of the anthropological literature on rearing practices and, as far as I am competent to judge, with much of the literature on infant psychology based on Meadian and Vygotskyan premises. This is particularly clear in the reference to children 'learning in a cooperative and imitative relationship to other more experienced companions', a topic we will return to in the part of Section 5.3 devoted to 'Scaffolding'.

Access to knowledge depends on the nature and quality of the individual's participation in social life, that is, on their *social identity*, as well as on their state of knowledge at a given time and on the appropriateness of the cognitive processes activated.

If we follow Clyde Kluckhohn's famous adage that:

> Every man is like all other men, every man is like some other men, every man is like no other man (in Kluckhohn and Murray 1961, p. 56)

then the social sciences, by definition, focus on the second set of characteristics – what we have in common with some of our fellows: men and women in groups. And what we have in common with some others is, again by definition, learnt, and what is learnt is subject to variation as regards both its contents and its modalities. This is why any theory of 'culture' is necessarily a theory of communication, of the ways in which a group survives *qua* group, preserves its identity, by transmitting its knowledge to new members. We learn society: 'le social pense en moi'. Man exists in society only to the extent that society exists in man. See the diagram in Figure 2.2 on the social learning process.

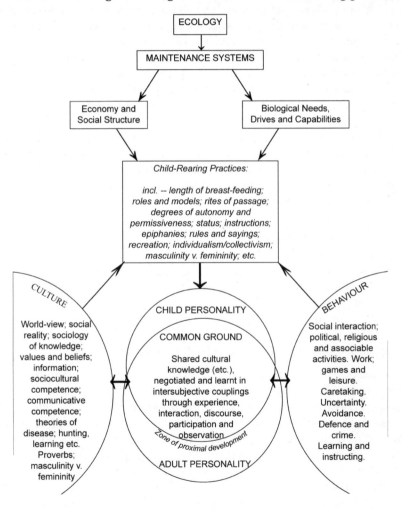

Figure 2.2 An anthropological model of social learning (After Riley 1990)

As we saw at the very beginning of this chapter, the term 'culture' is notoriously polysemic. Adam Kuper's recent book *Culture: The Anthropologist's Account* (1999) demonstrates and deplores this fact, whilst at the same time acknowledging that 'culture' is the essential, the defining notion of modern anthropology. The approach adopted here is that culture is knowledge, in the widest possible sense, including the traditions and history of the group, its common sense, beliefs, values, attitudes and language. Culture is the knowledge members of a society need if they are to participate competently in the various situations and activities life puts in their way. It includes such things as knowing how to fish or dance, how to use a telephone or a credit card, how to drive a car or a bargain, and how to talk. Learning these capacities implies a capacity to learn, and it is precisely this capacity to learn which determines the limits of anthropology.

Interaction and discourse play the primary role in the transmission and distribution of cultural knowledge. The child's personality develops progressively into that of a competent adult through social interaction with other members of society. Discourse, language in use, provides the tools for the negotiation of meaning in the context of such *intersubjective dyadic couplings*. This expression refers to interactions involving two participants who have established a state of shared meaning, that is, communication (illustrated in Figure 2.3).

Consider the following two examples of adult–child discourse:

F: ... and my students gave me a globe.
D: A what what's that what's a globe?
F: It's oh you know it's a sort of map ...
D: Like that? (pointing to a framed map fixed on the wall)
F: ... only no only it's round like a ball with a map printed on it and it's on a foot.
D: Can you turn it?
F: Yeah
D: Oh I know we've got one at school in the Head's office.

This exchange is totally banal, yet miraculous. It exemplifies our species-specific capacity to share meanings. At the beginning of the passage, the little girl did not know the meaning of the word 'globe'. By the end, she was able to say 'Oh I know'. This knowledge is only a minute part of what she will need to know to become a competent adult, but that will certainly be the cumulative effect of all the interactions she participates in during her childhood. It is also worth noting that she has already acquired the knowledge and skills necessary to negotiate meaning in this way: she was able to prevent her father from continuing and to pinpoint the source of her communicative

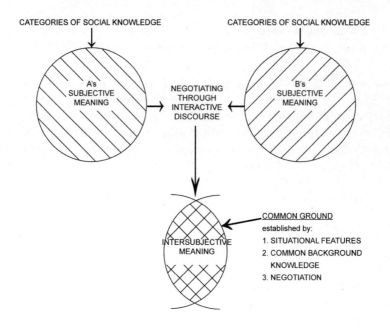

Figure 2.3 Communication and intersubjectivity

problem ('what's that what's a globe?'). She formulated a first hypothesis as to what her father was referring to ('Like that?') which, though incorrect, helped to exclude certain semantic features (rectangular, fixed to a wall) from her search. Her father, too, is actively involved in the negotiation: he starts with a class statement ('a sort of map') which is based on what he thinks his daughter already knows. He also uses an analogy ('like a ball') and provides information about a distinctive feature ('it's on a foot'). This narrowing of focus enables the child to form another hypothesis, which she tests by using knowledge that her father has not provided ('can you turn it?'). The communicative practices to which he has recourse (they are in fact compensation strategies and will be discussed further in Section 4.4) are manifestations of the father's role and identity, of what 'being a father' means in his culture.

In the second example, Father and small Daughter are together in their living room. Father is watching soccer on TV:

F: Foul! Foul! Honestly ...
D: What what's that? What's a foul?
F: It's when you do something you're not allowed to, you do something against the rules, he ...

D: Did he put his hand on it?
F: ... he no he kicked the player on the ground. Honestly!
D: That's not nice.

This extract is very similar to the first, in that the two participants negotiate the meaning of a word that was unknown to one of them. There is a difference, however, and it is an important one, because in this case the child is also acquiring 'culture' in the form of the values of the word 'foul', and an appropriate attitude to the transgression of rules and of the complex bundle of moral criteria and practical behavioural precepts we sometimes refer to as 'fair play'.

Individuals are members of society, which means that their cognitive functions and structures mirror those of the social knowledge system which have been enumerated above. They include:

ACQUISITION

Individuals progressively extend the range of meanings and knowledge available to them by participating in social interactions and by assimilating new information, problem-solving and decision-making. In doing so, they develop a cognitive orientation to experience, including learning styles and strategies.

COGNITIVE CATEGORIES

Individuals, as members, use socially-warranted criteria for the classification of situations, objects, genres, people, emotions, knowledge, etc. The organization and operation of such criteria may be variously described as 'representations', 'beliefs', 'personal constructs', or 'prototypes' which form the *eidos*, the individual's image of society and the world.

MEMORY

Knowledge and experience are stored in linguistic, discursive, eidetic and schematic forms such as lexical items, narrative structures, myth and symbols. They are organized largely by association, and retrieved on the basis of tropes, particularly metaphor and metonymy. Memory is largely constitutive of the self as a site for the-past-in-the-present essential to a sense of identical continuity.

SOCIAL IDENTITY

Social or public identity is the sum of the numerous social sub-groups (sex, age, profession, religion, etc.) to which an individual may belong and of which he or she is a recognized and competent member. Situationally salient facets of social identity, i.e. roles, are manifested by the performance of sets of verbal and non-verbal acts and communicative practices, requiring specific forms of knowledge for their competent performance and ratification and recognition by relevant others.

EIDOS

Individuals have 'world-views', i.e. sets of ideas, beliefs, representations, values and attitudes which form the interpretative repertoire they call on to organize and make sense of their experience.[2]

PRAXIS

All appropriate participation in social activities is knowledge-based: the individual acquires the linguistic, communicative and cultural competence, including both forms and norms and the parameters of variation, which are relevant to and constitutive of their social identity and self. In any interaction, the individual occupies a specific discursive position which permits the enactment of roles which are the dynamic and punctual manifestations of social identity. The communicative skills and practices acquired during childhood interpersonal communication provide the resources for the interpersonal dialogue which is the primary identity formation process.

2.4 'Culture' as knowledge: cultural markers

The knowledge established, categorized and circulated within the social knowledge system will be referred to here as 'culture'. However, this certainly does not mean that all members of a given society 'have the same culture': they cannot know all and only the same things, because their participation in society varies. Individuals acquire and construct their personal cultural repertoires on the basis of the interactional opportunities available to them. A country-dweller and a town-dweller, a doctor's child and a labourer's child, a Muslim and a Catholic will have access to participation in different ranges of interactions. Since cultural knowledge is extremely diverse, two individuals in the same society may come to have very different cultures. In other words, acquiring culture is not like serving oneself from a soup tureen, where every bowlful has identical contents, it is more like lunching from a vast smorgasbord. Each of us puts together, through choice or chance, a personal selection of the dishes, but there are far too many for everyone to have everything. We each construct our own culture, just as we construct our own language, on the basis of the materials available to us.

Culture, then, is not limited to a set of works of art (*Othello*, Guernica, Beethoven's Ninth) or artefacts (masks, combs, cricket-bats, looms, ploughshares). It consists of the totality of social knowledge and is distributed differentially. This approach has been an anthropological commonplace for more than a century, as we saw in the definition from Tylor quoted earlier.

A more recent, widely-quoted definition emphasizes the cognitive element even further:

> As I see it, society's culture consists of whatever it is one has to know or believe in order to operate in a manner acceptable to its members ... Culture, being what people have to learn as distinct from their biological heritage, must consist of the end-product of learning: knowledge in the widest sense of the term. (Goodenough 1957, cited in Cerri-Long 1999, p. 88)

To be learnt, culture has to be transmitted and any society that fails to pass on its knowledge to future generations fails to reproduce itself. This truism leads directly to a less obvious conclusion, namely, that any theory of 'culture' is necessarily a theory of communication, of the structures and functions of the social knowledge system and of the practices which instantiate it. This justifies the introduction of communicative and interactive criteria into a definition of culture:

> Culture is the sum total of the information, beliefs, values and skills one needs to share and apply in the society and situations in which the individual lives: what I need to know in order to 'make sense' in and of those situations in the same ways as my fellows and to communicate and behave in ways they find appropriate. The communicative practices through which culture is transmitted are themselves part of culture.

(We will discuss this topic further in Section 3.3, on communicative practices.)

There are three broad categories of cultural knowledge: *know-that, know-of* and *know-how*.

Know-that consists of what individuals believe to be true: their political and religious 'philosophies' and values, their 'theories' of disease, physics, child-rearing or hunting, their versions of geography and history and so on. This forms what we might call *relatively permanent background knowledge* and is the individual's version of 'how the world works'. It is closely akin to the philosopher's *Weltansicht* or the sociologist's *habitus*. More detailed examples include:

French cuisine is the best in the world.
If you get wet feet, you'll catch a cold.
Spare the rod and spoil the child.
Politicians are either left- or right-wing.
It's the rich what gets the gravy.
1066 and All That.
It's wrong to lie.

In brief, then, we can categorize such ideas as relatively permanent background knowledge.

Know-of consists of current events and preoccupations: what is going on in the society in question, who's who, who's doing what, the news, who has just been elected mayor, got married, started a new TV series, what is the state of the market, the crops, the weather, and so on:

Guantanamo Bay and the 'war against terrorism'
the crisis in Darfur
the new baker's shop; this winter's bus timetable
the neighbours' son's wedding
this year's Man Booker Prize winner

In this case, we may speak of relatively ephemeral background knowledge.

Know-how consists of the individual's skills, capacities and competencies, their effective mastery of reasoning, behaving and speaking in appropriate ways, or more simply how to do and say things in the ways things are said and done. Specific examples could include:

how to fish, dance or row
how to use a hoe or saw, a telephone or a credit card
how to ride a horse or bicycle or drive a car
how to choose a spouse
how to thank, greet, tell a story, address a superior

This pragmatic or procedural knowledge, then, covers practical reasoning, practical action and communicative practices.

A simple but powerful indication of the close relationships between culture, language and identity is to be found in the cultural markers, where culture is directly encoded or lexicalized. Of course, it can be argued that, since a language is itself a cultural system, all words are cultural – but some are more cultural than others. These cultural markers are, as it were, the lexical tip of the cultural iceberg.

CULTURAL MARKERS

Acronyms and abbreviations:
DIY, IRA, Quango, Ms, EU, UNO, TUC, B&B, IBM, softporn, bedsit, mod cons, BBC, SAS, UFO, PM, MP, GP, Lib Dems, PC, HP, IT

Places:
Sandhurst, Wembley, The Tate, Camp X-ray, Salt Lake City, The Lake District, Oxbridge, Southend, Whitehall, Westminster, Scotland Yard, Twickenham, Lords

Organizations:
Meals-on-Wheels, Barnardo's, Oxfam, NSPCC, RSPCA, Samaritans, Neighbourhood Watch, CND, Shelter, PTA, ASH

'Days':
Poppy Day, Guy Fawkes' Night, Good Friday, Boxing Day, Boat Race Day, Pancake Day, Halloween, St. David's Day

Dates:
1066, 1815, '14–'18, 1952
September 11th, March 17th, November 5th

Characters:
Dick Turpin, Dr Who, Goldilocks, Florence Nightingale, Russell Crowe, Osama Bin Laden, The Teletubbies, Good Queen Bess, Bad King John, Jack the Ripper, David Beckham, Peter Pan, James Bond

Signs:
Use hard shoulder, Pay and display, Blind summit, Pub Grub, Tow-away zone, Open to non-residents, Sale, Checkout time

Newspapers:
the *Sun*, *The Times*, the *Daily Express*, the *Independent*, the *Daily Mirror*, *Private Eye*, the *Universe*

Games:
Tiddlywinks, darts, bar billiards, snakes and ladders, fag-cards, it, ludo, conkers, marbles, hopscotch, dodgems, helter-skelter

Three further quick points on the subject of cultural markers: first, they may form extended patterns on the basis of domains of reference, often with figurative meaning. For example, the domain 'cricket' provides a metaphorical set of guidelines and criteria for behaviour, often carrying moralistic overtones:

It's just not cricket.
Play the game.
Keep a straight bat.
to be on a sticky wicket
to bowl someone a googly

(See also Section 3.5, Rearing practices)

Second, they can be extremely regular: a case in point would be the way in which French towns are associated with a very varied but highly specific set of historical or gastronomic references:

Bordeaux: wine
Commercy: madeleines
Dijon: mustard; cassis (blackcurrant cordial)
Montélimar: nougat
Rheims: champagne
Vaucouleurs: Joan of Arc
Verdun: 1914–1918
Vichy: Government in occupied France; pastilles; mineral water

Such expressions can be used for social categorization. For example, if I tell you that a third person 'reads *The Times*' the implications are very different from the statement that he or she 'reads the *Sun*'. After all, 'Top People Take *The Times*'.

Speakers will often use references of this kind to make indirect comments on their own or other peoples' identities and, in the way that some people use the signs of the zodiac, as a way of explaining and predicting behaviour and temperament.

Third, references of this kind are often extremely powerful symbols. For example, in September 2006, the leader of the extreme right-wing National Front in France, Jean-Marie Le Pen, chose to go to the town of Valmy to celebrate the anniversary of the Revolutionary Army's defeat of the Prussians. On the face of it, this was strange, because the National Front is inimical to revolutionary universal values such as internationalism and human rights, and they had certainly never shown any interest in Valmy previously. But in a speech of typically sophisticated bluster, Le Pen argued that France was once again threatened by a horde of foreign invaders, that the French should unite to resist them, that the nation's moral fibre and economic structure was being sapped and – inevitably – that French culture and identity were being threatened. On the grounds that there is no such thing as bad publicity, he must have been more than satisfied by the storm of outraged protest that followed.

Together, these three forms of knowledge form the individual's *cultural competence*, the sum total of the beliefs, information and skills which one needs to share and apply in the society and the situations in which one finds oneself: it is what I need to know in order to 'make sense' in and of the society and the situations in the same way as my fellows. Making sense, that is, includes both behaving and speaking in a rational and comprehensible way, and being able to understand and interpret the behaviour of others. (The notion of 'competence' will be developed in Section 2.5, below.)

An easy way to understand this point is to analyse newspaper cartoons, partly because the range of situations they depict is extremely wide and partly because the genre itself is culturally loaded: not all societies have them and when they do there is considerable variation in topic and taboo. Moreover, because cartoonists usually hope to address large audiences, it seems reasonable to suppose (that they suppose) that the knowledge required to understand their work is widespread.

One cartoon I am particularly fond of is set in a comfortable solidly middle-class dining room. The table is set for a candlelight supper for two and a bespectacled, balding man who is wearing a flowery apron with a feather duster tucked into the pocket is just lighting the candles. Behind him, standing with their backs to the fireplace are two portly middle-aged women, one of whom is his wife, presumably, as her portrait is hanging on the wall. She is saying to her friend: 'The only demand he makes is that I refer to him as a Male Chauvinist Pig occasionally'.

To get the point, we have to be able to recognize the setting – the kind of room, the furniture and numerous details such as the bottle of wine in a cooler beside the table, the table napkins, and so forth. But we also need to recognize the kind of relationship that is implied by the event we call 'a candlelight supper', to understand the meaning of the expression 'Male Chauvinist Pig' and to realize that men who fall into this category do not usually go around cooking dinner, wearing flowery aprons and carrying feather dusters. Our expectations, based on previous knowledge and experience, are not met, and in particular the linguistic classification of an aspect of the man's identity seems completely incongruous.

In another cartoon, a Landrover towing a horse-box has stopped by a signpost in a country lane. The driver is a man wearing a tweed cap and next to him is a woman wearing a headscarf. He is looking at the

44

signpost, which says 'Fadham 3' and asking his companion 'What's that in furlongs?'.

All the details, from the kind of vehicle to the occupants' headgear and the name on the signpost, point to a horsey, home-counties setting. But this time, the caption, instead of contradicting our expectations about the characters' identities, confirms them to the point of absurdity, since the word 'furlong' is now almost entirely restricted to horse-racing. (Specialized vocabulary as an index of social identity is further discussed below and in Section 3.4.)

What would a man from Mars or a language learner need to know to understand these messages and their contexts?

The first thing to notice is that it is quite impossible to be anything like exhaustive in our replies: culture-as-knowledge permeates every situational nook and cranny, every word of a cartoon. It includes:

1) the ability to recognize the *genre* (i.e. to distinguish cartoons from other literary or iconic forms such as sonnets or advertise-ments);
2) the ability to predict the *key* of the message (i.e. humour rather than instruction, say);
3) the ability to recognize the visual and spatio-temporal aspects of the *setting* (suburban dining-room, flowery apron, headscarf, etc), and
4) the ability to interpret the *discourse* (including communicative practices, presuppositions, implicature and cultural markers).

The final point on this list calls for brief comment. There have been several attempts to model interpretative procedures on the basis of quasi-philosophical maxims or principles. These include Donald Davidson's Charity Principle (1990), which states that as we cannot have access to a speaker's beliefs other than through the interpretation of his or her utterances, the only possible way of proceeding at the beginning of an exchange is to assume that he or she shares the same beliefs as ourselves. Brown and Levinson have elevated their model of politeness to a high level of generalization. But certainly the best-known approach is that of Paul Grice (1975), which, within the framework of a general Principle of Cooperation, proposes four interpretative Maxims, namely those of quality, quantity, relevance and manner:

Quality: speakers' utterances should be true to the best of their knowledge. They should not say anything for which they lack adequate evidence.
Quantity: speakers' utterances should be as informative as is required for the purposes of the conversation, neither more nor less.
Relevance: speakers' utterances should be clearly related to the matter in hand.

Manner: utterances should be perspicuous: they should be orderly and brief and should avoid obscurity and ambiguity.

Empirical ethnolinguistic observation has raised serious objections to this approach, since there are endless examples of speakers regularly violating the maxims in many different cultures. There are two ways of explaining this: either we say that, far from being universal, Grice's Maxims simply reflect the local values and interpretative procedures of his own community. Or we consider such cases as instances of flouting, that is strategic manipulation of the rules for communicative effects and purposes – which, it has to be said, is an integral part of Grice's theory.

When I was working in Malta, I set my heart on buying a red shirt. The owner was standing outside a menswear shop, so I asked him if he had a red shirt. 'Yes of course.' I entered the shop and found every kind and colour of shirt imaginable: white, blue, Hawaiian – except for red. Annoyed, I walked out. However, when I recounted this incident to Maltese friends, they were half-annoyed, half-amused, half-scandalized by my behaviour. To them it was completely obvious that the shopkeeper was simply inviting me to step inside, so to describe him as a liar (as I did) only demonstrated my lack of shopping competence as a foreigner and as a man.

As I have already mentioned, knowledge is distributed differentially in society. In fact, the number of people who possess a particular item of knowledge can vary from the whole of the community in question to a single dyad. There are things 'everybody knows' and things that are 'between you and me'. There is a clear tendency for the number of people who know an item to correspond with the number of people belonging to a specific social group. However, it is only a tendency, for two main reasons: first, it is possible to know one item without knowing all the others which are necessary to be, and to be recognized as, a competent member of the group in question, or to know something about that group. Knowing that Muslims do not eat pork does not suffice to make one a Muslim.

Second, it is quite possible to have a considerable body of knowledge in a given domain but still to be disqualified from recognized membership by some other facet of one's social identity, gender or colour being the most obvious examples. In 1861, Elizabeth Garrett achieved first place in Middlesex Hospital's qualifying examinations, although she had been ostracized and harassed throughout the course. (The examiners did not realize that the examination papers submitted by 'E. Garrett' were by a woman.) She was requested by the hospital authorities not to reveal her results and caused great scandal by refusing to comply: her application to matriculate at London University was turned down. A determined woman, to say the least, she went on to take the examination for membership of the Association of Apothecaries and was again successful. Aghast at their oversight, the members of the Association passed a retrospective statute excluding women from the profession. She finally qualified formally as a doctor in Paris in 1870. In the same year, male students rioted to prevent a handful of women taking the University of Edinburgh's medical examination. A path was cleared for them by force, whereupon a flock of sheep was driven into the exam hall after them (Schama 2002).

Despite their possessing the required competence and knowledge these women were refused membership of the groups in question on grounds of gender. So much is obvious, but the question remains as to why this should be so. Male chauvinism and professional jealousy, evidently, but underpinned by a variety of knowledge-related concerns: the belief that women's intellects were unsuited to scientific modes of thought, but also that knowledge of human anatomy was indecent, that there were certain things that women, by their very nature, should not know.

Consider the following example:

A: What will you have to drink? A drop of sherry?
B: I'm driving.
A: Coffee, then?
B: That'd be lovely.

The main items of knowledge necessary to interpret this exchange as the participants did can be summarized as:

You must not drink and drive.
In this context 'drink' refers to alcoholic beverages only.
Sherry is an alcoholic beverage.
Coffee is not.

This, then, is knowledge that every competent adult member of the society in question is expected to know – common or general knowledge. Another example of this type of knowledge distribution can be seen in a notice in a shop window:

Open on Sundays.

You will agree, I think, that this does not mean that the shop is closed the other six days of the week. But it is only our knowledge of the real world – knowledge which this notice presupposes is possessed by everyone – that allows us to reach this conclusion.

Now consider the following exchange:

A: A gin and tonic and a pint of Guinness, please.
B: It's ten past eleven.
A: What? A gin and ...
B: It's ten past eleven. You heard.

In this case, A is a foreign visitor in a London pub and he lacks a vital piece of information that 'everyone knows', namely that it is forbidden to serve alcoholic drinks after 11pm. (My French colleague returned to our table with a puzzled frown: 'Philip, what is happening? When I ask for a drink, she tells me the time'.)

Let us now go to the opposite end of the scale of distribution of knowledge, the dyad. Here, by definition, we have cases where the knowledge in question is restricted to two people:

A: What's for supper?
B: It's my yoga night.

Now we are all capable of interpreting this exchange. Indeed as competent adults, we can probably find a number of different interpretations:

On yoga night, they always eat a frozen pizza.
On yoga night, it's A's turn to decide on the menu and do the cooking.
On yoga night, B brings home a Chinese take-away meal.
On yoga night, they eat out.

And so on. What we cannot do, however, what we cannot know, is which interpretation is the right one. Here is a similar example:

A: What's for supper?
B: Chicken soup.
C: Why isn't Emily coming home?
B: Marie-Cécile's playing this evening.
A: Oh, right. Where's the bread?
B: It's Thursday.
C: I'll go down.
B: Don't forget the dog.

However, in this case, three members of the same family share various items of knowledge. Some of them are 'things everyone knows', others are restricted to family members:

Emily is A and B's eldest daughter. She does not like chicken soup, whereas both A and C, a sibling, are very fond of it. So A, who does most of the cooking, only prepares chicken soup when she knows Emily will not be eating at home. The reason for Emily's absence is that her best friend is

48

playing in a concert: A, B and C all recognize the name and know that she plays the piano, not volleyball.

A's query about bread elicits the information that it is Thursday. This is relevant, since, as everybody knows, all French bakers' shops have to close one day a week, and as people living in A and B's neighbourhood know, it's Thursday as far as their local baker is concerned.

A and B make a habit of storing a frozen baguette or two, since, as everybody knows, they are quite edible when defrosted and bread is an essential part of any meal. Their freezer is in the basement and the tins of dog-food are piled next to it. To save C making two journeys, B reminds her of this, because, as all members of the family know, they feed the dog upstairs in the kitchen.

In this example, there are at least three levels of distribution: there is knowledge which is restricted to family members, knowledge which is shared by everyone living in that neighbourhood, and there is what everyone knows. Each kind of knowledge corresponds to an aspect of the social identities of the individuals concerned: family, community of residence, nation. So between the extremes of dyad and the community as a whole, we have innumerable levels and figurations: sports clubs and trades unions, professions, political parties, religious groups, each with their own knowledge base, each a facet of social identity.

Conversation, and in particular the kind of conversation we often denigrate as 'gossip', is by far the most important channel for the constant reaffirmation of shared values. Those values are cultural values and when we gossip we are continually referring to them to assess things, ideas and people, such as our neighbour's garden, our neighbour's politics or our neighbour's spouse, positively or negatively. These complementary 'pat on the back' or 'tut, tut' assessments are the very substance of social solidarity, that is, the feeling of sharing common cultural identities and values, of 'belonging'.

Cultural values, however, are not 'out there', like trees or hills in a landscape: they only exist for as long as they are applicable and applied, in and through language. It is the practice of gossip, then, which maintains the group's identity and its common sense, its social reality. We do this by constantly defining and refining what we mean by (and how we feel about or value) specific social facts. Unlike trees or stones or any other physical objects, but like the dragons in *Discworld*, social facts only exist because we will them to do so, because we believe in them and behave as if they did exist: they are cognitive constructs which provide the rules and materials for our daily behaviour. By and large, social facts tend to come to the surface of discourse, in the form of words or expressions. Here are a few examples:

an appointment
promotion
a lie
our street
marriage
honour
a committee member
getting the sack
a purchase
the offside rule

The referents of these words are real. We 'make' appointments. And if we fail to keep them there are real repercussions: a friend might refuse to speak to us, the doctor threatens to strike us off his list, we fail to get the job.

Social facts require a consensus between a minimum of two people as to some aspect of meaning and behaviour. Very often, then, when we use such words or expressions in our talk, we expect our listeners to show their solidarity by assenting to the value-judgements we build into them: the poet in all of us wants to express and share how we feel about or perceive some aspect of reality.

a fair swap/a bargain/a rip-off
a good boss/a right bastard
a bright kid/a yob/a nerd/a delinquent
a straight answer/a rude reply
a real laugh/an absolute disgrace
a proper funeral

The second reason why gossip is prototypical of all discourse is that it provides the main mechanism for the management and distribution of knowledge and information.

Knowledge is distributed differentially. We do not all know the same things, partly because we do not all need to know the same things, partly because we do not have the same chances to learn. Culture is not some monolithic block which we 'have' or 'don't have'. According to the nature and quality of the social interactions in which we participate, we have access to different kinds of knowledge. This social distribution of knowledge is largely paralleled by the social distribution of language – and the two are largely constitutive of social identity. These points are very easy to demonstrate: consider the following expressions:

the Old Man's Gardens
a flash butt weld

a double top
phoneme
fascine
booze cruise
meals-on-wheels
squash
adabiatism
caption
mandamus
bur-chervil

These are all English words, in the sense that they are 'in the dictionary'. Yet it is highly unlikely that any single person knows them all. It is also unlikely (given that you are reading this book) that you don't know any of them. But what is it that determines not just how many and in what detail but which particular combinations of these items you know? The main influence is your social identity. You are much more likely to know *caption* and *mandamus* if you are connected in some way with the legal system, *the Old Man's Gardens* if you spent your childhood near the Royal Hospital, Chelsea, *bur-chervil* and *fascine* if you are interested in botany and historical architecture respectively, a *boozecruise* if you are in the habit of driving vanloads of cheap alcoholic drinks across the Channel, *adabiatism* if you are a physicist.

Examining the two evaluatory functions of gossip I mentioned above is difficult, since it involves looking at the relationships between notions which are themselves already extremely complex. These notions are culture, language, ethnic group and social reality. It might be helpful to schematize these relationships as in Figure 2.4.

The diagram in Figure 2.4 can be read platonically to mean that any

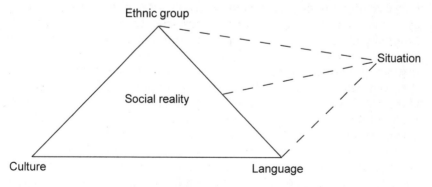

Figure 2.4 Ethnolinguistic triangle

given situation is specified or determined by a configuration of underlying ideals and norms, that a situation is only the ephemeral manifestation of social reality. It can also be interpreted as meaning that every individual involved in a situation can appeal to various kinds of knowledge in order to classify and interpret the situation and to select the behaviours appropriate to it. But to do so, of course, the individual must be, and be seen to be, *competent*.

2.5 Knowledge, identity and competence

Over the past fifty years, oceans of ink have been spilt on the notion of competence. There are good reasons for this, since any theory of action and any theory of language must be predicated, explicitly or otherwise, on some form of explanation of the relationship between action and actors, language and speakers. Even those theories which are based on the belief that it is possible to separate the two are in fact making extremely strong claims or assumptions about the nature of language which will have major implications for how it is acquired and used (often the very topics which they are designed to avoid).

In parallel with this development of our views of the acquisition and learning processes, there has been a corresponding development in our understanding of the types of outcomes, the kinds of knowledge and skills language learners are hoping to possess or attain, the *competence* which they are expected to demonstrate. Three successive uses of the term can be observed: linguistic competence, communicative competence and sociocultural competence (Brown *et al.* 1996).

Linguistic competence is Chomsky's term for the ability of a native speaker to produce or recognize correct sentences in a language. This ability is the dynamic expression of an ideal native-speaker's knowledge of the underlying system of rules (the units, morphological, syntactic and paradigmatic structures, functions) which form the internal code. It has often been pointed out that Chomsky's opposition between *competence* and *performance* is similar to de Saussure's distinction between *langue* and *parole*. Both are interested in studying the irreducible structures of language, 'la langue en elle-même et pour elle-même', and to do so these structures must be disembedded from their context of situation and dissociated from any form of variation, social or individual. Chomsky's ideal native speaker-hearers are a grammarian's clones, members of a perfectly homogeneous speech community and their sentences are produced in an interactive and socially sterile vacuum. It is not difficult to understand why such a view of competence should result in form-focused work such as grammar drill and grammar-translation exercises. Chomsky's learner is in his own image and likeness, a grammarian, neither more nor less.

Communicative competence is Dell Hymes's (1970) challenge to the structuralism of de Saussure and Chomsky. It can be defined as the ability to adapt one's utterances to the situation, or, in Hymes's words, as 'The rules of use without which the rules of grammar would be useless'. Our speech varies according to who we are and who we are speaking to, where and when, and what about. Communicative competence requires knowledge of the sociolinguistic norms governing variation and enables speakers to speak in situationally appropriate ways. In this perspective, the learner is seen as a language user, someone who wishes to perform certain speech acts. The Communicative Approach to language learning and teaching, as developed, in particular, by the Council of Europe (2001), is a systematic attempt to implement these ideas. Again, given this perspective, it is not surprising to find that this approach makes use of pairs practice, games, authentic materials, simulations and role-play, all of which can contribute in one way or another to the contextualization of language.

The concept of *sociocultural competence* brings together our knowledge of language with our knowledge of the world, our world, the society, situations and culture of which we are members. It is also important to emphasize the fact that an essential part of sociocultural competence is what we might call learning competence. Every society has its vision of the competent adult, a concept of personhood, and adopts appropriate rearing practices (see Section 3.5) aiming to reproduce individuals who will fit satisfactorily into the social mould. Taken together, these form a theory of what human nature is and how you become an accepted member of society, a theory of communication and of learning or acculturation. Since different societies have different views of human nature and different expectations as regards the competent adult, their representations of the learner, learning and what is to be learnt also differ.

These three approaches to competence are not incompatible. Schematically, one could say that linguistic competence means being a grammarian, communicative competence means being a speaker and sociocultural competence means being a member. Rather, the three can be imagined like Russian dolls, nesting inside one another, so that sociocultural competence includes communicative competence which, in turn, includes linguistic competence.

At the beginning of this chapter, I argued that the principal mechanism of the social knowledge system is language, since it both encodes and stores culture-as-knowledge and provides the means for

53

its distribution and transmission. In many cases it would be necessary to speak of languages rather than language, since most of the world's societies and most of the world's population are bi- or multi-lingual. (If you accept the guestimate that there are 6,000 languages in the world and divide that figure by 190, which is approximately the number of members of the United Nations, it is clear that even allowing for extreme cases such as India or New Guinea, with perhaps 1,100 and 650 languages respectively, an ideal 'average' country has to be depicted as at least bi-lingual.

This has important implications both for the functioning of the social knowledge system (two languages never pattern identically in socio-epistemic terms) and for those members of the society in question who use both or several varieties, who have, that is, some degree of *plurilingual competence*. Even if we describe this type of competence as simply the ability to communicate appropriately in more than one language variety according to social and situational norms, it becomes clear that, to reach any further understanding of those norms and situations, we need a framework for describing the overall linguistic economies of multilingual societies. Moreover, in the context of a discussion of competence, it is important to bear in mind that the nature of a linguistic economy will to a very large extent define and constrain the forms of social identity and personhood available, since it generates the social spaces and discursive positions which serve as their coordinates.

For the student of the identity formation processes, however, there is a major problem here. Despite the vast, rich literature on both the sociology of language and individual bilingualism (Fishman 1980; Fasold 1984; Romaine 1995; Hamers and Blanc 1989; Harding-Esch and Riley 2003), not only does no such descriptive or classification framework exist, there is not even agreement as to the definitions of and relationships between some of the most fundamental terms in the field.

Take, for example, the terms 'multilingual' and 'plurilingual'. If you consult technical discussions of sociolinguistics or works of reference, you will find that these two terms are sometimes treated as synonyms, or that they are used to refer to different phenomena: some authors prefer to use 'multilingualism' for social contexts such as 'a multilin-gual town/country', reserving 'plurilingualism' for a form of individual sociolinguistic competence. And sometimes you will find the opposite. The *Dictionnaire Larousse de Linguistique et des Sciences du Langage* (1994) states that 'multilingualism is synonymous with plurilingualism' and adds that 'certain countries such as Switzerland have national plurilingualism'.[3] For David Crystal in *The Cambridge Encyclopedia of*

Language (1997) multilingualism is 'Said of a person/community with several languages' and the entry for 'plurilingualism' is simply 'See multilingualism'. Romaine (1995) uses the term to apply both to social contexts and to individuals, referring for example to a person as having been 'raised multilingually'. Similarly in the *Routledge Encyclopedia of Language Teaching and Learning* (Byram 2000) one reads that 'the term (bilingualism) is often used to include trilingualism and multi-lingualism' – and one looks in vain for an entry for 'plurilingualism'. Neither Hamers and Blanc (1989) nor Mackey (1976) use either of these terms. Similar confusion can be shown for almost any other term used in this field.

The oceanic depths of sociolinguistics are full of the wrecks of taxonomies which have been launched on the wave of a fashionable theory only to be sunk forever by a broadside from the following theory. So it is with some trepidation that I propose the taxonomy summarized in Table 2.1.

Table 2.1 Categories of co-existence of language varieties

	Societal without complementary functional distribution	Societal with complementary functional distribution	Individual competence	Individual discursive or textual performance
Coexistence of two varieties	Societal bilingualism	Diglossia	Individual bilingualism ('bilinguality')[4]	Code-switching
Coexistence of more than two varieties	Multilingualism	Polyglossia	Plurilingualism	Heteroglossia

I would justify this suggestion on the following grounds:

- It is based on the existence of a number of sociolinguistic criteria and oppositions which are generally accepted as fundamental (even if, as we have just seen, there is terminological chaos).
- It provides a starting-point for examining the relationships between bi- and multilingualism and the identity formation processes.

The following sociolinguistic criteria are appealed to:

- The fact that it is useful for practical as well as analytic purposes to distinguish between the coexistence of two varieties and of more than two varieties.

- It is essential to distinguish between the coexistence of language varieties within a society and within an individual. There is no simple, one-to-one relationship between the two levels: theoretically, at least, it is possible to conceive of a multilingual society entirely made up of monolingual individuals.
- The distribution of varieties within a society may operate on a functional basis, or not.
- Since certain individuals use more than one variety, there are necessarily types of situation and discourse where they change from one to the other, where they overlap or enter into contact. Code-switching can take many forms and fills a wide and varied number of functions.
- The ecology of multilingualism is so complex and shifting that different forms may occur within the same society's structures or praxis. If we are to describe the specifics of such cases, it is essential to recognize these distinctions.

Each of these terms represents sociolinguistic phenomena, all of which have attracted considerable attention and discussion over recent years. It would be quite impossible to summarize that literature in any detail here; instead, I will give a brief gloss on each and, where possible, an indication as to how they may relate to social identities.

Societal bilingualism

This term refers to the coexistence within a society of two language varieties. A language variety is a set of linguistic forms having the same distribution with respect to one or more social criteria such as religion, topic, functional domains, age, sex, region and so on. 'Variety' is preferred to 'language' which is a political rather than a linguistic concept, and also because linguistic change accumulates progressively along geographical, social, functional and diachronic axes ('dialect continua') which makes the delimitation of 'a language' problematic, since it is impossible to identify linguistic criteria to establish where one 'language' ends and another begins. In some cases, the two varieties may be considered as full and independent languages (often because both have been standardized, as is the case in the Swedish-speaking areas of Finland, for example). In others, one of the two varieties is considered as a language whilst the other is relegated to an inferior position (dialect, patois, etc.) or neither the one nor the other is a standard language. (The standardization process and its implications for the identity formation processes will be discussed in Section 5.3.)

Official societal bilingualism should not be confused with actual societal bilingualism: the proportion of bilingual individuals in an officially bilingual country may be relatively low, and there may be many bilingual people in an officially monolingual country, like France. This is the result of social discontinuities, due, for example, to the fact that the groups concerned occupy separate territories (as in Belgium, Switzerland or the countries of the former Yugoslavia). Since the varieties in question may have very different statuses and functions, the forms and patterns of bilingualism, whether social or individual, tend to vary considerably with immediate implications for the types of personhood and configurations of social identity made available. The bilingual individual will be a member (though sometimes a sub-category of member) of both speech communities.

Community membership is both a principal category of social identity and a resource and site for further categories. However, it is important to remember that not only does linguistic competence vary in degree, but it is rarely the sole criterion for recognition of social groups and individuals. Moreover, the objective degree of similarity and mutual intelligibility between two varieties is by no means directly correlated with recognition and ascription of group identities. As cases such as Ireland or Malta demonstrate, speakers of English, whether monolingual or bilingual, may have very robust, autonomous and local community identities. The men of Gilead slaughtered the Ephraimites, whom they identified by their inability to pronounce the initial voiceless palato-alveolar fricative in the word 'Shibboleth' (Judges 12: 4–6), making a simple phonemic opposition into what was literally a matter of life and death. And Portuguese children, it is said, 'have to learn not to understand Spanish'.

What has been said about societal bilingualism also applies to multilingualism, the coexistence of three or more varieties, though there is of course an arithmetical increase in the number of community identities available. Indeed, in many cases the proliferation and survival of numbers of distinct varieties can only be explained in terms of the affirmation of group identities. Salisbury, describing the immensely complex sociolinguistics of New Guinea, shows that completely unnecessary interpretation was often used as a way of affirming group identities. For example:

> One Emenyo man ... spoke Dene on almost all occasions within his own village. He was an important man and when speaking in Emenyo village he used Dene and was not translated; when speaking publicly in any other Komunku-speaking village he used Dene and was translated; when speaking privately with me when no-one else was about he used Siane, but when groups were

57

> present he used Dene and it was translated to me ... The village luluaï or headman often spoke to me without an intermediary in Siane ... yet on many occasions he would not begin speaking until an audience was present, and after his speech would turn to a bystander and indicate that he should translate into pidgin before I could reply ...

He concludes:

> ... we must interpret repetition and the translation of speech as a linguistic means of emphasizing the importance and public nature of the discourse. (Salisbury 1962, pp. 54–5)

One of the most striking examples of multilingualism as a resource for the affirmation of group identities – and one which has consequently attracted considerable attention from sociolinguists and ethnolinguists (Sorensen 1972; Jackson 1974; Hudson 1996) – is provided by the Vaupés Indians who inhabit part of the Amazonian Basin in Colombia. Each of the twenty tribes in the region speaks a distinct variety and the Indians themselves insist they are mutually unintelligible. They share the same culture, are few in number (some 5,000 when the studies by Sorensen and Jackson were carried out) and have a *lingua franca*, Tukano. Moreover, the tribes are organized into five phratries of groups of four which are exogamous, meaning that all men have wives who speak a variety other than their own, and that conversation in the phratrie longhouse is highly multilingual, as potentially at least all sixteen languages spoken by the four other phratries might be represented there. All individuals speak at least three varieties and some as many as ten. Taken together, one might expect all these factors to lead to some kind of linguistic homogenization, but this is not in fact the case. Instead, the men will regularly begin speaking in the tribal variety as a sign of tribal affiliation.

Diglossia

This is a form of standardized societal bilingualism, characterized by the complementary distribution of the functions of two language varieties: each of the varieties is used in a closed situational repertoire, with no overlapping. In outline, there is a relation of superiority/ inferiority between a high variety (H) and a low variety (L): H is more prestigious, standardized and written, official and formal, learnt in a dedicated institutional setting, and is symbolic of national and religious identity; L is local, acquired informally and expresses social solidarity. For example, sermons in a church or mosque, university lectures, or radio news bulletins are given in H, but L will be used for instructions to a worker or a TV serial (Ferguson 1959; Fishman 1980).

The Arabic-speaking world is a striking example of diglossia (and in some cases, triglossia), where H is *al-fusha* and L is *al-ammiyyah*, as well as Haïti, where there is a diglossic relationship between standard French (H) and a creolized variety (L). Similar situations are to be found in Germanophone Switzerland (H: Standard German or Hochdeutsch, L: Swiss German or Schweizerdeutsch).

Diglossia is the central fact of the knowledge systems of the societies in question, since the functional specialization which is its defining characteristic, taken together with the High variety's overwhelming dominance of the written form, means that all scientific, religious and academic domains, all 'serious' literature will be formulated in that variety alone. If, as Francis Bacon has it, 'knowledge itself is power', the importance of social implications of this state of affairs could hardly be exaggerated. In particular, whereas L is the language of conversation, acquired in the family from birth, H has to be learnt, studied. Since access to schooling may be reserved for members of an elite or a sex, the competence and power these domains convey and confer will not be accessible to 'monolingual' L speakers, nor will membership of the epistemic communities and social groups which are based on them. Specific social identities are reserved for H-competent language users only. (Diglossia is in reality an extreme form of the stylistic variation which is to be found in all societies which possess a writing system and a standard language (see Section 5.3).)

Polyglossia

This term refers to a form of standardized societal multilingualism where at least three language varieties coexist on the basis of complementary functional specializations.

The Grand Duchy of Luxemburg may be considered to be such a case, since French, German, Luxembourgeois, English and Portuguese all occupy fairly clearly demarcated functional niches. A glance at a national newspaper, the *Luxemburger Wort*, shows consistent patterning of language and domains: French is used for political and cultural issues, German for the financial news, Luxembourgeois for birth, wedding and death announcements, special offers in the supermarkets, sports. Yet despite the fact that from the second year of schooling onward French and German not Luxembourgeois are the languages of instruction, and that they also dominate in professional contexts, many Luxemburgers continue to refer to them as 'foreign languages' and government surveys report that 90 per cent of domestic oral exchanges are in Luxembourgeois.

Individual bilingualism

When we define individual bilingualism as the coexistence of two or more varieties within the same person, the presence of the word 'person' immediately alerts us to complex issues of identity. Unfortunately, discussions of individual identity at any level, from the most technical to the most naive, have almost invariably been based on monolingual norms and models, and on a unitary view of identity itself. This perspective is directly related to the rise of nationalism in nineteenth-century Europe and to the ideology of the nation-state, symbolized and reified by a language.

> Bilingualism inevitably results in intellectual inferiority; this is the pessimistic conclusion by all authors who have studied the problem at first hand ... The harmfulness of bilingualism can be explained: on the one hand, the effort required to learn a second language seems to reduce the quantity of intellectual energy available for the acquisition of other knowledge, and on the other hand, the child finds himself pulled to and fro between two systems of thought which are different from one another and he adulterates them both, depriving each of them of their originality and thereby depriving himself of centuries of the resources accumulated by his predecessors in each language. As Mr Laurie so rightly says, his intellectual growth is not doubled, but halved: he has great difficulty in firmly establishing integrity of mind and character. (Pichon 1936, pp. 101–3; my translation)[5]

In the second half of the nineteenth and first half of the twentieth centuries, this approach received zealous support from certain psychologists. The bilingual individual, whose loyalty to the state is already clearly suspect, was shown to be defective in moral and intellectual terms. Since the end of the Second World War, however, the pendulum has swung the other way. Since almost all the research in question was carried out by psychologists interested in measuring 'intelligence' and was largely uninformed in linguistic or sociocultural terms, there is little point in summarizing it here. Readers looking for a clear and authoritative discussion of our present state of knowledge regarding the cognitive development of bilingual children are referred to Bialystock (2001). (A less technical overview will be found in Harding-Esch and Riley 2003.)

In its simplest and commonest form, this approach amounts to viewing the bilingual individual as being the equivalent of two monolinguals in terms of both language identity and competence: a schizophrenic with perfect mastery of both varieties. This view is still so widespread, even among educationists, that it is worth spelling out the principal sociolinguistic objections to it:

- No one individual ever speaks even one language 'perfectly', in the sense of knowing all technical vocabularies, genres or regional, historical or stylistic variations.
- In general, bilinguals practice functional and situational specialization regarding their language choice. They use one language in certain situations – at work, for example, or when writing, or when discussing a particular topic – and another at home, or in church, and so on. They do not necessarily occupy the same discursive positions or social spaces, play the same roles, in both languages.
- The conditions of acquisition or learning of the two varieties and the specific situational and functional configuration which results determine the individual's form of (bilingual) competence and the principal constituents of his other social identity.

Plurilingualism

This term is used when referring to an individual who is capable of using appropriately several language varieties. As in the case of bilingualism, the plurilingual individual possesses a specific form of communicative competence which consists in managing his or her linguistic repertoire according to a wide range of situational and cultural factors and parameters including domains (the roles, statuses and identities of participants; acts, strategies and genres; channel and modality; tonality; aims; conversational principles and implication). However, the differences between monolingualism, bilingualism and plurilingualism are quantitative rather than qualitative: even the most 'monolingual' of individuals is constantly making similar decisions and choices, but precisely because they operate intralingually, they are considered to be stylistic differences, or differences in dialect or register, and not as differences between two languages. The circularity or reflexivity of this underlines the extent to which social representations and attitudes to language variation and varieties determine the perception and classification of plurilingualism.

Code-switching

I recently moved house for the first time in over twenty years. Amongst the treasures I found in the attic was a recording of a spoof interview I

61

made with Katja when she was twelve years old. To understand it, you need to know that Katja is a serious musician and was studying harp at the Conservatoire: all her musical knowledge and experience have been lived and acquired in French. You also need to know that her father is as bad at music as he is at maths:

F: In the last lesson you had, what was it?

K: I learnt about the *temps binaire* and the *temps ternaire*.

F: Oh, what's that? What's the *temps binaire*?

K: Well, it's a *temps* with two *temps*.

F: Uh huh. And the other one, what's that?

K: The *temps ternaire* is a *temps* with three *temps*.

F: Hmm. Suppose so. Good. What else have you done?

K: Lots of things.

F: Tell me about them.

K: The *gamme chromatique* and the *gamme mineure* and the *gamme majeure*.

F: Oh, what are they?

K: Well, the *gamme chromatique* is a ... a normal *gamme* with a *ton* in between each note, a *demi-ton chromatique*.

F: Uh huh. And what's the other one?

K: A *gamme majeure* is a *gamme* with two *demi-tons diatoniques* and a *gamme mineure* is a *gamme* with three *demi-tons diatoniques*.

F: Uh huh.

K: And the *demi-ton chromatique* is when it's for example *do–do dièse*. And the *demi-ton diatonique* is *do–ré bémol*.

F: Oh, yeah.

For some people, this kind of switching is clear evidence of incompetence and split identity and Katja's bilingualism should be banned or prevented. What such people fail to realize is that this impression of linguistic incompetence is the direct result of her musical competence. If she did not know about music (like her father, say) this gap in her English vocabulary would never come to light. Indeed, one could argue that the surest way to prevent this kind of behaviour would not be to do away with her bilingualism, but to do away with her *music*.

Nor is her identity split. She just happens to be a musician in French and, so far at least, has never needed to express herself in English on that subject. Her identity is a bilingual identity, one which she can use as a resource when speaking to another person who knows both languages.

When a bi- or plurilingual speaker changes from one language or language variety to another within an utterance or exchange or between two situations, he or she is implementing a strategy which facilitates the expression of an extremely wide range of functions and attitudes. These include compensating for a lack of lexical or syntactic resources, topicalization, affirming personal identity, including or excluding the interlocutor from a social group, humour, and so on. Since the 1960s, code-switching has been intensively researched by linguists, psycholinguists and sociolinguists (overviews will be found in most general texts on sociolinguistics and bilingualism; more detailed studies include Gardner-Chloros 1995; Heller 1988).

In an important early study, Blom and Gumperz (1972) examined code-switching patterns in Hemnesberget, a small community in northern Norway. They were able to show that, far from being random, such patterns were a highly systematic resource for signalling social meaning. The two varieties in question were Bokmål, one of the two forms of standard Norwegian, and Ranamål, the local dialect. Bokmål is historically associated with the aristocracy and governing elite, with Danish-leaning tendencies (Norway was part of the Danish empire from 1380–1840) and expresses national, cultural, political and eco-nomic ideas and values: it is learnt at school and used in church. Ranamål is symbolic of local values and is acquired at home. To this extent, the Hemnesberget situation resembles diglossia. However, whereas in diglossia the choice of variety is situationally determined, in Hemnesberget other social and interactional factors also need to be taken into account, since individuals and groups are free to make tactical choices to express their own attitudes towards the values vehiculated by each of the varieties. In these circumstances, general expectations of functional specialization become a communicative resource, since they can be met, flouted or commented upon. For example, students home from university switched from Ranamål to Bokmål if topics related to non-local values were introduced, while artisans, merchants and managers expressed their strong adhesion to local values through a consistent use of Ranamål except in church.

Moreover, as Geirr Wiggen (1997) points out, to understand fully these micro-level meaning-creating processes, we need to attend to the Norwegian sociolinguistic situation as a whole. At macro level, where the relations and oppositions between all language varieties can be seen as a set of resources for generating social meaning, this means taking into account Norway's other standardized variety, Nynorsk.

Although Bokmål was to all intents and purposes Danish, 'the majority of the people maintained their popular dialects quite unmarked by Danish, due to their illiteracy'. In the nineteenth century,

> under the influence of Romanticism it seemed important to Norwegians to establish a Norwegian national language through

which the Norwegian 'folk spirit' might express itself. Since the only established written language in Norway was Danish, the Norwegians had to search elsewhere for a truly non-Danish as well as non-Swedish linguistic basis for establishing the uniquely Norwegian standard expression. That basis was found in the popular dialects. (Wiggen 1997, p. 949)

Nynorsk is based on the empirical dialect studies of Ivar Aasen (1813–96) as summarized in his *Dictionary* (1850, 1873) and *Grammar* (1848, 1864). It was originally called Landsmål – 'the language of the country' – but this was changed to Nynorsk in 1929.

Aasen's motivations were nationalistic, social and educational. His standard was not based on any specific dialect. Rather, it was an attempt to find linguistic common denominators while at the same time wherever possible he avoided Danish or Swedish forms, often preferring archaic Norwegian terms. He was consciously and explicitly trying to model both national and personal identities:

> Nynorsk was meant ... to connote a Norwegian national adherence, and to lend a platform to the ordinary man and woman for the development of linguistic and cultural self-respect and local engagement beyond the local and private spheres. (*ibid.*, p. 950)

There have been numerous reforms of both varieties, but all efforts to produce a single common standard have been in vain. At the end of the twentieth century, the positions of supporters of the two varieties seem further apart than ever. Schools are free to choose the variety they use, but in 1993 only 17 per cent of primary schools had opted for Nynorsk. Bokmål plays a predominant role in higher academic institutions, the army and the prestigious parts of private enterprise:

> ... so while N(ynorsk) so far has remained a variety associated with ordinary people, with rural Norway, B(okmål) has maintained those connotations of power and erudition previously adhering to Danish ... Ridiculing N(ynorsk) is a popular sport in B(okmål) strongholds like the Oslo area and in socially upward mobility circles elsewhere. (*ibid.*, p. 954)

As Blom and Gumperz showed, and as subsequent studies (Trudgill 1995) have confirmed, choice of language variety remains a major resource in Norway for the expression of local and national identities, values and attitudes at group and individual level, these social meanings being generated by a systematic series of oppositions between varieties. Macro-level oppositions are instantiated and maintained in interactional episodes. However, in the course of an interaction, individuals may choose to code-switch for a variety of communicative reasons.[6]

One of the most important identity-related functions of code-switching mentioned earlier is its use to signal the exclusion or inclusion of an interlocutor from group membership. I recently attended a conference where I was the only native speaker of English, all the other participants being speakers of either Norwegian or Swedish. I have little difficulty in following Swedish, which I have been fortunate enough to learn through the marital method. However, as I went from room to room or group to group, I found that my presence sufficed to make all other participants switch to English, and this continued despite my trying to point out – in Swedish – that I could understand.

It is interesting to note that code-switching, which has traditionally been denigrated in many educational settings, both in the second-language classroom and in cases where the language of instruction is in competition with a local variety such as Alsatian or Breton, has begun to attract more favourable attitudes and treatment in recent years. Several reasons can be given for this development, all of them related directly or indirectly to issues of identity. These include the adoption of a policy of multiculturalism; a better understanding of the nature of bilingualism and its relation to self-image and educational success; the proliferation of various types of bilingual education, perhaps the most striking European example being the support for CLIL – 'Contact and Language Integrated Learning' emanating from both the European Commission and the Council of Europe (Marsh and Langé 1999); and the problematization of the native speaker as the model for second language learning.

Heteroglossia

This term, which we owe to Mikaïl Bakhtin (1981), refers to the coexistence within a single text of a multiplicity of language varieties or registers. In Bakhtinian stylistics, interlinguistic difference (i.e. differences between two languages) and intralinguistic difference (between genres and sociolects, for example) are relatively unimportant when compared to intertextual relations, of which heteroglossia and code-switching are major manifestations.

Plurilingual competence

After this brief survey of related terms, we are now, hopefully, in a better position to discuss what constitutes individual plurilingual competence. Perhaps it is easiest to start with a negative definition: such a competence is *not* a neat bundle of separate competences, one for each language, uniform with respect to domains and degree of mastery. Instead the level and the nature of an individual's competence varies from one variety to another according to his or her participation in specific categories of situated social interaction, to the ways in which varieties and domain patterns interrelate, and to the types of communication functions, practices and norms they call for (Coste *et al.* 1997b).

It is for these reasons, as we have just seen, that the most immediately striking aspect of plurilingual competence is code-switching/heteroglossia. Moreover, with the exception of truly diglossic or polyglossic situations which leave participants with no choice whatsoever, participants will necessarily have to negotiate and accommodate concerning the definition of the situation, choice of variety and their respective roles and identities. This is another reason why any analysis of either competence or identity must necessarily take into account the general sociolinguistic characteristics of the society in questioning the kinds of distinctions we have just reviewed. Language, as we have seen, is the principal mechanism of the social knowledge system, and both competence and identity are knowledge-based.

Finally, a crucial but often neglected constitutive element in competence is that, to be effective, it has to be legitimated (this will also be developed in the discussion of 'recognition', in Section 4.2). It is not sufficient for the individual to have the relevant capacities and intentions: he or she must have the right to perform the acts and to play the role in question of which these acts are the manifestation. Roles have to be socially warranted. This is true of any social interaction, but for the bi- or plurilingual person, the necessity to affirm specific aspects of his or her identity in ways which are appropriate to the situation in question can very easily become problematic because of the relatively higher volume of variants and modalities involved. It is essential for bilinguals to develop what one might call 'membershipping competence' in their various varieties if they are to be accepted in their intended roles, although the perceptions and attitudes of the interlocutors are also crucial in the inclusion or exclusion of individuals in and from social groups of all kinds.

Notes

1 Gandhi provided the perfect riposte: when asked what he thought of English civilization, he replied 'I think it would be a good idea'.
2 This term is not intended to carry any of the pejorative, Marxist-type connotations associated with 'ideology'. It is more in tune with Bacon's 'idols'.
3 In fact, many English speakers still refuse to accept the term 'plurilingual-

ism', but the language policy of the Council of Europe and its publications and translations are gradually propagating the term.

4 I have not adopted the perfectly cogent suggestion put forward by Hamers and Blanc that we should keep 'bilinguality' for the level of the individual and 'bilingualism' for the social level, simply because most authors prefer the paraphrases 'individual bilingualism' and 'social (or societal) bilingualism'.

5 Le bilinguisme est une infériorité intellectuelle; cette conclusion pessimiste est celle de tous les auteurs qui ont, sur du matériel concret, étudié la question ... Cette nocivité du bilinguisme est explicable; car, d'une part, l'effort demandé pour l'acquisition de la seconde langue semble diminuer la quantité disponible d'énergie intellectuelle pour l'acquisition d'autres connaissances, d'autre part et surtout, l'enfant se trouve ballotté entre des systèmes de pensée différents l'un de l'autre, et il les adultère tous les deux en les privant de leur originalité et en se privant par là même des ressources accumulées depuis des siècles par ses prédécesseurs dans chaque idiome. Comme le dit fort bien Monsieur Laurie, sa croissance intellectuelle n'est pas doublée, mais diminuée de moitié; son unité d'esprit et de caractère a beaucoup de peine à s'affirmer. (Pichon 1936, pp. 101–3)

6 To complete the picture, it should be noted that despite their differences adherents of Bokmål and Nynorsk are being obliged in many ways to adopt a common, conservative approach in order to resist the pressures caused by the entry of yet another variety into the equation: commercial Anglo-American.

3 Identity

As kingfishers catch fire, dragonflies draw flame;
  As tumbled over rim in roundy wells
   Stones ring; like each tucked string tells, each hung bell's
Bow swung finds tongue to fling out broad its name;
Each mortal thing does one thing and the same;
  Deals out that being indoors each one dwells;
  Selves – goes itself; *myself* it speaks and spells,
Crying *'What I do is me: for that I came'*.
       Gerard Manley Hopkins, *As kingfishers catch fire*.

3.1 Identity studies: some issues and approaches

A few years ago, I was strolling down the High Street in the French town of Nancy, where I have lived and worked for much of my life. It was June, and Rue St Jean was congested with tourist cars and caravans. My attention was suddenly caught by one particular vehicle, a minibus. The reason why I noticed it was that it bore the name, the crest and the Latin motto of a British university.

The minibus was being driven by a middle-aged man and there were about a dozen passengers, all of them young people around nineteen or twenty years old. A teacher and his students, obviously.

As I drew level with the bus, the teacher-driver lowered his window and asked for directions, in French:

> 'S'il vous plaît, monsieur, auriez-vous la gentillesse de m'indiquer le chemin le plus direct pour aller à la Place Stanislas.'
> ('Excuse me, but would you have the kindness to tell me the quickest way of getting to Place Stanislas.')

Now I don't know why, but I felt very awkward about speaking French to a compatriot, so I answered in English:

> 'Sure, left at the second set of traffic lights, you can't miss it.'

I could never have imagined the effect this would have. The students burst into laughter, rolling around slapping thighs and shoulders in great amusement, possibly because they interpreted my replying in English as a criticism of their teacher's French, which it certainly wasn't meant to be.

The teacher, who was visibly nettled, glared at me and said:

'But how do I know I can believe you if you answer me in English!'

In other words, before even beginning to interpret my message in terms of vocabulary, grammar and so on, he wanted to check on my identity, on the social and epistemic framework: was his interlocutor competent? Was I really a member of the social group (French residents of Nancy) who could be relied on to possess the information he wished to obtain? By replying in English, I had thrown doubt on the identity he wished to ascribe to me. And when it comes to the interpretation and legitimation of illocutionary forces, identity is the most important felicity condition of all.

For over 2000 years, 'identity' has been regarded as a philosophical aporia, a problem so deep that we can hardly formulate the questions, let alone the answers. Some idea of just how knotty a problem it is can be gathered from the fact that not only is the debate as intense now as it was in the times of Aristotle or Aquinas, say, but it is still essentially about the same issues and concepts – and they are still just as intractable and just as important: the mind/body/soul/brain problem, the monadic as against the multiple self, or the relationship of the individual to society, the survival of the soul after the body's physical extinction – all those dualisms, Cartesian or otherwise, along with solipsism, relativism, determinism and various other -isms that want to get in on the act. However, I would like to suggest that, to some extent at least, in the social sciences – precisely because they are *social* – some of these problems can be side-stepped or, as the philosophers say, 'bracketed'.

Philosophers are interested in 'conditions of sameness', criteria for saying that an entity, a human being, say, or a stone, continues through time (Noonan 1989 is a clear and accessible study of philosophical approaches to this and related questions). What criteria can we appeal to in order to show or believe that a given entity at a given point in time is the 'same' as a given entity at a different point in time? Again, if identity means something like 'the continuing existence of an entity', what are the conditions necessary to ensure continuation and how can we know that it has indeed taken place? And what is the relationship between physical identity and personal identity? Despite the efforts made over many centuries, and after seemingly endless discussions of challenges to simplistic one-to-one body–mind relationships such as Siamese twins and brain-transplants, reincarnation and resurrection,

70

no one has ever managed to establish any physical phenomena which would provide an adequate explanation for the constitution of personal identity.

One reaction to this conundrum has been an appeal to psychological factors as constitutive of personal identity. For Locke, the crucial factor is memory, and clearly this is an argument which resonates with the knowledge- and experience-based approach which has been discussed in the previous chapter: 'you are what you know'. In this perspective, the individual is seen as a site for knowledge, which is stored in memory and which underlies the competence which determines and is determined by participation in social activity. However, it is important to note that Locke was careful to distinguish between memory of facts and memory of experiences. This is a distinction which certainly has repercussions on the characteristics of the identity in question, but not in the sense that it establishes a dichotomy where factual memory is irrelevant and only experienced memories are relevant.

The appeal to memory as the crucial criterion for the constitution of personal identity has been extremely influential over a wide range of social sciences and sociopolitical agendas: a stock of common memories is fundamental to the rationale of almost any kind of minority rights or identity politics movement, as can be seen in the bourgeoning oral history projects or, indeed, in the widespread use of interviews and anecdotes as a source of data. For many people, whether specialists or not, the intuitive pull of this line of argument is magnified by the lens of their own experience: for example, those who have watched an elderly relative slowly losing their memory often cite their 'loss of their identity' as the most painful part of the process. As an acquaintance of mine remarked:

> 'I lost my mother three years before she died. Once she had lost her memory, we didn't share anything any more, she just wasn't Mum any more, not the same person, because she had no past, no shared memories.'

However, it has to be said that there are some important objections, or at least limitations, to this approach: in particular, memory is not infallible. Were I to ask you what you did on the day after your seventh birthday, the chances are (unless you are an astonishingly precocious eight-year-old, perhaps) that you would be unable to remember. Does this mean that you are no longer the same person as that little boy or girl? And then there are mistaken memories and false memories. I was born in Kent, to where my mother and elder brother had been evacuated in 1939. As a very small child, I went to sleep listening to the deeply comforting rumble of bombers on their way to and from Germany. One night, as my mother put me to bed, I asked her what the noise was. 'That's the Battle of Britain', she replied. Well, she did no such thing, of course. It is a historical impossibility. But I remember it clearly. 'Ah, yes, I remember it well.'

For many philosophers, though, discussion of 'criteria for the constitution of personal identity' is almost synonymous with 'a waste of time', because although any such criteria could provide evidence for the existence of something we might wish to *call* personal identity, they tell us nothing about what it actually *is*. In this view – which in many ways is simply the man in the street's 'Well it's obvious, isn't it? Everyone knows what identity is, so where's the problem?' – personal identity is an unassailable and unanalysable fact. This is one reading of the Cartesian ego: 'I think therefore I am', a purely mental entity, the sole certainty in a universe of doubts. And it is a universe of which 'I', Ego, is the centre, not God or Nature. When Lear tells Cordelia 'Nothing will come of nothing', it may be the most fundamental heresy of all – because the deity is precisely that, something out of nothing, self-created – but it is one destined to become the new orthodoxy: Descartes' 'I' is both the source and the product of the self. Giambattista Vico's concept of 'Maker's knowledge' – the theory that only the creator of an object can fully understand its nature – resonates to this fundamental in Descartes' thought. Both were to become the targets of postmodernist thunderbolts for their espousal of the unitary, essential self. Interestingly, Isaiah Berlin, in his comparative study of Herder and Vico's thought (1976), says that Vico was the very first to propound notions corresponding to modern understandings of culture and commonsense knowledge, which would seem to indicate a distinction between public and private spheres of knowledge which would become commonplace in discussions of the self and personal identity in the following centuries.

In highly schematic form, the biography of the Self in Western thought seems to fall into three main phases which one might label, rather unenlighteningly, Pre-Enlightenment, Enlightenment and Post-Enlightenment. The Pre-Enlightenment phase is one of great length and complexity, so much so that it might be regarded as little more than a crude pedagogical convenience, as a way of moving on to the interesting bit, the Enlightenment. Nonetheless, if we accept the argument that a characteristic of the Enlightenment was a new sense of self, we are logically obliged to ask in what sense was it new, how do modern selves differ from those that preceded them?

If we manage to avoid the pitfall of imagining that the modern sense of self differs from all previous representations of personhood in one and the same way, irrespective of their social, historical and cultural contexts, it becomes tenable to see the Renaissance as marking the emergence of modern individualism, a quest for self-determination and self-knowledge. The authentic, autonomous individual, free from religious and political ideology and from social convention, is no longer a sinner whose soul depends on the church for salvation, but Hamlet's 'paragon' who is 'noble in reason' and 'infinite in faculties'. First Protestantism, with its emphasis on soul-searching and private reading, then secular rationalism reshaped the foundations on which selves are based. Capitalism is the expression of the new individualism in the economic sphere (Weber 1904/1920; Tawney 1926): the self-made man is first of all a man-made self. Samuel Smiles' nineteenth-century panegyric to the work ethic and the new heroes of capitalism and science is tellingly entitled *Self-help* (1882) and the fundamentals of Adam Smith's economic theory are accurately summarized in the expression 'enlightened self-interest'.

In similar vein, when President Herbert Hoover wanted to define the essence of Americanism he described it as 'rugged individualism', and most other presidents, when attempting to encapsulate the American vision of personhood or citizenship, have done so on the basis of the economic rewards for individual effort: Theodore Roosevelt, for example, 'wish(ed) to preach, not the doctrine of ignoble ease, but the doctrine of the strenuous life' (1899) and he believed that 'The first requisite of a good citizen ... is that he shall be able and willing to pull his weight' (1904, p. 85), adding in a speech on another occasion that:

> A man who is good enough to shed his blood for his country is good enough to be given a square deal afterwards. More than that no man is entitled to, and less than that no man shall have. (1904, p. 224)

It is also entirely consistent with this view of the person as a unitary active agent and citizen that he regularly railed against 'fifty-fifty Americans':

> A hyphenated American is not American at all ... Americanism is a matter of the spirit and of the soul. Our allegiance must be purely to the United States. We must unsparingly condemn any man who holds any other allegiance. (1915, p. 457)

The American and French revolutions were both largely motivated by concepts of the rights of man which were entirely incompatible with monarchical divine right, or any other form of absolutist rule. Society was the result of the voluntary association of free men, citizens, not subjects, and democracy is a process of self-determination at both the social and the individual levels. Geertz summarizes and defines the ideology of individualism, egocentric autonomy, as one in which the person is seen as

> A bounded, unique, more or less integrated motivational cognitive universe, a dynamic center of awareness, emotion, judgement, and action organized into a distinctive whole and set contrastively both against other such wholes and against its social and natural background ... (1983, p. 59)

The malleable self, as opposed to the fixed and unitary view of identity inherited from much Christian theology which was and is so common, makes change and progress possible through its activism in the spiritual, political, economic and scientific spheres, improving things, whereas the whole thrust of Pre-Enlightenment society was directed at the maintenance of the God-given status quo, since by definition any change could only be regression. Individuals, denied social mobility and playing only a limited and fixed range of social roles, with only a passive responsibility for their souls, living in a world whose epistemic contours were almost entirely delineated by revealed knowledge, simply did not experience the conditions necessary or conducive to self-reflection. Hence, almost certainly, the common perception that in the constitution of medieval selves (for example) it is collective identities which are preponderant.

One of the clearest manifestations of the shift to Enlightenment views of the self is the emergence of new literary genres. This is not surprising, given the relationship between identity and discourse which we have been examining: changes in identity necessitate the development of fresh forms of discourse to express the new positions in question. The modern novel may have long, deep historical roots, but there can be little doubt that its emergence as a prominent or even dominant genre in both quantitative and qualitative terms largely parallels the spread of Enlightenment thought and practices. This is particularly true, of course, as regards the *Bildungsroman*, a novel which sets out to describe and analyse the trajectory of a young protagonist during which he or she acquires maturity and sensibility through reflection on sometimes bitter experience. What is being 'built' or formed in such works is the individual as an individual through a process of self-discovery.

The literary historians recognize Goethe's *Wilhelm Meister's Apprenticeship* (1795) as prototypical of this genre, though Anglophone readers will probably be more familiar with cases such as Dickens's *Great Expectations* (1860), in the course of which Pip discovers that the self-image on which he has come to base his views, values and relationships – succinctly put, he has become a snob – is

74

extremely flawed. Obliged by events to revise his view that his money and social position are the natural if mysterious result of his own personal qualities, he attains a far greater depth of self-understanding. But it is also important to note that in successive scenes, Dickens systematically uses a series of binary oppositions – respectable/ criminal, rich/poor, town/country, home/abroad, gentry/bourgeoisie – to frame and investigate the social factors which form the contexts in which Pip's experience and identity are shaped.

The *Bildungsroman* overlaps with two other genres: the first is children's literature, including both works for and works about children and childhood: the Victorian period is characterized by a sudden and immense outpouring of publications of this kind, indicating a new awareness of and interest in childhood that was itself a reflection of the new individualism. This has to be seen, however, as the culmination of developments which had begun in the early modern period, leading to what Philippe Ariès (1960, English translation 1962) has described as 'the invention of childhood' and the nuclear family. Although some of Ariès's arguments have been seriously challenged (Gottlieb 1993), others, such as the progressive specialization of children's clothing, games and sleeping accommodation, are clearly indicative of the emergence of a new category of identity. (See the discussion on the formation of Victorian selves at the end of this chapter.) The second is confessional literature, itself a sub-genre of biography and autobiography, which had been developing from the Renaissance onwards. For example, the celebrated goldsmith and sculptor Benvenuto Cellini (1500–1571) has left us a particularly vivid picture of himself, as authorial modesty in the presentation of self and the stylistic conventions and discursive positions through which it is transmitted had not yet developed (English translation 1956). Boasting is the most transparent form of self-presentation. Autobiographical literature increased exponentially from the eighteenth century onwards. Rousseau is a key figure in all these lines of development. His *Confessions* (1782) is probably the first major example of detailed secular self-examination and introspection made public, initiating a genre which is still in full flood. With sin transformed into a psychopathology, the way is open to the discovery of the unconscious, to Freud and to Surrealism. The urge to tell all, to reveal one's self, even when such self-exposure can only lead to moral condemnation and social ostracism, runs via Hazlitt and the decadent poets of the nineteenth century (names which come to mind are Swinburne and Baudelaire) into the innumerable accounts of self-degradation by writers described by Roy Porter (2003, p. 11), in a moment of apt alliterative artfulness, as 'latter-day drunks, drifters, drug-addicts, drop-outs and depressives'. The search for the authentic self reaches its extreme form in the figure of the Romantic poet or artist as outsider, as outcast, rejecting conventional thought and morals and willing to talk or write about it.

Identities multiply or are metamorphosed as new discursive positions are staked out: to Porter's list, we can add numerous other types, such as bohemian, *flâneur*, dandy or hippy, as well as near-archetypal fictional creations like Frankenstein's Monster, Dr Jekyll and Mr Hyde and Dracula.[1] At the same time, an audience is being created: readers, of course, but also therapists and, latterly, counsellors. In the past half-century or so – neatly coinciding with Kaufman's (2004) dating of the emergence of modern self-consciousness, as cited in the Introduction – one of the most remarkable features has been the proliferation of the discourse of counselling, of counselling services of every kind and, of course, of counsellors. Nothing could exemplify more clearly the reflexive relationship between discourse and identity than the rapid penetration of counselling into every social nook and cranny, especially if we include quasi-synonyms such as advising, guidance and coaching, as a flip through the Yellow Pages will confirm: family and marriage; drugs, alcohol and substance abuse or dependency; a great diversity of post-traumatic stress (victims of accidents or crimes; bereavement; war service, etc.); bullying; anger control; eating disorders; obsessive behaviour disorders; self-assertion; shopping, fashion; life-style; careers and employment; language learning.

When it comes to theories of the history of identity, the acid test is the treatment reserved for identity cards. There is very general agreement that the multiplication, standardization and generalization of identity documents is a characteristic of modern societies, and, in particular, of nation-states and that this phenomenon has been steadily increasing in intensity over the past two and a half centuries. Equally clear is the fact that successive technological innovations have systematically been harnessed to provide more accurate, detailed, reliable and unfalsifiable forms of document: printing, photography, fingerprinting, anthropometric and biometric techniques and electronic chips, for example, as well as increasingly efficient and rapid computer-based retrieval, support, collation and information-sharing systems, all backed up by more and more powerful surveillance systems such as closed-circuit television and the monitoring of all forms of telecommunications. This, as I say, is generally accepted, but it is a state of affairs that is open to widely differing, indeed contradictory, interpretations.

On the one hand, it is possible to argue that these are manifestations of a continuing process of refinement of identities and the emergence of the distinctive self, tangible evidence of an underlying tectonic shift in the configuration of identities and of an increase in individual self-awareness. In this version of history, the identity card is the outward sign of inward self-affirmation, with society forced to take more and more sophisticated measures to keep abreast of increasing individualism. The teleological assumptions of orthodox nineteenth-century history result in an epic journey where mankind wakes from a long night of collective medieval torpor to march towards the dawn of the Renaissance, making heroic and unbroken progress until, well, us and now actually.

For others, though, and here we must count the postmodernist philosophers, and in particular Foucault (1966) and Althusser (1971), this narrative is, not to put too fine a point on it, a massive con-trick. Far from freeing the individual from the shackles of medieval obscurantism, the Enlightenment project is simply a way of transferring power and control from the Church, where it was justified by religious ideology based on revealed knowledge, to the State, where it is justified by humanism and reason (or as they would have it, 'humanism' and 'reason'). For them, humanism is the new hypocrisy, another ideology maintaining the power of the elite – the bourgeoisie, not the clergy, this time – by a process of mystification which convinces individuals that they are free, when all the time they are being slotted into the State's administrative and bureaucratic systems more and more precisely. And one of the major instruments of State control – along with the police force, the school system and taxation – is the identity card, or rather the system of surveillance and control of which it is the visible tip. If individuals are described there in greater and greater detail – from genealogical and biographical data down to the whorls on their fingertips, the patterns of their irises or their gait – it is indeed so that they can be 'recognized' and 'identified', but on whose terms? Certainly not on their own, as anyone who gets caught fabricating their own identity card or their own identity soon finds out.

Of course, it is possible to resist, but it is also dangerous or criminal or both, hence our perennial fascination with many of the stock figures of modern fiction. It is striking that deliberate and dangerous ambiguity of identity is a common trait to an otherwise highly disparate group of figures, including what are probably the two most important categories in popular literature, spies and private detectives (who are usually 'masters of disguise'), as well as con-men and 'gentlemen' burglars, imposters and frauds, anybody with some kind of unconventional sexual orientation, wizards and witches, superheroes-in-hiding, orphans and adulterers, escaped convicts, immigrants and extra-terrestrials, day-dreamers – the list seems endless.

This point about individuals who resist the identities which others wish to impose upon them provides us with a major objection to the postmodernist, post-Enlightenment version of the history of identity, according to which individuals are merely discursive constructs, texts or carriers of ideology: such an account is completely deterministic. It is also extraordinarily condescending and it flies in the face of the facts, discursive and otherwise. It is condescending because it assumes that only the authors of such texts have the ability and the intelligence to see that they are the target of social pressures. It is also logically vulnerable on the bases of both *tu quoque* and the Cretan liar: if all discourse is merely ideology whose meaning is independent of authorial intent, and if all discourses are equally 'true' (which is tantamount to saying that there is no such thing as truth), why should we believe these authors when they tell us we are merely social automata? And it is inaccurate because, as we will see in more detail in the section on membershipping strategies, resistance is part of our daily lives, is recognized, prized, even celebrated. Ordinary people are quite capable of challenging and even changing the identities which other individuals and institutions try to impose upon them. That, after all, is what all those minority rights movements are about.

However, we must not throw out the baby – insights into the ways identities are constructed in and through discourse – with the bathwater – unwarranted and politically motivated over-generalizations about individual lack of awareness and powerlessness.

In a sense, the whole aim of anthropology is to ask 'What does it mean to be a human being?' What, that is, are the parameters and limits, the degrees of variability, of human nature? So it is not surprising to find the self, personhood and identity at the very centre of anthropological inquiry, with its sister discipline, ethnography adding the question '– and what does it mean to be French, English or Cantonese?' (Sperber 1985 is an illuminating discussion of this distinction.) Together, then, these disciplines examine the essential and local forms and processes shaping 'identity'.

Most people working in this area would agree that the agenda for modern anthropological discussion of selfhood and personal identity was set by Marcel Mauss in his 1938 Huxley Memorial Lecture, 'A category of the human mind: the notion of person; the notion of self'. Mauss puts forward a theory according to which there existed in the past bounded societies consisting of totemic clans, each clan having a fixed stock of names transmitted by recognized procedures, the bearer(s) of a name being reincarnations of their predecessors back to mythical times and dancing out the fact at rituals. These he called 'personnages'. These identities were often symbolized by masks – 'personae'.

Children are recognized as reincarnations of particular ancestors: The individual is born with his name and his social functions. The number of individuals, names, souls and roles is limited in the clan and the line of the clan is merely a collection of rebirths and deaths of individuals who are always the same. (in Carrithers *et al.* 1985, p. 5; see also Allen 1985, pp. 26–45 in the same collection of papers for a detailed discussion of Mauss's theory.)

> ... the clan is conceived of as being made up of a *certain number of persons*, in reality of 'characters' (*personages*) ... the role of all of them is realy to act out, each insofar as it concerned him, the prefigured totality of the life of the clan.

Perhaps the best way of understanding this reincarnation/name/personnage idea is to look at aristocratic societies, where one is born into a title and its properties and functions: The Ninth Lord Shawfield of Effingham inherits the name, rights, duties and property of numbers one to eight by right of birth. The title and the kind of identity it indexes precede and survive the individuals who bear them and are unrelated to their abilities, temperaments, qualifications, and so on. Mauss cites examples of such societies in Africa, Polynesia, Malaysia, North America and Australia, but pays closest attention to the Romans, who gave the persona a legal and moral status: slaves could not be personae, as they had no legal existence, and in some societies the old, the infirm, the young, and (unmarried or childless) women might be excluded. The age at and conditions in which the individual attains personhood also vary from one society to another. There are even societies where the individual only becomes a full person at death, as we shall shortly see.

Mauss argues that the concept of a form of identity which survives the individual after death was picked up by the Church (via Aristotle) as the idea of an immortal soul. However, the Christian apologists added the notion that all individuals, not just those recognized by society as personae, but children, women and slaves, possessed metaphysical and moral value, that persons were sacred. In the seventeenth and eighteenth centuries, sectarian movements developed a philosophy of this person, the self, positing and examining ideas of individual freedom, conscience and agency, ideas that influenced the big gun philosophers like Leibniz, Descartes, Spinoza, Hume, Berkeley, Fichte, Kant – and led to the Declaration of the Rights of Man and the French Revolution. Anticipating in detail, and with far more evidence, certain ideas of Michel Foucault and the postmodernists, Mauss insists that this interest in the notion of an autonomous self is a characteristic of modernism and unique to Western thought.

In the seventy years since it was published, Mauss's theory has been extremely influential and there have been many anthropological studies of the concepts of person and self and of the construction of identity in specific societies. (I know of no single-volume survey of the whole field, but useful general discussions will be found in Lévi-Strauss 1977; Shweder and Levine 1984; Levine 1992; Giddens 1991.) However, in 1985 Joan la Fontaine published an article 'Person and individual: Some anthropological reflections' which provides us with an extremely useful set of examples and a cogent review of Mauss's ideas, and extends the theory with her own powerful suggestions concerning the main source of variation in the concept of the person. She discusses published ethnographies of four traditional societies (full bibliographical details will be found under the reference to La Fontaine), all agricultural peoples without centralized political institutions. There are many differences between them, but

> ... overall they resemble one another in their concepts more than they resemble the individualist West ... in these four societies, human beings are seen as composite creatures; in all four, the individual human being is composed of material and immaterial components ... concepts of the person serve to identify and explain a wide range of behaviour, emotions and events. None of the concepts are strictly comparable with the concept of person which characterises individualism, for the elements are not unified into a whole which of itself has significance. (La Fontaine 1985, p. 126)

All four concepts are based on different ways in which the individual participates in tradition.

For the Tallensi of Ghana, for example, a human being has *sii*, which is not life itself, but which constitutes the living body as a unique identity, an individual in our terms. An individual's possessions are imbued with their *sii*, taboos prevent conflict between the *sii* of an eldest son and his father. *Siis* attract and repulse one another, giving rise to likes and dislikes. *Sii* vanishes at death. The living body distinguishes persons (*niriba*) from ancestors, ghosts and non-human spirits. The immaterial aspects distinguish men from animals (except for some sacred crocodiles, since they are manifestations of the ancestors, therefore persons).

Individuals are distinguished from one another by their distinct *sii*, not by names for they identify individuals with 1) an event in the life history of his family (the public name) and 2) an ancestral guardian (the private name). A 'personal identity shrine' embodies the fate already prepared for its owner and is associated with a set of ancestors; it thus distinguishes him or her as an individual but in terms of a place in a system of social relations. 'A human being's unique identity is thus determined from the first by his place in society.' The quality *yam* (wisdom, good judgement), which is located in the abdomen, increases with age and enhances its owner's personhood.

The concept of person here refers to a 'moral career'. The completed person, whether Tallensi or Lugbara or Taita (two of the other groups she discusses), is the product of a whole life:

> In Western societies, the conferring of a name serves to achieve the same end: personhood and individuality are thus identified from the beginning. But for the Tallensi, personhood is finally validated at death. It is the completion of a proper life which qualifies an individual for full personhood, for marriage and the birth of children are essential prerequisites ... no individual qualities of behaviour or temperament can disqualify a parent from person-hood; conversely, no matter how loved and admired an individual may be, if he or she fails to fulfil the ideal pattern of life and leaves no children, then full personhood has not been attained. (*ibid.*, p. 128)

She concludes that Mauss's theory has been validated by subsequent ethnographic work. The concept of the social personality allows us to see Tallensi, Lugbara and Tait ideas as concepts of the person seen as the sum of statuses. However, the concept of the person in individualism is different, the *personne morale* does not refer to statuses (Mauss uses 'personnage' for that). In individualism, the concept of person implies a general moral status accorded to human beings by virtue of their humanity, which recognizes their autonomy and responsibility for their actions. As Mauss says, it is the extension into the moral sphere of the unique nature of the individual. By contrast, the Tallensi, the Taita and the Lugbara do not generalize, they particularize and personhood varies according to social criteria which contain the capacities of the individual within defined roles and categories. In this perspective, personhood is seen as a status reserved for defined categories of people, parents or men, and those who are not persons are individuals.

In the West, where the dominant ideology is individualism, society is represented as being constituted of autonomous equal units and the institutions which reflect this vision are based on a rule of law, framed by the state, where persons are citizens, with all people, even rulers (ideally), being subject to law. As Weber pointed out, this principle is the defining characteristic of bureaucratic organization. The main features of such structures are a clear distinction between office and office-holder, and hence between the individual and the social role, and the allocation of authority on the basis of fitness for office, fitness being of course a quality of individuals. The equality of persons and competition for office are thus integral to the structure of Western society. Hierarchy and inequality are conceptualized as attributes of social roles; all individuals are equal as persons.

By contrast, the Tallensi, the Taita and the Lugbara base their concept of society on tradition, a tradition established once and for all in the distant past. 'Society' is the projection over time of the original founders, heroes or ancestors of the tribe and its internal and external boundaries are established by a systematic genealogy which relates living people to these original beings. In such a society each new baby has a position defined at birth.

La Fontaine's conclusion is that the Western concept of the individual is unique. However, as this summary of her article shows, so is every other society's.

A number of social psychologists have arrived at similar conclusions, but by a very different route. At the beginning of the twentieth century, Cooley set out his theory of the 'Looking-glass self', which became a hugely popular and influential metaphor for the genesis or construction of the self:

> A self-idea ... seems to have three principal elements: the
> imagination of our appearance to the other person; the imagination
> of his judgement of that appearance and some sort of self-feeling
> such as pride or mortification. (Cooley 1902/1964, p. 184)

Despite this recognition of the role of social factors in the emergence of the self, Cooley insisted that the self remained both active and assertive. Although he found Cooley's general approach too introspective, these ideas were taken up by the sociologist George Herbert Mead, who argued (Mead 1934 and *passim*) that minds and selves can only emerge as a result of communicative interaction, and that what is called 'the mind' is in fact an internal conversation based entirely on language and social meanings. We can see this in terms of an 'I' and a 'Me', where both are part of the 'self', but where the 'I' is the individual as having consciousness, and the 'Me' is the individual as an object of that consciousness, including the internal, subjective representation of the Person, the site of social identity.

From the 1960s onwards, this theory has been resurrected and developed by social theorists in various forms and combined with ideas borrowed from a very diverse group of thinkers, including psychologists (Bruner 1999), sociologists and linguists, who share this vision of discourse as the primary mechanism of socialization and the construction of selves. A clear and influential synthesis has been drafted by the neo-Marxist Ian Burkitt who, in his study *Social Selves: Theories of the Social Formation of Personality*, argues that:

> The self is social in its entirety. Only if we begin from the study of

social relations can we truly understand how individuals are social selves ... social life is the source of individuality and human beings only develop as truly human within a social context. (1991, p. 215)

This affirmation obviously has important implications for any kind of constructivist approach, where cognition is seen as a socially mediated activity, since it provides a bridge between interpersonal and intrapersonal, showing that 'social' and 'individual' aspects of cognition and the identity formation processes, far from being unrelated or even contradictory, are the distal and proximal motions of one and the same mechanism.

Burkitt's formulation may well strike you as overly deterministic, so it is important to remember that certain of the membershipping strategies discussed in Section 3.4 are clear evidence of our individual ability to resist, negotiate and manage our identities. In addition, metalinguistic activity of almost any kind can be seen as strategies for the reconfiguration of identities, for redefining the speaker's *ethos* or self-image (see Section 5.1).

There is, then, an increasing weight of evidence drawn from disciplines across the board that identity is socially constructed, that our sense of self can only emerge as the result of communicative interaction with others. Children raised outside society do not acquire language, though they have the capacity to do so, and for that very reason, they fail to form selves.

Since both anthropologists and social psychologists insist on the importance of language and discourse as the mechanism for the construction of identities, it is not surprising that linguists should have been keen to examine in real detail just how that mechanism functions. At least three major lines of investigation have been opened up. The first concerns the role of language as a component of ethnic identity and there is already a copious literature on this topic, much of it related to multilingual communities (Fishman 1980, 2001; Haarman 1986. See Section 2.5). The second, an offshoot of anthropological studies of rearing practices, deals with the ways adults speak to children in different cultures according to social expectancies of competent adult persons (Ochs and Schieffelin 1984; Andersen 1991). This will be the topic of Section 3.5 below.

The third, relatively recent and relatively neglected line concentrates on deictics and address systems in general and pronouns in particular. An especially interesting and detailed study is Mühlhäusler and Harré *Pronouns and People* (1990). They examine the pronominal systems of dozens of languages from all round the world and present convincing evidence that they vary in the social space, positions and functions allocated to the 'I' and that these correlate with variations in the ways in which identities are conceived and configured, represented and enacted. 'Identities' are constructed appropriately through the acquisition of certain practices, particularly those involved in taking and assigning responsibility: individuals have to learn a local theory of personhood which is to a large extent both summarized and instantiated in the pronoun system and other communicative practices.

For example, following Mauss and La Fontaine, they hold that the Western notion of 'Self' as the embodied self, the self-within-the-skin, where the physical and the psycho-social are co-terminous, is by no means universal and that this is revealed in language, particularly in the words and systems expressing social deixis. They reject previous, linguistic approaches such as Bloomfield's on the grounds that they attempt to explain pronoun choice purely in grammatical terms, as if no other forms of knowledge were necessary, which is demonstrably untrue: use determines form and pronominal systems develop according to the social demands made on them. Grammarians have focused on the anaphoric functions of pronouns and neglected their deictic and indexical functions.

Despite widespread belief to the contrary, not all languages have pronominal systems with three 'persons' and two numbers. Grammatical descriptions are still limited to the traditional view that only three persons are possible – the person speaking, the person spoken to and the person spoken about, where the Speaker is always the central, unmarked category – but the existence of such genres as baby-talk in English or certain kinds of doctor–patient discourse ('How are we today?') and of hearer-oriented languages such as Inuit Potowamini shows that this is not the case. There are languages where 'self' may include close members of one's family, and there are languages, such as Iaca (New Caledonia) for example, which have sets of pronouns marked for different tenses, which contradicts Western notions of physical continuity. There are languages such as Inuit and Japanese which are group- rather than speaker-oriented, so that individuals speak first and foremost as representatives of their collectivity. This seems to explain partly at least the Inuits' well-documented collective behaviour: when one laughs, all laugh, when one cries, all cry.

All in all, pronoun choice and use can be observed to vary according to a wide range of social parameters, including the spatial and social distance of the addressee from the speaker, gender, kinship status, social status and age group or generation. Even in cases where number is a factor, the use of the plural is by no means always determined by the arithmetical facts: the first-person plural is often not a real plural but an index of respect and distance, and it can also serve to include or exclude the addressee. Membership and membershipping are frequently more important than number.

Mühlhäusler and Harré put forward a 'Thesis of double location' according to which a person, being an incorporated being, located in a specific socio-temporal context, including physical objects and socio-historical events, necessarily has a point of view. At the same time, the person is also situated within a deontological framework of rights and duties, and therefore has a sense of moral responsibility. The individual's identity is the product or meeting point between these sets of relational structures. Local theories of personhood are summarized and instantiated in the pronominal system and also expressed through other communicative norms and practices.

It is interesting to note in this respect that the technical linguistic terminology used in the discussion of these topics and of argumentation – terms such as 'discursive position', 'local knowledge', 'topos', 'social deixis', 'double location', and so on – is based on the same conceptual metaphor (perhaps 'Opinion is place' would capture its essentials) as those used in everyday conversation and that some of them (e.g. 'position' or 'point of view') are common to both genres. Expressions such as:

> I see (or hear) where you're coming from.
> Je te vois venir. ('I know what you're leading up to.')

are metaphorical conflations of the individual's physically incorporated, phenomenological and spatio-temporal nature and of his or her location in the social, epistemic and moral matrix, which supports both the Mühlhäusler and Harré 'thesis of double location' and the wider observation that specific languages express local theories of personhood.

My own attention was drawn to this issue by a Burmese student of mine as early as 1985. Although he was a specialist in French, he confessed to me that he was having problems because he found French 'such an impolite language'. Somewhat surprised, I pressed him for details or examples.

> 'The word "je",' he replied. 'In my language, I have an "I" for when I am superior or inferior to you, for when I am pleased with you or angry with you, so that when I speak French, I always feel like a bull in a china shop, never respectful, never expressing my attitudes appropriately.'[2]

In this context, it is interesting to note that the French pronoun *on* can, subject to multiple syntactic and pragmatic constraints, be used as a substitute for *any* other term in the pronominal system, a fact which should be kept in mind when we are dealing in generalizations such as 'the Western sense of self'.

It is indicative of the importance which identity has taken on as a central concept in so many areas of modern life and thought that it has come to be the subject of investigation over a wide range – possibly, even, the totality – of the social sciences: anthropology, sociology, social psychology and linguistics are the disciplines to which one is most likely to appeal in a study of the relationship between language and identity, but other major disciplinary areas such as politics and history are also directly concerned with identity issues. Moreover, the establishment of university departments such as Women's Studies, Black Studies and any number of cultural, ethnic and language studies, such as Jewish, French or Maori studies, bears witness to the energizing, focalizing effect which the concept continues to have in academe. Strangely enough, although the existence of such disciplines and departments is clearly postulated on the notion of identity, there is to my knowledge no department of Identity Studies, in the sense of a department which would be devoted to the investigation of identities right across the board and from a multiplicity of disciplinary angles. Still, I have taken the risk in my section heading of suggesting that there would definitely be a place for such an interdiscipline and there certainly exist already a small number of research centres dealing with identity theory and processes as such, rather than using the concept as a fresh and insightful way of establishing the contours of a discipline.

3.2 Social identity: you are what you know

As we have seen, philosophers can discuss 'identity' as a quality which entities 'have' without reference to other entities, since it is intrinsic. To put it simplistically, a stone does not need another stone to tell it what it is. Socially speaking, though, 'identity' is a quality which is ascribed or attributed to an individual human being by other human beings. We *do* need other people to tell us who we are, and, as we shall shortly see, they do so all the time: waiters and doctors, siblings and bus conductors, colleagues and friends all constantly bombard us with instructions concerning the positions and roles we occupy or which they wish us to occupy, what groups we are and are not members of. And, as we shall also see, we ourselves jockey for position, sending out a stream of identity claims.

We also change from role to role. In what sense is it the 'same' person who is present in successive situations? Here, clearly, the linguist's and the philosopher's concerns coincide, though we will be placing the emphasis in this book not so much on the self as on social identity and the social processes through which it is established, attributed, negotiated and manifested. And it is also our interest in identity as social process which precludes us from appealing to reductionist approaches where identity can be defined and discussed in vitro as it were, decontextualized and, above all, desocialized. In social terms, identity can, by definition, only be treated with reference to others, since others are its principal source. Discussing social identity as if it were an intrinsic quality of one person makes about as much sense as discussing the sound of one hand clapping. I take this to be the point of Berkeley's dictum *Esse est percipi* ('To be is to be perceived') and of Sartre's 'Il suffit qu'on me regarde pour que je sois ce que je suis' ('It only needs someone to look at me for me to become what I am.') Socially speaking, identity is as much the product of the gaze of others as it is of our own making. We will return to this point under the headings of role (Section 3.3) and ethos (Section 5.2).

Again, one of the few things most people working on identity agree about is that a principal source of difficulty lies in the fact that the term is used in two very different ways, as illustrated in Figure 3.1.

On the one hand, we use 'identity' to talk about what makes individuals just that, individual. What makes 'me' *me*, as opposed to all other individuals, the agent of my actions, the continuing locus of my thoughts and memories, separately embodied in a numerically and physically distinct organism, which self-reports using the pronoun 'I', which is subjective and private and which has a proper name.

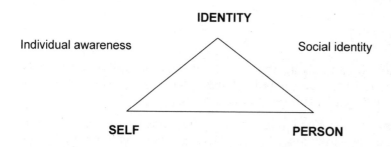

Figure 3.1 Identity, Person and Self

Table 3.1 Identity, self and person

Self: Numerical identity (*which* individual?)	Person: Social identity (*what sort of* individual?)
Private, subjective	Public, social
Reports as 'I'/'me'	Addressed as 'you'
The agent of my actions	A set of roles
Essential individual	Member of groups
Continuity of memory: Diachronic locus	Participant in interactions: Synchronic focus

On the other hand, we use 'identity' to talk about what makes this individual like other individuals in terms of shared characteristics, memberships, the 'you' that others address and construct, report on and to (see Table 3.1). For instance, when we say:

Gloria Peason is a 40-year-old mother of three who works as an accountant for Investeuro, votes Liberal and is an active member of the Ramblers Association

we have categorized Gloria in terms of her

- age cohort
- gender and family
- occupation
- political affiliation
- residence
- leisure activity

Here, then, we are talking about *social identity*, the sum of all the sub-groups of which the person is a member. All these categories are related to language in at least three different ways:

1) They are encoded in language: expressions such as 'accountant', 'mother' and 'Liberal' are selected from the repertoire from which identities can be constructed, different languages and societies having in varying degrees different repertoires.
2) These different aspects of Gloria's identity are likely to influence indexically the ways she talks and the ways people talk to her – as mother, accountant, rambler, and so on. Her communicative practices, the vocabulary and grammar she uses, will vary according to the particular role she is playing at any given

time. They are the dynamic enactment and expression of her identity.

3) Gloria is a member of more than one speech community. In other words, she might enact different memberships in different languages. Gloria Peason is also Mrs Lopes. She met Manuel her husband whilst on holiday in Madrid. They use Spanish at home and because of her language skills Gloria is regularly called on to help in the Foreign Exchange department. Like all bilinguals, she code-switches between her languages according to the specific roles she is called upon to play, according, that is, to the situationally salient aspect of her identity.

We can generalize schematically, though by no means exhaustively, from Gloria's example as in Table 3.2.

Table 3.2 Parameters of social identity

Figuration	Aspect
male, female	Gender
teenager, pensioner, middle-aged	Age
deaf, hearing	Audition
Londoner, Liverpudlian	Residence
lawyer, welder, cashier, bus conductor, bookseller	Occupation
Plymouth Brethren, Muslim, atheist, R.C., C. of E.	Religion
Green, socialist, conservative	Politics
chess player, swimmer	Pastime, sport
married, single, divorced	Marital status
Jamaican, Irish, Pakistani	Ethnicity
speaker of Urdu, Spanish, Arabic, English	Language(s)

There is, I am aware, an important objection to the approach to identity in interaction which I am adopting here. Do terms such as those I have used above to illustrate the parameters of social identity have referents which enjoy some sort of independent existence or are they purely and simply social constructs? Essentially, the question concerns the relationship between social structures, as identified and labelled by social scientists, and intersubjective couplings, as they are formed by individuals. In this particular context, then, it concerns the relationship between the 'figurations' I have used as descriptive and analytic terms, and the actual categories and perceptions constructed and used by participants in communicative events. What evidence do we have that these terms have any kind of psychological reality? Just as some have argued that *langue* is an invention of grammarians and *culture* has been invented by anthropologists, terms such as 'religion' or 'occupation' might be no more than just that – terms, expressions serving an analytical and highly reductive purpose in the theoretician's world of disourse, but not forming any part of a set of systematic correspondences with events in the participants' world. In brief, are such things real, and are social scientists and the person in the street talking about the same things?

It is important to note that, in this case at least, the social scientist's terms largely coincide with those used by participants in real-life interactions. Whereas most people get through life satisfactorily without ever using or needing expressions such as 'determiner in a nominal group', it is an objectively observable fact that they do frequently need and use expressions like 'religion' and 'occupation'. Studying how they use them and bringing the social scientist's understanding of the terms into line with that usage, doing discourse analysis, may be difficult and complex, but it would also be pointless unless based on the belief that there are systematic correspondences between what people say and their vision of reality, on the one hand, and between their individual vision and other people's visions on the other. As we saw in the last chapter, the individual can only exist in society to the extent that society exists in the individual.

One answer to this conundrum is to be found in the Durkheimian notions of the social representation and the process of *exteriorization*. In a nutshell, Durkheim argues that institutional forms of any kind are social constructs, but to be social they need to be exteriorized. These exteriorized constructs (linguistic, monetary or educational systems, genres, and the like) impose constraints at all levels of human activity, specifying both their variables and their degrees of variability. It is in and through this power to impose constraints that institutionalized social constructs are dissociated from the contingencies of specific instances of interactive discourse, becoming independent social structures because they are seen as such. They include, I would argue, both the parameters of social identity and the communicative virtues (see Section 5.2, below), seen as semantic prototypes, flexible resources for making the judgements on which the discursive process of social construction depends. Together with *automatization* and *phenomen-alizing* (Bruner 1999), it is this cyclical process of exteriorization which makes communication possible and which specifies the forms and modalities of negotiation.

As I mentioned earlier, any of these categories of identity can correlate with language, though not necessarily in the same ways, of course. One of the most strikingly familiar examples is the close relationship between 'occupation' and vocabulary. Individuals demonstrate their membership and knowledge of trades, professions, gangs, political movements and the like by their use of technical terms and jargon. In a general way, that is, you are much more likely to know and use domain-specific terms if you are a practitioner in the domain in question.

> ekphrasis
> phoneme
> manga
> quinto acuto arch
> chromatic scale
> mandamus
> a double top
> blog
> podcast

You know *ekphrasis* if you are an art historian or critic, *phoneme* if you are a linguist, *a double top* if you are a darts player. You are what you know: 'identity' is made of knowledge and language is both what we know and how we know it. But these are over-simplified, one-to-one examples. After all, our knowledge of a term and a domain can be a matter of degree: a *quinto acuto arch* and a *chromatic scale* are just 'some kind of' arch or scale to most people, but to architects and musicians they are far more specific terms. The closer we are to the centre of the group – the 'community of practice', as Etienne Wenger (1998) puts it – the more meaningful the term, because it is more richly grounded in personal knowledge and experience, in identity and life. The more peripheral our participation in the group's activities, the vaguer the meaning.

This throws fresh light on the role of the cultural markers we discussed earlier, since it shows that the specific selection of those markers known to an individual will be related to the repertoire of communicative situations in which he or she participates, so that knowledge and language on the one hand and role and identity on the other can be seen as mutually defining. It should be emphasized, however, that this is true of all communicative practices, not just the use of cultural markers. As we shall see (Section 3.3), the performance of any communicative practice requires linguistic and pragmatic knowledge, which is distributed differentially, the patterns of distribution iconically delineating the spaces and boundaries which determine identities.

To cross those boundaries, then, relevant knowledge and competence is a necessary condition. But it is not a sufficient one, as social identities, by definition, must be recognized and legitimated by others and they may have reasons for not wishing to do so. If they are in a position of power of any kind, therefore, they may refuse to recognize a speaker's claim to membership of the group in question.

Many years ago, as a youngster living in London, I would occasionally 'go for a day in the courts', sitting in Bow Street or one of the Inns and enjoying the colourful, often dramatic entertainment they provided free. On one occasion, a young woman who was suing her doctor for incompetence (an extremely rare event at that time) was being cross-examined about her symptoms, and said:

'I coughed up a lot of sputum.'

At this, the judge gestured to her to stop and said to her barrister:

'Mr Smith, ask her where she learnt that word.'

Mr Smith did as he was told.

'In hospital,' was the reply, which Mr Smith relayed to the judge.
'In hospital, m'lud.'
'Then tell her to leave it there,' said the judge. ' "Spit" or "phlegm" will do.'

It was clear to everyone what was happening. By using a technical term, the young woman had had the effrontery to lay claim to knowledge and to an identity which the male, middle-aged legal and medical professionals felt they had to deny and which, since they were in positions of power, they were able to flatly reject by removing her right to use the discourse in question. She also lost her case. But presumably, as lawyers say, *post hoc sed non propter hoc.*

3.3 Communicative practices, roles and acts

It is a matter of simple observation that people frequently coordinate their behaviour. Explaining how they do so, however, is a task of such complexity that it has led some to believe that communication is either an illusion, a mystery or an impossibility. Evidently, this is not a response that social scientists can endorse, since their various disciplines are all predicated on the existence and the investigation of forms of coordination: what makes society possible? 'Language' is not the only answer to that question, but it is certainly the most important resource for creating the conditions and implementing the acts necessary to establish intersubjectivity and to coordinate action.

The study of linguistic forms of coordination has shown that they are subject to cultural variation or, if you prefer, that they are part of culture. We will call such culture-specific forms of language use *communicative practices*. They are the ways in which members of a given community exploit their linguistic resources (for the moment, we will set to one side other, non-verbal semiotic modalities, such as gesture, smoke signals or body adaptors such as clothing, tattoos or jewellery).

Physically speaking, all normal human beings possess the same set of resources. Culturally speaking, though, groups of various kinds select, pattern and use those resources in different ways. For example, the phonological system of each language is a highly restricted use of our general phonetic capacities. Similarly, the forms and functions of messages, the modalities of interaction and the repertoire of communicative situations and genres and the parameters of variation of a community are a culturally specific selection of the totality of known practices.

A striking example, and one which brings these points together, is the phenomenon of whistled speech. Cowan (1948, p. 280) reports on a whistled conversation between two speakers of Mazateco in Oaxaca, Mexico, who carried out a commercial transaction, buying and selling a load of corn leaves without exchanging a single spoken word. Mazateco is a tonal language and speakers, or rather whistlers, can reproduce the system of phonological oppositions in this alternative modality. Whistled speech is also found in the Canary Islands and I have personally heard claims that the mountain shepherds who use it can make themselves heard and understood over distances of up to ten kilometres, though I admit that this strains the bounds of credibility.

The main point I wish to make here, though, is that communicative practices – any communicative practices – do not just communicate messages, they also communicate identity. Speaking and communicating in cultural and group-specific ways proclaims membership of that culture and group. In parallel with the contents of their whistled messages, the Mazateco peasants or the Canary Islands shepherds are also proclaiming loud and clear their membership of their respective groups, their identities. This expressive or indexical function of communicative practices is always present to some degree, and this is as true of accent, vocabulary or grammar as it is of stylistic or pragmatic aspects of language use. Unfortunately, the identifying functions of language have been neglected by most theorists, with the exception of some who are interested in aesthetics or stylistics, in order to concentrate on the representative and communicative functions, on how we know and see the world and how we share that knowledge and vision with others (Joseph 2004). These are essential issues, but until we start to take the identifying function into account as well, our understanding of them will be at best incomplete and at worst highly distorted. Language variation is a systematic and iconic representation of social structures. Studied carefully, it provides a map which displays the contours and coordinates of the demographic, functional and epistemic patterns of distribution which constitute identities.

Communicative practices, then, include every formal or rhetorical variant, including, for example, the performance and realization of speech acts. It is now a commonplace of contrastive pragmatics that there is intra- and intercultural variation in the ways in which illocutionary forces are mapped across syntactic structures. The speech act *suggesting* can be realized in English in a number of different ways, for example:

> Why don't you talk to her about it?
> If I were you, I'd talk to her about it.
> I suggest you talk to her about it.
> Don't you think it would be a good idea to talk to her about it?

In Swedish and French it is possible to express a suggestion using a conditional structure that, for the sake of argument at least, we can regard as the same:

> Si on allait au cinema ce soir.
> Om vi skulle gå på bio i kväll.

The 'same' structure also exists in English:

> If we went to the cinema this evening.

However, although perfectly acceptable formally as a syntactic structure, such an utterance does not carry the illocutionary force of *suggesting*. If it occurred as part of an exchange, the addressee would treat it as an incomplete hypothesis. The use of this illocutionary strategy is, therefore, part of French or Swedish language self-expression. A very small part, admittedly, but the same affirmation could be made about any other form–function variant. In this case, the identifying function can be clearly seen in occasions of infelicitous use, or pragmatic failure:

French student of English: And if we went to the cinema?
English 'lecteur' (after a pause): What would happen?

The student's incompetence is perceived by the lecteur as expressing identities such as 'learner', 'foreigner' or 'French'.

To underline the importance of this point, let us look at a brief selection of examples of communicative practices:

Howzat!

This is the cry of the cricketer who is claiming that he has just dismissed an opponent and who is appealing to the umpire to ratify his claim. It is an act, therefore, that can only be appropriately performed in cultures and situations where that sport is played, and it is remarkable that the felicity conditions for the act, as formulated in the official rules, are dozens of pages long. The cry, then, is based on a specialized competence and is expressive of the individual's identity as a cricketer, as a member of a particular team, which may in turn be based on forms of local identities, and as a member of the wider culture and society within which cricket functions.

Tack för senast.

This Swedish expression means literally 'Thank you for the last time', and is used when you meet someone again for the first time after you have been their guest. Failure to do so is regarded as impolite, and the length of time which has elapsed between the two events seems to have no attenuating effect: when my wife met a cousin of hers she had last seen three years earlier, his very first words – after 'Hallo' – were 'Tack för senast'. As always, recourse to a group's communicative practices is a proclamation of, or at least a claim to, membership of that group, and in this case there are also implications concerning the actors' relative positions and roles of ex-host and ex-guest.

Bon appétit.

Despite the combined efforts of much of Europe's catering personnel, this expression has no real equivalent in English. (I am of a generation that considers substitutes such as 'Enjoy your meal' as impudent imperatives.) The use of this expression is role- and identity-related and, as an element in commensal symbolism, is a potent exponent of in-group identity, especially *en famille* or *entre amis*. Here, too, the use of a particular language, French, indexes cultural practices and identities in the same way as the cuisine may do.

I baptize thee in the name of the Father ...

The fact that the individual person is both named and admitted into membership in the church in this performative ceremony, or rite of passage, is indicative of its importance in the shaping of identities in the culture in question. The Christian theology of the soul is a theory of the person. Since all individuals have souls, they are of great and equal value in their own right. It is this vision, which will place the individual above society and its values, which are mere human creations, which is the basis of the universalizing systems of ethics and morality – the 'rights of man' – common to Western cultures.

In his seminal study of Mayan Tzeltal illocutionary practices, Brian Stross (1974) cites the following locally-recognized categories:

> talk in which the speaker spreads the blame, so that he alone is not blamed
> inhaled talk
> speech occurring at night or late evening
> speech by someone who comes to another's house and talks even though the other is ill

These are highly idiosyncratic, and recognizing them and the communicative practices which instantiate them is to commit oneself to a set of discursive positions which frame Tzeltal identities. But we must not allow our ethnocentric perception of their 'exotic' nature to blind us to the general fact that *all* communicative practices, whatever else they are doing, are expressive of speaker identity. For example, even a communicative practice as seemingly universal as the use of proverbs is still fully expressive of their identities when used appropriately by competent speakers, since they are both extremely condensed versions of cultural knowledge and values and are highly idiomatic, in the sense that they cannot be used or interpreted freely.

Sirhan (1993) studied the proverbs of the Vute of Cameroon 'with the aim of constructing a model of tradition as a process of communication'. He quotes the following proverbs, in translation:

> 1) Even if you really like meat, you don't eat your own lips.
> 2) The bush pig did not receive a tusk even though his maternal uncle did the sharing.
> 3) You don't throw stones at the place where you've hidden a calabash filled with palm-oil.

The meanings of these proverbs can only be guessed at by a non-Vute. Sirhan glosses them as follows:

> 1) is basically a version of the incest taboo;
> 2) expresses the fear that a person's nonchalant behaviour might cost him a golden opportunity;

3) is advice not to misbehave among the people from whom you received a wife.

As with cartoons, the quantity of knowledge necessary to interpret a proverb can seem to be completely disproportionate to its length. Sirhan explains (2), for example, as follows:

> In a matrilineal system such as the Vute's, property is inherited from the mother's brother. That bit of information is not in the text of the proverb ... Although, among the Vute, authority is in the hands of this kinsman, who previously had the right to sell his sister's son, the idea that maternal uncle and uterine nephew are interchangeable is strong. In fact, Vute kinship terminology has but one term (la) by which these two men can address one another.

> Compared to those of the warthog, ... the tiny tusks of the bush pig ... are obvious evidence that it has not been well endowed. We can understand why the Vute would be surprised if the very person responsible for your position in the world turned out to deal you such a meagre hand. But the story tells that, when goods were being distributed, the overconfident bush pig did not turn up in time. When it finally arrived, everything had already been dealt out. Now imagine an overconfident person, too sure of his prerogatives, who does not make the least effort to secure himself the best share. Two of his friends fear he will be lackadaisical, as usual ... (*ibid.*, p. 236)

– and so one of them turns to the other and quotes the proverb.

Appropriate interpretation and use of the proverb requires great competence and knowledge: the kinship system, the oral tradition and Vute values and attitudes. To possess that knowledge and display it, it is necessary to be – it *is* to be – Vute. This is one of the main reasons why members of such groups are not always eager to share their knowledge, mythology and language with outsiders, such as ethnographers: they see the knowledge written down, taken away and feel that they are the victims of identity theft.

British speakers of English might be surprised to learn how very odd practices such as wedding speeches or formal debates seem to most other Europeans. Again, the intense, fixed gaze of a Swede personally toasting another dinner guest – 'Skål!' – can be positively unnerving for a non-Scandinavian (but whatever you do, don't look away). In parts of West Africa, a socially inferior listener may systematically repeat final sections of a socially superior's utterances *sotto voce*.

As an informal demonstration of the diversity of communicative practices, readers are invited to reflect on the 'Questionnaire on communicative practices', below.

1) In your country, is it possible to tell by someone's accent whether they:
- are rich?
- come from a specific region or town?
- are members of a particular social class or have a particular occupation?
2) Do you have any proverbs or expressions about verbal behaviour? For example, in Britain people say 'Little boys should be seen but not heard' and in France 'Il faut tourner la langue sept fois dans la bouche avant de parler'.
3) What do you say when:
- someone gives you a present/you give a present to someone?
- someone sneezes, breaks wind or belches?
- you propose a toast?
- you invite someone to dance with you?
- you enter a crowded shop or room?
- you take leave of a friend?
- a friend is going to take an examination or their driving test?
- you start to recount an anecdote or tell a joke?
4) Are there any taboo subjects in your society?
5) What do you talk about when you meet someone for the first time?
6) Do you have any linguistic games, competitions or professions?
7) Are there any times when silence is obligatory?
8) Are there any differences between the ways men and women speak?
9) Is more than one language spoken in your country? If so, how do people decide which language to speak?
10) Do you have any expressions which are used at particular times or on specific dates (dawn, a birthday, an anniversary, the season, etc.)?
11) In a family gathering, who would have the right to speak first:
- a very old person
- the father or mother
- a child, the eldest son or daughter
- an uncle or aunt
- a visitor?
12) Do you have special forms of address for speaking to:
- a child, a childhood friend
- your employer or employee
- an animal

- your wife, husband, lover, mistress
- a stranger or foreigner
- a teacher, priest or member of the armed forces?
13) At table:
- do people talk a lot or not very much? What about?
- are children encouraged to talk when guests are present?
- what do you say when you begin to eat?
- how do you refuse another helping?
14) Do you use gestures:
- to show that you are or are not in agreement?
- to greet, insult, congratulate, thank?
- to ward off evil?
- to hedge or tone down the force of what you are saying?
15) How do you go about striking up a conversation with a member of the opposite sex?
16) Do you give 'human' names to certain kinds of animals or objects?
17) Do people in your country enjoy a lively exchange of views or even an argument? Or do they prefer to keep quiet when they do not agree?
18) Do you have any swear-words? Religious, sexual or other? And what are people's attitudes to swearing?
19) How do you conclude a bet or a deal?
20) How do you call or attract the attention of a waiter, barman or shop assistant?

I would now like to relate this discussion of communicative practices to what are generally recognized as two of the most important concepts concerning the negotiation and creation of identities, role and act. What I hope to do is to show how they relate to one another and to certain other characteristics of interactive discourse in culturally specific ways.

Role is defined as the occupation by an individual of a discursive position, conferring a set of socially warranted linguistic and non-linguistic rights and duties which legitimate the performance of certain categories of act: non-verbal, illocutionary and interactive. The enactment of a role is the dynamic expression of a situationally salient aspect of the individual's social identity.

Non-verbal acts are prototypically exemplified by a surgeon removing a patient's appendix, a policeman arresting a suspect or a barman pouring a drink. The right and capacity to perform such acts is usually granted after an institutional knowledge-based assessment of some kind and symbolized by documents such as diplomas and warrant-cards.

Illocutionary acts (Austin 1962; Searle 1969), without going into any detail, are acts such as greeting, inviting, thanking, asking for information, paying a compliment and so forth. If performed in compliance with the relevant felicity conditions, they serve to express and realize the actors' intentions and to produce specific effects on their interlocutors.

Interactive acts are those acts which realize and impose the interactive structure of the discourse. Fundamentally the interactive structure is to be understood and described in terms of who speaks to whom and when, that is, in terms of turns and their relative distribution. Basically, they are turns in communicative behaviour which enter into the structure of the discourse. If a participant's contribution is unheard or deliberately ignored, it is not a turn. Turns may be realized both verbally and non-verbally: a nod of the head or the utterance 'yes' can both realize a turn.

In the type of interaction analysed below, turns fall into three main categories: Opening (O), Replying (R) and Closing (C). This sub-categorization of turn is based on the concept of *Address*: by Address we mean that a speaker selects another participant or participants and imposes on them the right or duty to reply. Address may be realized verbally or non-verbally (Gremmo *et al.* 1976); in small-group inter-action it is almost exclusively non-verbal, being realized by eye-contact, gesture and orientation. An *Opening* turn (O) is one in which a Speaker (S) imposes on one or more other participant(s) the right/duty to reply: they are the Speaker's Addressees (A). When the Addressee avails himself of his right, his turn is a *Reply* (R) (the Addressee of an R-turn being, by definition, the Speaker of the previous turn). An O followed by an R gives us the minimum unit of interaction, the *Exchange*.

Once an exchange is completed, the Speaker (i.e. the producer of the O turn) can either initiate a new exchange with the same participant, or he can change Address, i.e. select a new Addressee, or he can perform a Closing turn, one in which no duty to reply is imposed. Change of Address and Closing both mark the boundary of the next-higher unit of interaction, the Transaction, which therefore has the structure O, R (1…..n) C.

When we talk about discourse rights and privileges, then, we are referring in particular to the rights to perform Os, Rs and Cs, to the right to Address and to the right to Interrupt. These rights vary considerably from interaction to interaction and from participant to participant: by stating the repertoire of a given participant's interactive acts, that is the types of turns he performs, we are describing a second important constituent of his or her role.

As an example of this approach to the description and definition of role, let us take a brief passage for analysis. The passage in question, which is authentic, is an extract from a lesson being given by a teacher of French to a group of immigrant workers. The demands we make on our analysis and our model are stiff ones: can we, by describing the discourse, make generalizations about the teacher's role and the students' roles in this type of interaction?

In this passage, the teacher was preparing a dialogue with his group: the target discourse was:

'Tiens, bonjour Bashir.'
'Bonjour Iovan.'

(Bashir and Iovan are names of characters in the textbook.)

Turn 1 Teacher
Ça va? Je commence maintenant. 'Tiens, bonjour Bashir.' Tu es Iovan, Ali.

Turn 2 Student 1
'Tiens, bonjour Bashir.'

Turns 3/4 Teacher
Très bien. Maintenant Bashir dit à Iovan: 'Bonjour Iovan'. Tu es Bashir.

Turn 5 Student 2
'Bonjour, tiens, bonjour Iovan.'

Turn 6 Teacher
Il ne dit pas 'tiens', c'est Iovan qui dit 'tiens, bonjour Bashir'. Maintenant Bashir dit simplement 'bonjour'.

Turn 7 Student 2
'Bonjour.'

Turn 8 Teacher
Il s'appelle comment?

Turn 9 Student 3
Iovan.

Turn 10 Teacher
(gesture to student 2 to try again).

Turn 11 Student 2
'Bonjour Iovan.'

Turns 12/13 Teacher
Très bien. Alors, tu es Iovan, tu es Bashir. Allez-là.

Turn 14 Student 4
'Tiens, bonjour Bashir.'

Turn 15 Teacher
Bashir.

Turn 16 Student 5
'Bonjour Iovan.'

Turn 17 Teacher
Très bien.

ILLOCUTIONARY STRUCTURE

1 *Framing*   *Performative*   *Modelling*
Ça va?   Je commence maintenant.   'Tiens, bonjour Bashir.'
Nominating
Tu es Iovan, Ali.

2 *Practising*
'Tiens, bonjour Bashir.'

3 *Evaluating*
Très bien.

4 *Modelling*   *Nominating*
 Maintenant Bashir dit à Iovan : 'Bonjour Iovan'. Tu es Bashir.

5 *Practising*
'Bonjour, tiens, bonjour Iovan.'

6 *Correcting*
Il ne dit pas 'tiens', c'est Iovan qui dit 'tiens, bonjour Bashir'. Maintenant Bashir dit simplement 'bonjour'.

102

7 *Practising*
'Bonjour.'

8 *Correcting*
Il s'appelle comment?

9 *Informing*
Iovan.

10 *Nominating*
(NVC: address and gesture)

11 *Practising*
'Bonjour Iovan.'

12 *Evaluating*
Très bien.

13 *Nominating*   *Directing*
Alors, tu es Iovan, tu es Bashir.   Allez-là.

14 *Practising*
'Tiens, bonjour Bashir.'

15 *Nominating*
Bashir.

16 *Practising*
'Bonjour Iovan'.

17 *Evaluating*
Très bien.

See also the analysis in Table 3.3

Before proceeding to interpret these two analyses, two points need to be made.

For the sake of argument, the reader is requested to accept the fiction that it is possible to make valid generalizations on the basis of such a small 'corpus';

I am well aware of the inadequacy of the labels used for the illocutionary acts: only after far more analyses of this type have been carried out will we have a more reliable taxonomy, and even then

Table 3.3 Interactional structure

Turn / Participant	1	2	3	4	5	6	7	8	9	10	11	12	13	14	15	16	17
Teacher	S	A	S	S	A	S	A	S	A	S	A	S	S	A	S	A	S
Student 1	A	S	H	H	H	H	H	H	H	H	H	H	H	H	H	H	H
Student 2	H	H	H	A	S	A	S	H	H	A	S	H	H	H	H	H	H
Student 3	H	H	H	H	H	H	H	A	S	H	H	H	H	H	H	H	H
Student 4	H	H	H	H	H	H	H	H	H	H	H	H	A	S	H	H	H
Student 5	H	H	H	H	H	H	H	H	H	H	H	H	A	H	A	S	H
	O	R	C	O	R	O	R	O	R	O	R	C	O	R	O	R	C

Legend: S = Speaker A = Addressee H = Hearer

O = Opening (a Speaker turn in which a participant is addressed, i.e. the duty to reply is imposed on him)

R = Reply

C = Closing (a Speaker turn performed by the same participant as the 'O', but in which no duty to reply is imposed)

operational consistency (i.e. different observers using the same labels for the same acts) will probably be the most we can hope for, since our present state of knowledge does not allow of a rigorous definition of such acts. Our ignorance of the hierarchical ordering of illocutionary values is an especially serious handicap: in the passage in question, for example, should 'Evaluating' and 'Correcting' be related to some macro-function such as 'Judging'? Or is 'Nominating' more closely related to 'Performing' (Specifying an Addressee) or to 'Directing'?

Turning to the illocutionary structure of this passage as shown in our suggested analysis, one is struck first by the preponderance of Teacher Acts. Note that this is not the same thing as teacher-*talk*, which has always been measured in purely quantitative, chronological terms. The realizations of acts may be of very different lengths (compare 6 and 8, for example). Nonetheless, the ratio of Teacher Acts to Student Acts in this passage is the same as that generally given for Teacher Talk to Student Talk, i.e. 2 to 1: of the 22 acts in this passage, 15 are performed by the teacher, 7 by the students. If we look at the passage in terms of types of act, we see that the teacher performs seven different types (Framing, Performing, Modelling (2x), Nominating (5x), Evaluating

(3x), Correcting (2x) and Directing), whereas the students perform only two types of act (Practising (6x) and Informing).

As can be clearly seen, almost all the Teacher Acts involve some form of control over the learner's behaviour. The importance of this aspect of role is underlined by the fact that *none* of the types of act performed in this passage are common to both teacher and student. Nothing could be a clearer example of role as the right to perform acts, i.e. as discursive positions. Readers are invited to test this against their own experience: it is just unimaginable that in a traditional class such as this, one of the students should start Evaluating or Correcting, or indeed performing any of the acts performed here by the teacher. They simply would not have the right: it is not their role.

When we examine the interactional structure of this passage, we are immediately struck by the teacher's degree of discourse control. This is directly related to his right of Address: he and he alone can select speakers. The students cannot initiate an exchange, they have to wait until they are addressed: their right to interrupt is correspondingly non-existent. They have extremely limited rights of Address. They cannot even address one another, they can only address the teacher. Consequently, only he can produce Opening and Closing turns. One consequence of this is his centrality: since all the discourse must go via the teacher, his share will be far greater than that of the students. All decisions concerning the activity are in his hands – when to begin and end a new phase of some kind, selection of participants, specification of their participation. The teacher's task of classroom management is clearly reflected in his task of discourse management. The most direct form of role-challenge possible in this situation would be to try to wrest control of the discourse away from the teacher, which explains why teachers have traditionally been so opposed to 'talking in class'. Of course, role is relationship: the norms on which the behaviour we have been studying rests have to be accepted by all participants. The roles of teacher and student, that is, are mutually defining because they are defined by and in interaction.

As can be seen from this example, one of the teacher's rights is to perform acts of discursive management or control: announcing performatively that the class is starting, selecting speakers or (although this is not exemplified here) silencing speakers. In certain situations, this right is given symbolic expression: the gavel of a committee chairperson for example. In *The Lord of the Flies*, William Golding describes his plane-wrecked schoolboys consciously devising such a practice:

Ralph ... lifted the shell on his knees and looked round the
sun-slashed faces.
'There aren't any grown-ups. We shall have to look after ourselves.'
The meeting hummed and was silent.
'And another thing. We can't have everybody talking at once.
We'll have to have "Hands up", like at school.' He held the conch
before his face and glanced round the mouth.[3] 'Then I'll give him
the conch.'
'Conch?'
'That's what this shell's called. I'll give the conch to the next person
to speak. He can hold it when he's speaking.'
'But-'
'Look-'
'And he won't be interrupted. Except by me.'
Jack was on his feet. 'We'll have rules!' he cried excitedly.
'Lots of rules! Then when anyone breaks 'em –'
'Whee- oh!'
'Wacco!'
'Bong!'
'Doink!'
Golding (1954, pp. 32–3)

If we look at a variety of discourse types, such as bargaining, teacher-
talk, highly specialized technical reports, books or articles containing
scientific vulgarization, gossip, news bulletins, weather forecasts, and
so on, and ask what they have in common, most linguists will reply
'Precious little'. This is a normal enough first reaction, since there are
obviously clear differences between them along most of the parameters
usually used to describe discourse. Some of these genres are written,
some spoken; some are spontaneous, others prepared; some are
interactive, others single-source. We would expect these differences to
show up clearly in vocabulary and syntax or in rhetorical and
interactive structure, and they do.

However, they also have something in common: they can all be seen
as variations on a theme. That theme is the way in which knowledge is
stocked, assumed and attributed, distributed and exchanged. In other
words, it is helpful to approach the categorization, analysis and
description of discourse on the basis of *social* rather than *linguistic*
questions. Such questions would include:

1) Who knows what? Is the knowledge common knowledge, or is it
    unevenly or differentially distributed? That is, is the discourse
    asymmetric?
2) If the discourse is asymmetric:

- is the main purpose of the interaction to share the knowledge, make it common and restore the informational equilibrium, or
- is the knowledge being used unilaterally by one of the participants, for example, for diagnostic purposes or to preserve some aspects of the status quo such as social control, or to make a financial profit. In other words, is the knowledge in some sense 'secret' or withheld?
3) If the knowledge is indeed secret, what are the communicative strategies and practices employed by participants in order to bypass this obstacle to communication?

In brief, what are the relations between social knowledge and the nature and quality of the individual's participation in an interaction? How do knowledge and identity relate to the individual's communicative practices?

Certain aspects of widely differing discourse-types are the result of the ways in which social knowledge is networked and negotiated, that is, their characteristic 'differences' are the results of variations in the ways in which knowledge is selected and distributed. Most work on negotiation or communication assumes that participants are invariably willing to disclose facts known to them fully, to make their knowledge freely available. Such a presumption is naive and obscures the primordial role of social factors in moulding discourse. Doctors do not always share their knowledge with their patients, nor do policemen interrogating witnesses, or examiners questioning students, or second-hand car salesmen selling dodgy vehicles. As these examples show, the reasons for withholding knowledge vary considerably. It may be to diagnose, solve or test (most social groups, whether formal or informal, use some form of evaluation of relevant knowledge as an entry qualification). One of the most common motives for withholding knowledge is that its possession confers an advantage of some kind, very often social or financial. 'Insider dealing' is by no means restricted to the world of high finance: ask for a spare part using technical terms ('A B25 flanged grummit') and you may halve your car repair bills. And knowledge is something we pay for every time we consult a lawyer or have the plumber in.

This approach contrasts with other approaches to discourse analysis, where the characteristic of 'being specialized' is seen as somehow inherent to a particular topic, vocabulary, grammar or style. Instead 'specialization' is regarded as social and relative: relative to the individual and to the way in which knowledge is socially distributed, an approach which can be paraphrased by asking 'Specialized?

Specialized for whom?' To take the simplest of examples: legal texts in English or French, such as the following, baffle me completely:

> I am prepared, for the purposes of this case, to assume (without necessarily accepting) that Section 70(1)(g) of the Land Registration Act 1925 is designed only to apply to a case in which the occupation is such, in point of fact, as would in the case of unregistered land affect a purchaser with constructive notice of the rights of the occupier; and it is to be observed that the words 'actual occupation' are used in Section 14 of the Law of Property Act 1925 and were used in Barnhart v. Greenshields (1953) 9 Moo. P.C.C. 18,34.

Such a text, though, is meat and drink to my elder daughter. To the objection that because she is a lawyer she must know things I don't know, I can only reply 'quite'. She, on the other hand, might well have problems coming to grips with a text on linguistics which I would regard as fairly basic. The perception of a text as specialized or otherwise depends, first and foremost, on the individual's state of knowledge.

In very general terms, common sense exhibits the following characteristics:

1) It is *socially transmitted*, learnt from parents, friends, acquaintances, teachers, arts, the media, literature. What you know is largely a matter of who you know.
2) It is *differentially distributed*: different people know different things. Any of the parameters of social identity (age, sex, profession, religion, etc.) can be a source of knowledge.
3) Knowing *how knowledge is distributed*, who knows what, is itself an important aspect of commonsense knowledge.
4) Commonsense knowledge is to a large extent encoded in language (vocabulary, grammar, metaphor, rules of practical reasoning).
5) The commonsense world is *perceived as objective* reality and we presume that others see it the same way: this is the 'natural attitude'.
6) Commonsense thought and reasoning are based on the natural attitude and natural language, that is, they are *context-dependent* statements rather than attempts to formulate 'objective' truths and therefore have little in common with formal logic or scientific argument. (Mannheim 1936; Schütz 1964; Leiter 1980)

These points help us to understand the relationship between commonsense knowledge and 'specialized' knowledge. In particular, they underline what might be called the communicative paradox: that while common sense is variable and we know it to be so, it is what we take for granted, the scaffolding of presuppositions we use when we construct discourse. By and large, it is only when we become aware of a discrepancy between what we know and what we assume our interlocutors know that we may have recourse to explanatory or compensatory communicative strategies (see Section 4.4 on compensation strategies).

For the moment, though, let us consider a communicative exchange from the point of view of commonsense assumptions. The scene takes place in a newsagents' shop. A is a customer, B the shop assistant.

A. *Newsweek?*
B. Sorry, tomorrow.

It would be possible to gloss this exchange by making explicit a few of the underlying assumptions:

A. I have come here because I know that this is the sort of shop where objects such as the one I want can usually be obtained. I have the money necessary. However, I am unable to locate the object in question. I am, therefore, addressing you in your role of sales assistant since that is precisely the sort of information I expect you to have.
B. I appreciate the fact that you have come here to obtain a particular article in an appropriate (buying/selling) way and that my role is to manage that exchange. However, *Newsweek* is published weekly on Thursdays. Since it is Wednesday today, I regret to report that I am unable to satisfy your request. Should you come back tomorrow, though, I will be willing and able to do so ... etc.

In such an exchange, there is an almost perfect congruity between the commonsense worlds of A and B, so that B's reference to an external condition is sufficient for A to understand why this request cannot be complied with, When the knowledge gap is wider, though, negotiation and explanation may be called for:

A. ... and at the end of the parents' meeting they decided to organize a kermesse. (1)
B. A what? What a ker ... what did you ...? (2)
A. Oh it's a a kermesse it's a traditional ... it's a sort of party for everyone connected with the school. (3)
B. A prize-giving ceremony. (4)
A. No [laughing] no, no we don't have those in French schools. It's games and dancing more. (5)
B. Do you sell things? (6)
A. Yes, cakes and lottery tickets and maybe things from people's attics. (7)

109

B. Oh, I know – that's very, that's funny, that's what we call a 'school fete'!
   (8)

At the beginning of this passage, A uses a term (an item of knowledge) which is not known to B (*kermesse*). B immediately indicates that there is a problem and tries to identify it for A (2: *A what?*) at the same time appealing for help. A responds by providing a descriptive paraphrase (3: *it's a sort of party*). On the basis of the information provided, B forms and formulates a hypothesis (4: *a prize-giving ceremony*) but for sociocultural reasons this is unacceptable to A (5: *no we don't have those in French schools*). A continues to provide supplementary information for B to work on (5: *It's games and dancing more*). B now forms a second hypothesis which he tests by asking A to confirm a further piece of identification (6: *Do you sell things?*) which A had not provided. A confirms this hypothesis (7: *Yes*) and illustrates it with more detailed examples (7: *cakes, etc.*). B is now confident that he understands what A means by 'kermesse' (8: *Oh, I know*) and demonstrates that this is so by providing a translation (8: ... *that's what we call a 'school fete'!*). The negotiation has been successfully concluded.

Two further points need to be made about this process of negotiation:

1) A tries to base his explanations on what he presumes B to know already: items like 'school', 'party', 'games' and 'dancing' as well as the fact that the first of these items only occurs with the others on special occasions. Had the discrepancy between A's and B's knowledge been larger, there would have been more to negotiate.

2) Both participants employ a variety of different strategies during the process of negotiation (requests for repetition and clarification, paraphrase, analogy, translation, etc.). These strategies are the primary linguistic mechanisms of negotiation in any face-to-face situation, but they acquire additional importance in exolinguistic discourse since they allow interactants to create – albeit fleetingly – a common culture.

The above example is typical of collaborative discourse, where participants negotiate a common meaning together. Such discourse belongs to the category of 'non-zero-sum games' (Riley 1985; Rapoport 1986) which allow players on both sides to make a profit, as opposed to 'zero-sum games' where there is a winner and a loser: the winnings of the one exactly balancing the losses of the other. Amongst the conditions which are necessary if a discourse is to be regarded as collaborative are the following:

1) Participants must wish to arrive at a common understanding or agreement.
2) They must be willing to share their relevant knowledge in order to improve the quality of their collaboration.
3) They must have at their disposition the communicative, cognitive and social resources necessary, that is, a set of strategies appropriate to the game in question.

Let us look at the communicative practices of bargaining. Here we have a situation where, for reasons which will be detailed below, participants are not nearly as generous with their knowledge as they are in 'non-zero-sum games'. Bargaining, in the sense in which this term is used in the discussion of 'bazaar economies', is not as common in Europe as it is in Asia, for example. This serves to underline the basic point that there is a direct connection between communicative practices and the distribution of information: when Europeans go shopping there is usually no bargaining or haggling since prices are displayed and fixed.

Nonetheless, even in Europe, there are certain situations where bargaining is appropriate: when you buy a second-hand car, for example, or an old piece of furniture; at auctions, or open-air markets, not to mention the small-ads in publications like *Exchange and Mart* which include the expression 'o.n.o.'. Knowing which set of communicative practices to employ in which situation requires a personal 'sociology of knowledge' which forms the basis of our communicative competence.

Bargaining can be defined simply enough as the negotiation of a price; the main characteristics of this type of situation are the following (Alexander and Alexander 1987):

- by definition, no pre-established prices are displayed or announced;
- buyers and sellers have different objectives: buyers want low prices, sellers high ones;
- these objectives are not necessarily contradictory, though, since other factors 'exterior' to the particular sale in question may have to be taken into account (the condition of fruit at the end of the day; 'clientelization' – will the buyer become a good regular customer or is he/she a 'one-off' tourist; a feast-day with special culinary traditions, etc.);
- this means that both zero-sum and non-zero-sum games are possible.

Under these circumstances:

- buyers will try to discover the current lower price-range before

111

starting the bargaining process: extensive search precedes intensive search;

- sellers will try to discover the quality of the buyers' information. Information is difficult to obtain: sellers compete with buyers, not with other sellers. The buyer can question other buyers and several sellers, i.e. they will conduct an extensive search before negotiations with one particular seller, but both groups have their own reasons for not wishing to divulge this information:
- buyers, because they do not wish to lose face and in the hope of exercising a downward influence on current prices, however small, will quote prices lower than the ones they really had to pay;
- sellers, because they do not wish to give away their lower price-range, will ask for higher prices than they are willing to accept.

This is what leads Clifford Geertz (1983, p. 30) to say that:

> The search for information – laborious, uncertain, complex and irregular – is the central experience of life in the bazaar.

and it is this situation which determines the communicative characteristics of bargaining discourse:

1) The overriding principle is that sellers try to confuse buyers as regards both the quality and nature of their knowledge and the current status of the negotiation.
2) The seller bids first if necessary.
3) Bids alternate.
4) 'Backward jumps' are forbidden; that is, the buyer cannot offer less or the seller demand more than their own previous bid.
5) Units may be changed ('Avocados are one euro each, but if you take a kilo ...').
6) The buyer can break off the negotiation, walk away and come back later.
7) 'Extras' may be added ('If you buy a dozen crayfish, I'll throw in the crown of dill for free').
8) Bluff: on both sides, participants try to give the impression that they are the best-informed and to establish personal superiority in the field.
9) Patter: the seller will sing the praises of his or her goods.
10) Either buyer or seller can change the object of bargaining (or the quality, etc.: 'By the way, have you seen my cucumbers?', 'Are you sure you wouldn't prefer something bigger?').
11) Bids should be honoured once they have been accepted.

Even a summary as succinct as this shows quite clearly that such negotiations operate on the basis of a social relationship where knowledge is not given away freely. It is this fundamental characteristic that makes the discourse 'specialized', rather than any inherent features of form or content. Indeed, such features can be seen as an expression of particular communicative relationships.[4]

A few years ago, I had the pleasant duty of organizing a dinner for a group of colleagues and their partners to celebrate a friend and colleague's sixtieth birthday. My wife and I visited several restaurants to make arrangements and we received a number of suggested menus and estimates. However, when it came to making a definite choice, we found the decision was by no means easy, since restaurant managers seemed to adopt strategies that made it difficult to calculate the value of their proposition and almost impossible to compare propositions with one another:

> Je peux vous proposer deux menus, l'un à 110F, l'autre à 150F. Pour 110F, vous avez trois plats et la boisson est comprise, mais pas le café. Par contre, pour 150F vous avez quatre plats avec un choix de fromages ou desserts, le café est compris, mais pas le vin, et je vous offre l'apéritif.

3.4 Membershipping strategies, phatic communion and greetings

3.4.1 Membershipping strategies

So, social identity is made up of a configuration of memberships and each membership is knowledge-and-language based. It is social, that is, constructed in our communicative dealings with others in intersubjective couplings. Each individual's identity is made from what some philosophers have called 'a moral narrative' (De Graaf 1994) or 'career', a communicative and epistemic autobiography consisting of the experiences and knowledge acquired as a member of that configuration of groups (see Ricoeur 1990).

To illustrate the ways in which speakers select situationally salient aspects of their addressee's identity, the philosopher Louis Althusser cites the case of a gendarme being called to the scene of a crime. His uniform and his revolver confer on him both symbolic and real power, so that when he shouts at a person running away 'Hey, you, stop!', that person becomes a criminal *because the gendarme says so*. The runaway, that is, is both the subject of and subject to the gendarme's discourse: 'Ideologies interpellate individuals'.

Or, in discourse-analytic terms, subject-positions are materializations of power relationships.

113

If that were all, as the postmodernists claim, it would be a very deterministic, very pessimistic account of personal identity. However if you look at discourse, at actual examples of situated communicative interaction, what you find is that the individual is consciously and constantly trying to affirm his or her sense of identity. Our attempts are not always successful, of course, and this can give rise to conflict, but the very existence of conflict disproves the thesis of absolute social determinism:

Who do you take yourself for?

Identity claims are techniques for selecting or imposing situationally salient aspects of identity (i.e. roles, see above) on addressees. Examples include:

Are you ready to order, sir? Open wide. Tickets, please. Next patient, please. Compare and contrast ... Place your hand on the Bible and repeat after me ...

Why do you Northerners (women, Catholics, teachers, etc.) always ...
You BBC luvvies are all the same.

Business Class passengers only. Staff only.

Pregnant women should consult their doctors before using this medicine.
There's a good girl.
'Corporal!'
Asylum seekers should go directly to desk C.
Non-EU nationals.

Symbols can also be used for the same purpose – see Figure 3.2.

In each of the examples in the list above, members of specific social groups are selected and subjected to the discourse of some external institutional or individual voice, coming at them from one discursive position with the intention of 'suturing' them (to use Althusser's grimly

Figure 3.2 Symbols: Disabled; Gents; Ladies

114

vivid image) into another. (Davies and Harré (1990) is a more rigorous and linguistically informed discussion of 'positioning'.) However, it has to be stressed that this is not the whole story, as individuals can use membershipping strategies to position themselves.

Here are some examples of what we might call *identity affirmation strategies* or *claims*: these are utterances in which individuals affirm their membership of specific social figurations or sub-groups in order to foreground them with reference to the matter in hand and thereby orient their audience's behaviour and expectations. In English, such claims are commonly, but by no means exclusively, made by using the expression *as an X, I ...*

Prototypical forms

I'm an X
I'm a teacher, a Rotarian
I'm one of those people who ...
(Speaking) as an X
Speaking as an anthropologist, a lifelong Arsenal supporter ...
As a single mother, a taxpayer, a beer drinker ...
We/us Xs
We are playing Chelsea this afternoon.
Us Londoners ...

Domain-specific discourse.

Any attempt to use a domain-specific discourse, including its lexis, will be perceived as in itself a claim to membership of the epistemic community in question by virtue of possession of the knowledge which delimits its boundaries.

'Domain-specific' in this context includes restricted or specialized knowledge or discourse of any kind, including legal or scientific texts, jargon or slang, and so on. Such domain-specific discourses operate as the boundary markers for epistemic communities, which have been defined above as knowledge-based social groups or figurations. Any boundary, physical or mental, has two principal functions. The first is to delimit the domain itself and to ensure that it retains its integrity and identity through the consistent play of oppositions which characterizes and differentiates all forms of discourse: the actual 'content' inside the surface delimited by these boundaries is in many cases in constant flux, as anyone studying, say, slang, biochemistry or the language of web operators knows only too well. The second is to distinguish between insiders and outsiders: using a domain-specific discourse is an identity claim. (See section 3.3 above)

115

Indirect strategies

> You're telling me!
> Is the Pope a Catholic?
> I'll have you know you are talking to someone who spent thirty years in India.
> Those of use who have the privilege of working in higher education ...

A subset of identity claims consists of *multilingual identity claims*, claims which are related to the negotiation of language choice and/or social identity as a bilingual. For example, if you go to Stockmann's, the main department store in Helsinki, you will find that most members of staff wear two or more little flags in their lapels – Finnish, Swedish, German and Russian, say. This is in fact a very direct form of self-identification as a multilingual – 'These are the languages I speak and in which I am prepared to provide service'. Other strategies of this kind include:

Keeping your options open

Although Finnish and Swedish (Finland's two official languages) are very different, there is a form of greeting which they have in common:

> 'Hei hei!'/ 'Hej hej!'

Use of this form is therefore 'unmarked', leaving interlocutors free to use either language or to continue to negotiate for a preferred choice.

Verification

A speaker who has a preference checks with his or her interlocutor to see whether it is acceptable:

> 'Får jag tala svenska?' (Can I speak Swedish?)

Given that Swedish speakers are very much in the minority except in a very limited number of coastal areas, it is usually a Swedish speaker who makes such a request – and who has to change languages when the reply is negative.

Multiple choice

A speaker who is unsure of an addressee's linguistic identity may use both languages, leaving the choice to the addressee, at the same time declaring their own identity as a bilingual:

> 'Päivää. Goddag.'

116

Interestingly, civil servants in contact with members of the public are being encouraged to adopt this strategy and to state the name of their department or service in both languages, in conscious imitation of Canadian practice.

Finland has possibly the best record in the world as regards the protection and respect of its native minority's linguistic rights, but even so a speaker who initiates an exchange in Swedish will often receive a flat reply in Finnish, as Finnish speakers assume that Swedish speakers are bilinguals. Since this is almost invariably the case nowadays, cases of conflict are extremely rare. Nonetheless, this kind of *code-switching* unmistakably reflects the relative power of the two speech communities, and it is a world-wide phenomenon. Identities are formed and negotiated within the macro-sociolinguistic structure of the society in question.

Bilinguals are people who use two languages, switching from one to another according to a vast array of social and situational factors. The analysis of code-switching patterns can, therefore, help us identify those factors, laying bare the interior workings of society by revealing just where the boundaries are between its constituent parts. It shows us where topics and domains begin and end, it delineates groups, it traces the contours of identities. Code-switching can, therefore, be used strategically by individuals for a variety of identity-related purposes: as an identity claim; to membership an interlocutor; for the inclusion or exclusion of others in or from a group; as an affirmation of group identity, and so on. Such practices can be extraordinarily tenacious: when I take the bus home from work, for example, I can hear a group of my students, third-generation descendants of North African immigrants, chatting in French, but code-switching regularly to the same handful of fixed expressions. As one of them said in a classroom discussion: 'My mother tongue is Arabic, but I don't speak it'.

Code-switching can index or change the identities of participants so radically that it can be used to redefine a communicative situation in its entirety. Here is something my younger daughter said during a parent–teacher meeting at her French secondary school. The poor child has inherited her father's gift for mathematics, with the result that she had an overall mark of 4/20, well below *la moyenne*, the statistical average expected of all French pupils, but often obtained by only a minority (– don't try to understand). Katja was being roundly condemned by her maths teacher. She tried to defend herself, but to no avail. Her teacher's verdict, the institution's verdict, was implacable: 'Pas d'excuses, t'es nulle.' ('No excuses. You're useless.'). (For a discussion of teacher–pupil discourse in France, see Section 3.5) Despairing of softening her teacher's hard heart, she switched from French to English:

117

'C'est vrai que j'ai pas la moyenne, but my marks are going up and I'm doing my best.' ('It's true that I haven't reached the average ...')

By switching in this way, Katja changed the whole situation, including her identity, and mine. She was no longer the school pupil whose behaviour is subject to the institution's objective evaluation, against which there is no appeal. She had excluded her teacher from the exchange and she was now daddy's girl, and as such able to appeal to quite different subjective and affective criteria, 'doing one's best'. And she had membershipped me as 'Daddy' instead of 'school parent'.

Membershipping strategies are by no means limited to spoken discourse. Indeed, it is interesting to note that some of the most subtle and interesting analyses have been carried out on scientific and academic texts by linguists and didacticians whose main aim is precisely to help learners acquire the strategies appropriate for acceptance as members of specific epistemic or disciplinary communities (Ventola and Mauranen 1996a, b; Cortese and Riley 2002). Novice writers, whether native or non-native, may experience considerable difficulty in doing so not only because of a lack of linguistic or scientific competence, but because they are unable to adopt the new discursive positions required. In my experience, this incapacity often manifests itself as an embarrassed lack of self-confidence, and I have been struck by the fact that several of my postgraduate students from widely differing backgrounds have described their problem as being due to the feeling that they didn't 'have the right' to use technical or 'academic' words or expressions.

A written genre in which membershipping strategies are particularly salient is the public service announcement or, more generally, the discourse adopted by the authorities to address members of the public. As we saw in our discussion of identity cards, to exercise its power and control efficiently, the state needs to identify, categorize and communicate with individuals. The repertoire of categories employed and the tonality of the communication will, therefore, often contain clear indications as to the types of identities available in a given society and situation and their related values and rights, and as to the relationship between state and individual, though of course genre conventions need always to be kept in mind: the civil servant who tells me that he is my humble servant may be a thing of the past, but modern, chummy phraseology of the 'thanking you for your understanding' type can still be just as much of a velvet glove on an iron fist.

With these precautions in mind, though, it is still very worthwhile examining public notices and announcements and comparing them across languages and cultures, as I hope the following examples will show. Saying that such texts are stereotyped to a large extent misses the point: except in cases of outright oppression, they express a consensus between governors and governed as regards the very social norms and values they convey. Whether the instructions, prohibitions, commands and exhortations they contain are actually heeded or not in a specific instance is a very different matter. Nevertheless, they clearly appeal to sets of culturally-defined presuppositions and expectations as to what is appropriate behaviour on the part of specific groups and as to how it should be indicated and expressed, encouraged or enforced. A clear indication of the strategies through which a society legitimates and manages a repertoire of social identities, and of the relations between the authorities and subjects or citizens, is given in the following two examples, to be seen in French and British buses respectively:

Les places numérotées sont réservées en priorité aux
Mutilés de guerre
Aveugles civils
Invalides de travail
Infirmes civils
Femmes enceintes
Personnes accompagnées d'un enfant de moins de quatre ans
et dans l'ordre ci-dessus.

'Please give up this seat if an elderly or handicapped person needs it.'

'Ouverture et fermeture des glaces:
En fonction des conditions atmosphériques, les glaces de l'auto-bus peuvent être soit ouvertes, soit fermées par le personnel au départ du terminus. Les voyageurs peuvent modifier en cours de route la disposition adopté au départ, mais, conformément aux consignes en vigueur, en cas de désaccord, il est donné satisfaction au voyageur qui désire que la glace soit fermée.'

'Please do not open the window beyond the point marked by the arrow as this may cause inconvenience to other passengers.'

One cannot help being struck by the considerable differences between these two sets of examples – the comparative brevity of the English notices, for example, or the presence of 'please' – though it is not easy to say how important they are or what they signify. Here are some of the reactions to them elicited from a small group of French–English bilinguals:

The French notices were variously described as:

'A peremptory appeal to authority.'
'Cartesian.'
'Exhaustive and precise.'
'Legalistic and unrealistic.'
'An attempt to be logical and clear in a social and emotional minefield.'
'Authoritarian, but in the public interest.'
'Based on the assumption that there is always a right answer.'
'Addressed to a group of quarrelsome nit-pickers.'

The English notices attracted the following remarks:

'A polite appeal to civic responsibility.'
'Moralistic, unrealistic.'
'Asking people to do something, not telling them.'
'Woolly.'
'An ineffectual appeal to individual decency.'
'Based on a sense of social solidarity.'
'Short, sweet and to the point.'
'No help at all if there's a problem.'

Such reactions do not have any statistical value, of course, but it is not unreasonable to note that the majority of comments draw attention to the nature and quality of the relationship between the individual and the authorities and that, whatever else may be going on, rights are being distributed on the basis of membership of specific social groups. It is also relevant to note that members of the first four categories cited in the first French example ('Mutilés de guerre ...' etc.) can be expected to carry identity cards attesting their membership of the group in question.

Although contrasting textual practices in this way clearly falls within the purlieus of what we now call the ethnography of communication, it is certainly not a new approach to intercultural comparisons. Indeed, it would be possible to establish a whole literary genre on the basis of this technique, one which would include the *Lettres Persanes, Major Thompson's Diaries* and *Gulliver's Travels,* as well as much non-fictional travel writing, science fiction and utopian or dystopian literature.

120

We could add a further dimension to this literary genre by adding to it works composed in certain writers' 'other' or second languages, francophone maghrebins, for example, or anglophone Indians, where mastery of the language as such does not preclude the assimilation and expression of ideas, cultural values and norms which are not usually associated with it, in the sense that they do not conform to the expectations of many of their readers. Rather than attempting to reduce the problems of hybridity and postcolonial literature to what would probably be vacuous generalizations, though, let us return to the field of public notices for a more manageable example. A few years ago, my wife and I took our grandchildren to Borgbacken, the splendid amusement park in the centre of Helsinki. So did several thousand other parents and grandparents, and we ended up parking in a slightly irregular fashion. At the end of our visit, we returned to our French-registered car to find the following letter in French attached to the windscreen:

> On behalf of the municipal authorities, I wish you a warm welcome.
> When driving in a strange place, even the most careful of drivers can unintentionally break the traffic regulations. You yourself have just broken the parking rules. I would like to ask you, before you stop next time, to make sure that stopping or parking is permitted. In most cases, a street sign will tell you what rule applies. If there is a parking meter, please make sure that you have inserted enough money for the time you wish to reserve. If you wish, come to the parking supervisor's office or to any police station for further information.
> In case of repeated offences you risk being fined.
> I am sure, however, that this offence was unintentional, and I wish you a pleasant stay in our country.
> The parking supervisor,
> Helsinki.[5]

Although my personal reactions to this message were by definition subjective ('The French police would never be so understanding or address a tourist so gently and politely', and so on), such an example is not merely anecdotal: after all, the authorities had gone to the trouble of translating and printing the text for distribution to members of a highly specific social group: French tourists guilty of traffic offences in Helsinki.

Social identity and language are related in a multitude of complex ways. First, there is the indexical information which all speakers provide, willingly or unwillingly, consciously or unconsciously, about themselves (we will return to this point in Section 3.4). Second, there are the types and combinations of illocutionary acts which speakers perform, and their specific instantiations, since these are manifestations of role, which confer on members of particular social groups the socially-warranted bundle of rights and duties necessary for their competent performance. Roles, that is, are encoded and constructed in and through discourse. They are situationally salient aspects of social identity, the dynamic enaction of characteristics which need to be foregrounded for the successful achievement of the matter in hand. However, precisely because they are socially warranted, that is, attributed and accepted by others, they may well have to be claimed and negotiated, particularly when interactants are not familiar with one another, not co-present or not collaborating in the construction of the discourse in question, as is usually the case with written texts, even if they are read aloud:

> Good evening. You are watching the BBC World Service. The news. I'm Philip Hayton ...

Third, there is the question of the degree of competence with which individuals are capable of producing and interpreting discourse which is formally, socially and epistemically appropriate to the matter in hand and specific to the domain, whether the domain is darts or plumbing, palaeontology or the Beatles.

Earlier, I defined social or public identity as 'the sum of the numerous sub-groups of which the individual may be a member (occupation, religion, sex, age, etc.)'. This definition highlights the nature of the problem we are dealing with: just how do individuals select and project the particular aspect of that complex and multiple identity which they consider to be appropriate to the matter in hand? My first answer, given above, was to say that 'Situationally salient facets of social identity, roles, are manifested by the performance of particular kinds of communicative acts, requiring specific forms of knowledge for their competent performance or interpretation', but in certain cases it may not be clear to the individual concerned exactly which facet of his or her identity is appropriate, which 'hat to wear'. This can clearly be seen when recourse is had to compensation strategies, such as:

> Are you asking me as a taxpayer, or as a member of the town council?

where the interlocutor is required to adjudicate and choose between two distinct and potentially contradictory facets, two worlds of discourse. Unsurprisingly, individuals will often justify a course of action as being forced upon them by the existence of this kind of contradiction: one thinks, for example, of Edward Gibbon's explanation in his *Autobiography* (p. 55) as to why he felt obliged to follow his father's orders and break off his relationship with a young lady:

> I sighed as a lover, I obeyed as a son.

Time and time again, writers and speakers go to great lengths to establish their credentials and negotiate their identities in this way: this is further confirmation of Gunnarsson's (1994) statement that writing and speaking need to be seen firstly as parts of an overarching set of communicative practices.

Lastly, it is also worth noting that flouting these rules for humorous purposes is possible: for example, I might say of my dentist's performance in the latest local amateur opera production:

> As an opera singer, he makes a great dentist.

As we have seen, knowledge is largely constitutive of identity and specific forms of knowledge confer specific aspects of identity. Individuals have strategic choices to make, however, in formulating their discourse: for example, they can either claim membership by demonstrating knowledge, or they can claim to have knowledge by proclamation of identity.

Here is a striking example of a straight claim to knowledge:

> No-one with a life of finite duration could hope to be an expert on the entire oeuvre of figures as prodigiously productive and diverse as Freud, Marx, Durkheim, Helmholtz, the contemporary structuralist or post-structuralist thinkers, or to have an intimate first-hand acquaintance with contemporary ethnological, anthropological, archaeological, etc. writing. *The only areas where I can lay claim to any kind of expertise are in twentieth-century American and European philosophical thought, the writings of post-Saussurean theorists and modern biology and medicine.* (Tallis 1997, p. xiii; my emphasis).

Even if we exclude for the moment those cases where normal procedures for the attribution of identity are deliberately flouted for dramatic or humorous effect, as in Shakespearean comedy, or farce, we are still left with a wide variety of potential dysfunctions for which no classificatory system as yet exists. Any future taxonomy will probably have to include:

1) Pragmatic failure (see Section 4.3); in this context it would largely be a matter of mistaken identity:

    Do you have those in a smaller size?
    Sorry, but I don't work here.

    It might be convenient to include here dysfunctions due to an ignorance of 'the way of the world', for example the ways in which roles, tasks and competences are distributed:

    I've come to see you about my local taxes.
    I'm afraid you've got the wrong person, I only deal with road tax.

2) Resistance: individuals who are the subjects of another's membershipping strategy may refuse to accept the identity or role being attributed to them. One of the commonest ways of doing so, it seems to me, is to lay a counter-claim to a different identity or role:

    Look, I'm the secretary here, not the tea-lady.

3) Contestation: we have probably all experienced at some time in our lives situations where the identity we wish to claim is either refused because the claim is not accepted (e.g. being accused of gate-crashing, or of being an imposter) or is rejected as incompatible with the matter in hand (e.g. being refused service in a restaurant because of one's ethnic origins or way of dressing). As one might expect in such conflictual situations, participants' discourse tends to become extremely direct, containing explicit challenges to identity:

    Who do you think you're talking to?
    Who do you think you are?
    Do you know who I am?

3.4.2 Phatic communion and greetings

Years ago, I came across a cartoon depicting a formal dinner party. The focus was on a bejewelled lady, who is turning towards her dignified gentleman partner and saying 'How small do you like your talk?' I think the point the cartoonist is making is clear enough, but let us try and tease out some of the various strands in what the lady is saying:

(i) by drawing attention to the fact that she is about to engage in small talk, she shows that she is fully aware of what she is doing and that she presumes that her interlocutor is too,

(ii) by indicating explicitly that her small talk comes in different sizes, she

124

shows that she has a range of subjects and strategies available which she will select from according to her partner's tastes and interests

(iii) so by doing all these things simultaneously and through one skilful metacommentary, she has in fact torpedoed the whole business because, in brief, she has flouted two major rules: not only has she said something unexpected – which in itself goes against all the rules of small talk, though not of humour, by any means – but by presenting small talk as trivial, superficial and so on she has robbed it of its serious, interpersonal function since it can only fulfil that function if conversational partners at least appear to take it seriously.

The expression 'phatic communion' is taken from the work of the anthropologist Bronislaw Malinowski (1884–1942), who wished to describe the social functions of language. Indeed, when Roman Jakobson came to write his more detailed studies of the functions of language, he tipped his hat to Malinowski by naming one of them 'the phatic function'.

Malinowski's contribution to social anthropology and linguistics is difficult to exaggerate: at the theoretical level, his is a major contribution to the development of functionalism and at the methodological level he overturned the procedures of armchair anthropologists such as Frazer, who relied on reports sent to Oxford by missionaries and explorers, to introduce fieldwork. The only way of obtaining an accurate understanding of a group's social reality is to become a member of the group, whilst still retaining one's anthropological expertise. This necessitates leaving the missionary's verandah and going to live in the village, participation in the group's activities of every kind, such as going hunting, attending ceremonies or tilling the fields, and above all learning the language. Previously, much anthropological and ethnographic work had been carried out via translation, but for Malinowski the aim of ethnography is 'to grasp the native's point of view, his relations to life, to realise *his* vision of the world' (Malinowski 1922) and this could only be achieved through detailed study of the ways in which language encodes culture and the ways in which language is used. This ethnographic theory of language was founded on two concepts: first, the notion of context of situation and, second, the view of language as a mode of action:

> The main function of language is not to express thought, not to duplicate mental processes, but rather to play an active pragmatic part in human behaviours. (Malinowski 1935)

Malinowski's theoretical work has been strongly criticized for its lack of rigour, but the profundity of his insights was so great that his work has to be regarded as essential to modern understandings of the pragmatic nature of language, as is witnessed by his use of the expression 'verbal act' well before Austin. Above all, though, he put real live individuals back in the spotlight of anthropological attention, rather than 'savages' or social automata. For Malinowski, cultures are functioning wholes. One can never isolate one aspect of culture from the rest to deal with it separately – pull at any loose thread and you will find yourself unravelling the whole of the social fabric:

> Malinowski's greatness lay in his ability to penetrate the web of theories to the real man, boasting, hypocritical, earthy, reasonable. (He had) an invaluable awareness of the tension which is always there between what people say and what they do, between individual interests and the social order. (Kuper 1973, p. 49)

Phatic communion can be defined as communication which is interactive but which is not intended to transfer information, either by seeking or conveying it. Instead, phatic communion has a social function, which is to establish or maintain contact, to show that the communicative channel is open, that it is functioning well and that the speaker is willing to use it. It is essential, therefore, in establishing social contacts and relationships and setting up the conditions necessary for intersubjective couplings. A very clear example is when we answer the telephone:

Hallo, 584 1452

we say, and in doing so we performatively indicate that we are willing and able to talk, and that the apparatus is working properly. We also identify ourselves by name or number, but it is worth noting that this is a not a universal communicative practice by any means. In France, the most common reply is:

Âllo. Je vous écoute. ('Hallo. I am listening to you.')

which can seem impolite and uncooperative to people from societies where the onus of identity is on the called and not the caller. This is not a trivial point, since it demonstrates that from the start phatic communion and greetings play a fundamental role in the negotiation of identities.

A similar example can often be heard on radio broadcasts, chat shows, for example, where listeners are invited to call in:

So if you want to call Nick Ross the lines are open ...

Obviously, the most common way of establishing contact is through some form of greeting:

Lovely day, isn't it?
How do you do?
Morning!
Alright?
Wotcher!
How's things?

It is easy to demonstrate the power and importance of phatic communion: all you have to do is just ignore a friend or neighbour, someone you usually greet. The result can be catastrophic – socially catastrophic, that is: it's not a matter of semantics, you haven't said anything. What you have done is to deny your neighbour's existence and identity by refusing to acknowledge him or her as a member of the group. No wonder we talk about 'cutting someone dead'.

The term is usually reserved for speech, but there are examples of phatic in writing, such as sending a postcard from your holiday: 'Having a lovely time. Wish you were here'. Greetings cards have the same function, even, or perhaps especially, those we send to old friends and acquaintances that we haven't seen for years and that we do nothing more than sign. In much of south-east Asia, visiting cards still play the important role in phatic contact – 'you know where to contact me if you wish to do so' – that they did in Europe in the nineteenth and early twentieth centuries.

Jakobson extended Malinowski's (1922) notion of 'phatic communion' – 'the predominance of contact over other factors' – to include what he called the phatic function, which characterizes what is said just (or mainly) for establishing, prolonging or discontinuing communication, for example when speakers check that the channel works, as in *Hello, can you hear me?* For Jakobson, greetings are seen as serving the phatic function, given that they do not have a 'content' (they are not 'about something') or when they do, their content does not seem to be their main purpose. The same is true of expressions about the weather said in elevators and other closed spaces where spatial proximity makes people feel (in many societies) that they should say 'something' (Duranti 1997, p. 286).

Greetings are recognized by ethnolinguists and anthropologists as constitutive of the person, social deictics situating individuals in their relative positions in the social matrix. They have a fundamental role in proclaiming personhood and identity. In Foley's words:

> Greetings are constitutive of the persons involved in the greeting ...
> the repertoire of language practices in a culture, embodied in the
> habitus of that culture's members, are both indicative and
> constitutive of its conception or local ideology of personhood –

127

what is a person and what are the types of person there can be?'
(Foley 1997, p. 261)

Moreover, as we shall shortly see, time spent in greetings can be used for the observation and classification of indexical information, much of which is highly relevant to categories of social identity such as sex, age, marital status, profession, ethnicity, and so on. Intuitively, it seems clear that identity claims and greetings have much in common, but to the best of my knowledge no systematic theoretical or empirical studies have been carried out which would permit us to establish a taxonomy of their respective epistemic functions, as has been done for various kinds of hedges, for example.

Greetings, then, refer reflexively to the conditions of communication, they indicate that 'informative', that is semantically and pragmatically rich communication is a possibility, is feasible. Later in the interaction, interlocutors may regularly repeat this message in the form of various kinds of feedback behaviours:

Yes, right, go on, really!

However, when I speak of 'the conditions of communication', I am referring to more than the fact that the channel is open. 'The conditions of communication' include the overarching social structures contextualizing the interaction in question. As we saw earlier in our discussion of societal bilingualism, this will include the macro-level patterns of distribution of language varieties with respect to communities and functions and the ways in which they impinge on specific instances of social interaction. What we find in those specific instances is that individuals are constantly stating or reaffirming their own and their interlocutor's positions with respect to the macro structures, that is, their places in society, their roles and their identities.

To illustrate this argument, let us look at a vividly instructive piece of work by Wendy Schottman, 'The daily ritual of greeting among the Baatombu of Benin' (1995).

The Baatombu form an ethnic group of approximately 500,000 people. They speak Baatonum, which is one of the Gur family of languages. The social structure of this group is both complex and rigid. This is an important point, because in a general way, the more complex and the more rigid a society is, the bigger the effort the members have to make to keep it that way. For example, they have to keep reminding themselves and others who is who and how things are, they have to quite literally keep things in order.

There are three classes in Baatombu society:

1) The Wasangari – nobles, the former warrior class
2) Commoners – farmers and hunters
3) Ethnic Fulani and Gando – descendants of prisoners of war – and 'abnormal' children.

In most European countries, it is sufficient to greet another person once a day. In fact, in some cases it might be unacceptable or at least a source of embarrassment to greet the same person twice. But whenever two Baatombu meet they have to greet one another:

> Every morning, each member of the compound and all close neighbours must be greeted ... and welcomed back (from the fields) with a greeting. They must be greeted when one runs across them ... life in a village is bathed in greetings, a multitude of repetitive exchanges of formulas ... (Schottman *ibid.*, p. 489)

But of course, when it is a 'first time' the exchange of greetings is longer: indeed, by non-African standards, it is extremely long. These lengthy exchanges have been described as greetings litanies, since they are composed of fixed expressions which are often repeated and which are performed in a monotonous chant, closely resembling the kind of ritual worship found in some kinds of religious ceremonies.

In any exchange of greetings, any greetings litany, there are two asymmetric roles – one of the participants is the Superior and the other Inferior. In the complex, rigid society there is almost no such thing as 'an equal'. Even identical twins have a Superior–Infererior relationship, though it is perhaps not the one Europeans would expect. The first-born twin is the Inferior, because in the African hunting tradition he has been sent out first by his brother to scout out the land.

Some greeting expressions can be used by both Superior and Inferior:

> Foo! (a general form of greeting)
> Good afternoon
> It's been a long time.

Some are reserved for the Superior role:

> How are the children?
> Are you well?
> Are things better?
> Are the members of your household in good health?

Some are reserved for the Inferior role:

> Alafia ('in good health')
> Ami ('Amen')

O, mm ('yes')

Again, in very general terms, the Inferior has fewer forms of greeting and often the exchange consists of a rapid, monotonous question-and-answer sequence that gradually fades away.

There are three main criteria for negotiating relative status:

1) Relative age
2) Kinship ties (there is no equality even for twins and your in-laws are superior
3) The possession of a power-conferring title ('goobiru', by no means restricted to the noble class).

Superiority is recognized by the inferior adopting a certain form of behaviour, *sekuru*, which literally means 'good shame' (but which might be translated by 'decorum'). Sekuru involves using those expressions which are reserved for Inferiors, lower posture, a lower volume and a fixed gaze away from the Superior. In Baatombu society, the Superior formulates the greeting and greeting questions, the Inferior replies (this is not always the case in Africa. In fact the main aim of Schottman's work was to answer the question as to why in certain ethnic groups it is the Superior who asks the questions, makes the communicative effort and in others the Inferior).

There is a limited set of rules governing the initiation of the exchange:

A visitor must initiate. 'Visitor' here means that a person is entering someone else's home, which, as we have just seen, occurs every morning as residents in the compound go round their neighbours and kinsmen, either before or after receiving a similar visit from them.

A traveller must not initiate. 'Traveller' here means someone who is coming towards the village, either from another village or, more frequently, from working in the fields or fetching water from the well.

The Inferior initiates. Obviously, in many cases, previous encounters between individuals have already taken place and their relative status has been negotiated and they know their positions, their places in society.

It should be emphasized here that Superior/Inferior does not imply contemptuous attitudes on the one hand or grovelling behaviour on the other. Both sides are expected to show respect for one another, and indeed the rules governing greeting litanies can be seen as politeness rules, preserving the face of both interlocutors, whilst at the same time protecting society.

Such a frequent, lengthy and complex communicative practice must be of some importance to the Baatombu. If we draw up a list of the functions it fulfils, we find first Malinowski's phatic function:

1) to establish social contact

The second and third functions (they are two sides of the same coin) are implied in Malinowski's approach, but perhaps brought out more clearly in Jakobson's:

2) to demonstrate that the channel of communication is open and present oneself as a potential communicative partner and ...
3) ... to indicate recognition of one's interlocutor as a potential communicative partner.

However, there are other functions which can only be understood in terms of the negotiation of identity. As we saw earlier, some of the most important parameters of social identity include age, sex, class, marital status, religion and occupation. It is striking to note how each of these categories can be signalled in terms of indexical information:

Age – grey hair, balding
Sex – beard, breasts
Class (social, economic) – accent, clothing
Profession – uniform, stethoscope
Marital status – engagement ring, wedding ring
Religion – Sikh's turban

Clearly we could go much further into the semiotics of identity: old school ties, hair-styles, slogans and messages on T-shirts, decorations such as medals, piercing, 'fashion statements' of every kind. As incorporated individuals, our bodies are sites for a visual discourse of identity and power. But remaining with phatic communion, one might object that phatic communication by definition does not transmit information. It doesn't – but it thereby leaves us free to assimilate this other, indexical information. When we are engaged in a phatic exchange, our attention is free not to wander but to make a reconnaissance. And as the old military adage has it, 'Time spent in reconnaissance is never wasted'. Phatic communion gives us just that – time. We need to know who we are speaking to or, in many cases, we would not be able to decide who they are and what they know already so that we can select and formulate our utterances appropriately.

So we can add three further functions to our list:

4) to provide indexical information for social categorization, that is, to signal various aspects of social identity

5) to negotiate the relationship, in particular relative status, roles and affectivity
6) to reinforce social structure.

Function 5 can clearly be seen operating if we look at the various forms of greeting and address a given individual uses according to his or her social and affective relationship with the interlocutor: 'Hallo there!', 'Good morning, sir', 'Good morning, Jones', 'Hi, sweetie-pie', 'Good afternoon, doctor', 'Yes, madam?' represent only a minute selection of strategies for signalling who we think we are speaking to and who we want to be taken for.

Taken together, then, Baatombu greeting practices are seen as a constant reaffirmation and maintenance of social structure and of the positions within that structure which the individuals in question occupy. They illustrate the general observation that greetings are the most common, condensed and direct form of Althusserian 'hailing' or 'interpellation'.

In formal terms, as regards length, tone and phraseology, phatic communion varies considerably. First, the sheer quantity of phatic can vary. According to various authors, the Apache (Basso 1972), the Paliyans (of Southern India) (Gardener 1966) and the Finns (Lehtonen and Sajavaara 1985) all prefer silence in certain conditions, but silence is not to be equated with ignoring someone. Silence can be nourished, as the Danes say. It can be companionable, relaxed and relaxing in ways which is rare in highly verbal societies, such as France. Finnish-speaking Finns have the reputation of 'having no phatic' and the article by Lehtonen and Sajavaara just mentioned is entitled 'The silent Finn'. Certainly, when I first went to live in Jyväskylä, a small town in central Finland in the mid-1960s, I was amazed at the almost total silence in which Finns would queue in a shop and then, when their turn to be served came, would carry out the transaction with the absolute minimum of words:

Litra maitoa. ('A litre of milk.')

That was it. No greetings, no thanks.

I have returned to Jyväskylä at regular intervals and although I have carried out no formal research I have formed the very strong impression that things have changed, that phatic exchanges are longer and more frequent, though I still have no clear idea how or why. All sorts of possibilities come to mind – the influence of foreign TV programmes and films, greatly increased interaction (tourism, business) with speakers of other languages, the conscious efforts of some interculturally aware language teachers, the training in 'communication' provided by foreign consultants to Finnish companies – all part of the process of globalization and of modernism's characteristic need to interact with strangers.

Again, as I used to try to find my way from one English class to another, I would often have to stop people in the street to ask for directions. Now most Finns in those days had simply never heard Finnish spoken with a foreign accent. The result was that they attributed my inability to articulate clearly and to find the right words to the fact that I was drunk. Old ladies would cross the road to avoid me, grown men would shake their heads knowingly. Indexical information can be misinterpreted, too.

It has been suggested that phatic communion is like grooming amongst the primates, and like that behaviour has been very important in the development of homo sapiens. Grooming behaviour allows the great apes and monkeys to affirm, to perform, their position in their social group, to maintain social structures, whilst at the same time bonding them closely together. Socially, then, grooming fulfils many of the functions of phatic communion which we have already identified. In addition, phatic communion prepares the stage for intersubjectivity, it is how we learn to 'do' intersubjectivity, if you like, to attend to others, to get others to attend to us, so that we can collaborate in sharing meaning, and we know that that is essential both phylogenetically and ontogenetically. The child who is deprived of phatic either by accident (wolf children, pathological conditions such as autism) or by design (deliberate experiments, abused and neglected children) is very likely to have major communicative problems, to have difficulty establishing intersubjectivity with others, i.e. difficulty in becoming a competent and acknowledged member of society. Small talk is a big deal.

3.5 Rearing practices

To meet the primordial requirement of survival, all human societies develop representations of their ideal, competent adult member and adopt behavioural strategies for reproducing individuals in their image and likeness (Jahoda and Lewis 1988). These *rearing practices* are framed within a folk theory or cognitive model of personhood and education, a set of beliefs, values and attitudes related to 'how you should bring up children' (Deloach and Gottlieb 2000). They aim, that is, to satisfy parents' and society's expectations concerning the individual's cultural competence, his or her ability to behave appropriately in the situations they are called upon to participate in. Since individuals do not all participate in the same repertoire of situations, nor play the same roles, since, that is, they occupy different positions in the social matrix, such folk models are necessarily theories about the kinds of identity available in the society in question as well as how they are to be formed and performed. And since different societies have different social structures and cultures, different expectations, the identities constructed within them differ.

By examining and comparing rearing practices, including both the way adults speak to children and the way they talk about bringing them up, we can obtain some idea, then, of their theory of personhood, of what those identities are and how they are constructed and attributed. Over recent years, considerable progress has been made in this field, the anthropology of childhood (Jahoda and Lewis *ibid.*), and in developmental sociolinguistics, the acquisition of communicative competence (Ochs and Schieffelin 1984; Andersen 1990). Parents not only wish to ensure the physical survival of their offspring, they also hope to ensure their 'social survival' by providing them with the culture and skills meeting local definitions of what it is to be an acceptable member of the society in question. In other words, every society has a theory of the person, of what it means to be a competent adult. The way we talk to children largely determines the kind of selves and persons, the kind of adults they become. However, the very different concepts of personhood and competence give rise to considerable variation in rearing practices, since different measures have to be used to reach different goals. To outsiders, these practices may seem wrong, cruel and unnatural, but to adult insiders they are simply common sense.

This does not mean, of course, that adults never discuss their rearing practices. In fact the very opposite seems to be generally the case, with young parents having long, animated and detailed discussions about such matters as development, diet and discipline, gender distinctions and clothing, sleep, play and personality, and so on, with one another and with the older generation. By adopting particular kinds of practices, the adults are shaping their own identities, too, being socialized through their new roles into such discursive positions as 'mother', 'father' or 'grandparent'.

Numerous studies of adult/child discourse have been carried out since the mid-1960s. As a very broad generalization, I think one can say that the earlier work was anthropological in the sense that under the influence of Chomsky cognitive psychologists and psycholinguists were looking for grammatical and cognitive universals, the architecture of the human mind and the ways in which it is reflected in language structures. Over the years, though, from around the mid-1970s, there has been a shift to more ethnographic approaches. This shift reflects developments in linguistics and in particular the challenge by Hymes,

Gumperz and others to the hegemony of studies of purely linguistic competence.

In a striking example of the way in which scientific research can be conditioned by extrinsic social factors, linguist mothers made a virtue out of necessity and produced doctoral theses on what was at first known as 'motherese', but which was quickly rebaptized as 'caretaker talk'. As gender roles were redefined, linguist fathers also discovered that the topic was both interesting and important, leading to the observation that there were clear differences between the rearing practices of different groups related to factors such as ethnicity, gender and class. Such variation could only be due to local social and cultural factors rather than to universal constraints on human psychology.

For example, in the 1960s, the leading ethnolinguists, Ron and Suzie Scollon, were called on by the US government to investigate a wide range of educational problems, indeed of educational failure, amongst the Athabaskan indians of Alaska (Scollon and Scollon 1981). After lengthy and detailed study of communicative practices, the Scollons concluded that the root of the problems lay in very different communicative practices, in very different attitudes to the value of speech. For the white, anglophone American teachers, speech is a good thing, silence is bad. 'It does you good to talk.' Talking easily is a sign of openness, talking fluently a sign of intelligence. However, for the Athabaskans, speech has very different roles and values. Speech in quantity is dangerous and demeaning, and talking about what you know is egoistic and boastful. In the classroom, this difference gives rise to contradictory communicative behaviours. The anglophone teachers busily fire away their questions, expecting the children to display their knowledge. But the children are inhibited from answering, since to do so would make them seem vain, competitive and boastful in the eyes of their peers. Social relationships are predicated on different views of the value and purpose of speech. Anglophones speak in order to get to know someone: Athabaskans get to know someone in order to speak. As you can imagine, this gives rise to misunderstandings and negative judgements. The anglophone teachers find that Athabaskan children are passive, lazy, unwilling to learn, unintelligent and having nothing to say. The Athabaskans find that the anglophone teachers are boastful gossips, empty vessels ... who are unintelligent and have nothing to say.

Rearing practices include both verbal and physical behaviours in adult–child interaction. The physical behaviours include breast-feeding and other direct contact; forms of restraint, reward and punishment; games and sports; work, tasks and errands; commensal, vestimentary, postural and kinesic norms and models, and they may play an important role in ceremonies and rites of passage. They are hugely important in determining the individual's sense of self (Porter 2003; Hanks 1996), but limited space means that in what follows I will be concentrating on verbal rearing practices, the ways we speak to children.

Adults adopt socialization routines aimed at shaping competent adult selves in conformity with local notions of personhood. Such cognitive or folk models necessarily entail a theory of teaching and learning – how you speak to children, what they need to learn, how they learn – as any theory of acculturation must include an account of the ways in which culture is transmitted.

In Bali (Deloach and Gottlieb 2000), a rigidly hierarchical society, speakers' and their interlocutors' respective ranks are always made fully explicit through titles and respectful forms of address. Since a newborn is the divine reincarnation of an ancestor during the first 210 days of life, adults adopt forms suitable for addressing a god, as well as ensuring that the child's head is held higher than that of any other person present. Every child has several names, including an ordinal name and a personal name which the parents may change if the child's behaviour deviates from what is expected of the bearer of that particular name. The parents' social position is specified and formulated with respect to the child: they are known as 'The father/mother of N'. Balinese notions of personhood, according to which the ideal self is calm, fatalistic and serene, require children to learn to control their emotions (their very physical health depends on this), which must never be expressed in public. To this end, when the child is approximately 21 months of age, the mother will 'borrow' a baby from a neighbouring family, lavishing on it affection and respect and ignoring the reactions of her own child.

Among the Kaluli, a highly egalitarian society in New Guinea, competent adults are those who can assert and defend themselves and their individual rights (Ochs and Schieffelin 1984; Foley 1997). The newborn is not considered as a conversational partner: when it is addressed by others, the mother holds the baby out facing towards them and answers on its behalf in a falsetto voice. To enable the child to become an assertive self, parents avoid simplification and baby-talk and give priority to teaching assertive illocutionary acts such as giving orders and teasing. It is important to note, though, that this is not for the child's benefit – the child has no understanding – it is for the benefit of those speaking to the child, for example, elder brothers and sisters, who are being socialized too, and who need to forge a strong bond with the infant. When a Kaluli child starts to speak, he or she has to be instructed. The method adopted is direct and explicit: the mother

136

produces an utterance and then orders the child to repeat it: 'say it like that'. However, mothers limit these instructions to asserting, requesting, teasing and reporting. They do not teach children the names of things, as we do in Europe: 'This is a dog.' 'That's a horse.' 'This is a car.' 'That's a bus.' That will come naturally and is relatively unimportant. What is important is a strong and independent child who can assert his or her rights, claim their due among equals.

In most Western countries, including the USA, it is common to find in books on childcare the advice that caretakers should speak to infants, 'provide them with a rich linguistic environment' as the catchphrase goes, from birth or even while the child is still in its mother's womb. Now this is perfectly good advice in context, but it should not be mistaken as a universal truth. It reflects the values we in the West attribute to speech. We bombard small children with nursery rhymes and stories, we provide running commentaries on what they are doing, we interrogate, we encourage them to speak, the earlier the better. All good preparation for the so-called communication society. But in Guatemala, a Mayan mother will put her small baby in a hammock in a dark recess in silence. And that baby grows up to be a perfectly competent member of his or her society, speaking the 'mother tongue' fluently.

Again, in most Western countries, children are encouraged to ask questions and adults are duty-bound to answer them. 'Why do birds have wings, Daddy?' 'Why are bananas yellow, Mummy?' This behaviour is so deeply-rooted in our society that some psychologists have even suggested that it is universal, genetic, a phase of development that all children go through: 'the why phase'. But if we look at other societies, we see that it is nothing of the kind. There are very many cases where children are not expected to question adults directly, because it would be impolite to do so, or a challenge to the adult's authority and superior social position. The child who asks a question is told 'You have eyes, use them', or is referred to another person, an elder brother or sister, for example, who is expected to give answers. Now this is extremely interesting those of us who are teachers, because it may go some of the way to explaining one of the major differences in educational practices, which is the difference between those societies where classroom teaching is based on questions-and-answers and those where it is not.

Signe Howell (1988) describes the rearing practices of the Chewong, an aboriginal group living in the Malay Peninsula rainforest. She argues that the concept of 'self' – 'what it means to be a human being' – is central to cognitive development:

> The process of acquiring knowledge can be delineated only by
> eliciting socially agreed expectations of what it is that a child is to
> become. (Howell 1988, p. 147)

How a 'child' is changed into an 'adult' is best revealed by 'perceived'
shortcomings in small children. By emphasizing how children fail to
measure up to certain standards, the Chewong express the characteristics of humanity in negative rather than positive forms. All strong
expressions of emotions are regarded as potentially destructive and
controlled by numerous rules which are constantly referred to. There is
no formal machinery of law and punishment, just the rules and
superhuman retribution. The Chewong avoid conflict and acts of
aggression. Indeed, extravagant behaviour of any kind is in general
suppressed, with children being allowed two emotions, fear and
shyness.

'Children' become 'adults' after marriage, on the birth of their own
first child. Children learn knowledge from adults, and adults learn
knowledge from superhumans. The concept of knowledge (*haeratu*) is
enormously important and the acquisition of knowledge is one of the
three main factors (together with the assimilation of elements of 'self'
and the growth of the body) which contribute to the transition from
child to human. There is no simple opposition between 'practical' and
'theoretical' knowledge. Children are 'not knowing', that is, they do not
know the rules and they do not understand the implications of their
acts. They need, therefore, to be both protected and educated by adults.

There are no gender differences in names, toys or roles, and there is
no competitiveness. However, education – learning to be your 'self' – is
based on two distinct approaches. First, there is knowledge which has
to be asked for and which one learns best from example and individual
initiative. Second, there are the rules governing behaviour, which are
learnt best by specific, enforced instruction, where rules have names
and are constantly called out to children: 'Don't touch (etc.) or a tiger
(bogeyman) will get you'.

Joanna Overing (1988) carried out fieldwork among the Piaroa, a
jungle people dwelling along tributaries of the Orinoco in the Guiana
Highlands of Venezuela. They live on some fifteen territories, each of
which is led by a wizard who controls knowledge and keeps disease and
death away. However, this power is not coercive: indeed, the wizard
preaches against coercion. He is a knowledgeable teacher of virtues
such as autonomy, equality and tranquillity. Personal autonomy is
valued very highly: one is free to hunt or not as one wishes, or to prefer
to do something else, such as making artefacts. It is regarded as very
rude to comment on such decisions and especially on their relative

worth. The overall aim of education is to learn the wizardry to lead a tranquil life. There is no physical punishment of children: strong anger is expressed by silence. There are no real stages in development, since the individual is constantly in transformation, and anyway one can be 'mature' in one aspect and a child from another point of view.

The Piaroa have a highly developed theory of mind. They stress the value of autonomy, moderation and intelligence and regularly discuss the relationships between reason and the emotions, between reason, knowledge and madness or reason, consciousness and behaviour. They distinguish between two main forms of knowledge, *ta'kwanya* and *ta'kwakomena*. *Ta'kwanya* refers to the acquisition of cultural capabilities: it includes the knowledge and capacity for using customs, language, social rules, rituals, cuisine, etc. *Ta'kwakomena*, on the other hand, refers to the acquisition of one's own consciousness of and responsibility for such capacities. It is one of the most ordinary words in their language.

This research clearly illustrates the ways in which different social knowledge systems give rise to different informational economies, leading to different patterns of socialization and a diversity of communicative practices. The forms of social reproduction necessarily correspond to the ideological structures they are reflexively expressing and maintaining. That is, the way we talk to children determines the kinds of learners they become. 'We' here is to be understood as referring to the set of discourse voices to and of which the individual is subject.[6]

Children's selves and their social identities, then, are shaped in and through discourse: we tell them who they are, and how to behave in ways appropriate to their position in society according, for example, to the sex, class and religion they belong to. We say things like:

1) Big boys don't cry.
2) Nice little girls don't use words like that.
3) *Boy*: Silly bastard!
   Teacher: No bad language in school! I've told you before.
4) *Girl*: We played volleyball yesterday, us against the boys.

These examples of gendered communicative practices require a considerable amount of unpacking, but the thrust is clear enough. In Britain, and in a number of other countries, 1) is a common saying. In effect the adult is saying to the child 'If you want to grow up to be a real man, if you want me to consider you as an adult, then you must stop crying'. The little boy's gender and identity is being socially constructed through direct social pressure in the form of parental discourse.

However, there are wider ramifications. Boys are opposed to girls, so this statement is also saying that (big) girls *do* cry. The question arises, then, if boys don't cry, and girls do, is there something that boys do and girls do not? And the answer – in many societies, at least – is, yes: boys swear, girls don't. Boys swear, girls cry. The ideology underlying such a practice is that boys, males in general, have a more powerful discourse than girls, and that the expression of a girl's identity is based on the emotions, not on reason. The fact that the woman teacher in 3) reprimands the boy for swearing in no way contradicts this argument. Male 'tough speech' thrives on such institutional (and feminine) prohibitions, since flouting them proclaims the gender difference in the clearest possible way. And in 4) one could argue that the gender distinction has been imposed by the institutional 'voice'.

5)   You can't play with that child, he's a Catholic/Protestant.

Prohibitions of this kind perpetuate the social discontinuities which delineate the borders between different constituents of group or social identity.

6)   What did you do at school today?
7)   Don't interrupt, don't answer back.
8)   *Teacher*: Listen, Christopher, if you've got a question, ask, but don't sit whispering behind your desk lid.

Amongst the educative practices employed by adults are those which inculcate the rules of turn-taking (which is itself part of the address system, see 1), above). Who has the right to speak, where and when? In 6), the child is expected to reply. In 7), he or she is told pointedly that adults should have the last word. In 8), the teacher is reminding a pupil of one of the fundamental rules of classroom language, which is that pupils are only allowed to speak when they are spoken to by the teacher, and that even then they must choose the teacher as their addressee. 'Talking in class', that is, means talking to another *pupil*, which is as much a transgression as *not* answering the teacher.

9)   *Neighbour*: Good morning, Mrs Nolan. Hello, John.
     Mother: Good morning, Mr Greenway. John, what do you say?
     John: Good morning, Mr Greenway.
10) *Child*: Can I have another biscuit?
     Mother: Can I have another biscuit what?
     Child: Can I have another biscuit please.
     Mother: That's better. There we go. And ...?
     Child: Thank you.

These are typical examples of European rearing practices for teaching politeness and greetings, essential indicators of social relationships and

140

social deixis. The child is being instructed concerning his position in society and how to indicate that position discursively. In 9), the mother first provides a model of the appropriate performance of an act and then prompts her son to repeat it, which in this case means selecting a locution which is socially acceptable for greeting an adult, male, neighbour and selecting the correct form of address ('Mr'). In 10), the forms of polite requests to an adult are being inculcated.

11) *Teacher*: Why don't you use a green crayon?
    Child (after some hesitation): Because it's blue?

Confusion all round! What has probably happened here is that the child has misinterpreted the adult's act of *suggesting* as a *request for information* (because of the interrogative-negative structure used). This case of pragmatic failure will require some repair work for the negotiation of meaning – *if* the adult is willing to invest the necessary time and effort. This will, of course, usually be the case when the adult is playing the role of teacher, but as we have seen, this is not a cultural universal, by any means.

12) *Teacher*: What's the difference between a horse and a pony?

The philosopher Isaiah Berlin once said that all philosophy begins with one question: How is this like that? I take him to have meant that thought involves going beyond the level of single, material objects, by abstracting qualities and establishing categories. Questions of this kind are meant to help the child to develop such cognitive categories. Once again, though, it should be noted that this Socratic or maieutic practice – the teacher already knows the right answer, this is knowledge guidance or testing, not a genuine request for information – whilst it is very deeply rooted in the European pedagogic tradition, is not a cultural universal.

13) *Mother*: No, Christopher, you don't watch the telly until after you've done your homework.

Through their discourse, adults express their values and inculcate children with them. In this case, priorities are being established between different kinds of activities on the basis of the work/duty versus play/pleasure dichotomy. This is not merely theoretical, though: the adult's behaviour will have immediate effects on the child's behaviour in the short, but also, possibly, in the long term.

14) *Child*: No school today?
    Mother: Silly! It's Saturday!

Adults will expect children to develop the interpretative skills necessary for going from what is *said* to what is *meant*. As we saw in example (11), this includes the identification of indirect illocutionary acts, but here we have a clear example of an adult calling attention to the role of background knowledge in implicature. All figurative language also makes similar requirements on children, including the major tropes of metaphor, metonymy, irony and synecdoche.[7]

15) *Teacher*: So what could the chimpanzee do to reach the banana?
Child: He could use a stick, miss.
Teacher: That's right, very good. But what about the prisoner?
Child: He could use a rope, miss. No, he could ... no, I know, he could ask the chimpanzee to –
Teacher: *Listen*, Christopher, think a bit before you answer.

This is a typical example of the tripartite structure of European classroom discourse, with the teacher initiating (usually with a *request for information*), the pupil responding (by *giving information*) and the teacher closing the exchange (*confirming, evaluating*) and then re-initiating the whole process. (This structure is the logical consequence of the norms of turn-taking mentioned under 8), above.) In the second exchange (beginning with 'But what about the prisoner?'), the teacher also displays the impatience with non-serialist cognitive styles which characterizes much Western schooling, with its preference for analytic and reflective modes of behaviour (Duda and Riley 1990; Riley 1988a)

16) *Father*: How was school today, love?
Child: I got nine in arithmetic.
Father: That's really good!

One of the main ways adults orient and select children's behaviours is through praise and encouragement (and their opposites). (See Section 3.5) This example depends on shared or 'background' knowledge and values: nine is only 'really good' in a system where marks are awarded out of ten (as in England, say) and not twenty (as in France). And arithmetic, or more generally mathematics and science, is often regarded as more difficult and more worthwhile than other subjects.

17) Headings in a school timetable: Environmental Studies, R.I., History ...

As we saw in Chapter Two, any society necessarily possesses a social knowledge system, that is, a set of functions and structures for knowledge management. This system underpins institutional discourse, as can be seen by glancing at any school timetable, and is subject to intercultural variation. 'Environmental' studies often occupy an important place in English school timetables, but as far as I can tell they do not have any equivalent in France. Nor, for obvious but profound structural and political reasons, does 'R.I.' (Religious Instruction, still largely obligatory, as the Anglican church is established as the national faith in Great Britain). History is taught as a separate subject in Britain, but in France it is always in tandem with geography ('Histoire-géo').

18) *Child*: Please miss, I ain't got no paper.
    Teacher: Speak nicely. You haven't any paper.

The outcome of the standardization process is not just a set of correct or stigmatized forms, it is a set of *behaviours and attitudes towards language* which are usually learnt or acquired by children in interaction with adults (Downes 1998; Ryan and Giles 1982). When the child's first language variety is regarded as socially substandard, this interaction may well be conflictual in nature. Despite massive institutional intervention, backed up by powerful sanctions, substandard varieties persist precisely because they are the major forms of expression of the identity of members of the social groups in question. Teachers are the major agents in enforcing and maintaining the norms and position of the standard variety. This is a perfectly legitimate role, since mastery of the standard is a necessary, if not sufficient, condition for access to the knowledge and power it vehiculates: if, as we saw (Chapter Two), language is the main mechanism of the social knowledge system, it is the standard form which dominates in almost all public affairs, scientific, political, religious, educational and artistic. What is not legitimate is the denigration of children's non-standard varieties on the grounds that they are ugly, illogical or simply inferior. Apart from being sociolinguistic nonsense, such an approach tends to be self-defeating, since it inevitably calls up defensive reactions on the part of the children whose identities are under attack. (See Section 5.3 below on 'Standardization'.)

It is particularly surprising to Westerners to learn that there are a number of societies where adults do *not* speak to children, or not directly at least, because children are not considered to be potential communicative partners or to have achieved personhood, or where no attempt is made by adults to simplify their discourse.

In most English-speaking countries, even people who abhor baby-talk unconsciously adapt their speech to children in a number of ways. These include:

short utterances
avoidance of anacoluthon
lexical selection, denomination
higher pitch, wider intonational range
attention signals, exclamations, frequent use of names
reformulations, expansions, explanations
slow delivery
onomatopoeia
gestures and facial expression
model dialogues and accentuation of turn-taking structure

Together, these behaviours form or manifest a very powerful and very profound set of beliefs about language and language learning, one which we could roughly summarize as being based on a discursive process of *simplification* and a form of transfer we might call in a circular way *teaching*. This is so deeply ingrained into us that we think it is both essential and natural, and it has been observed that in Western societies these same modifications can be seen to occur even between children of different ages, with children as young as four years old modifying their speech along these lines when talking to children of two years old, for example. Moreover, these same features can be observed in the behaviour of many Western language teachers in the foreign language classroom. These are the areas of classroom behaviour that official, conscious teaching methods simply do not reach. In other words, we unconsciously bring into the classroom discourse based on a set of beliefs about language and learning, summarized in the list above, which may not be shared by our learners. This certainly seems to explain, at least in part, why students in Thailand, say, find the classroom language and behaviour of some foreign teachers to be shocking, improper and artificial, completely over the top, when the teachers themselves believe they are behaving naturally and appropriately.

Snow (1977) has a delightful example of a mother simulating interaction with her infant by attributing intentions to the child's involuntary movements:

Mother: Hello. Give me a smile, then. (gently pokes infant in ribs)
Infant: (yawns)
Mother: Sleepy, are you? You woke up too early today.
Infant: (opens fist)
Mother: (touching infant's hand) What are you looking at? Can you see something?
Infant: (grasps mother's finger)

Mother: Oh, that's what you wanted. In a friendly mood, then. Come on, give us a smile.

This kind of behaviour will be familiar to European readers. In Samoa (Ochs and Schieffelin 1984), however, mothers and caretakers behave very differently. Until babies start to crawl, they are regarded as 'non-conversational' beings and no attempt is made to interpret the noises or the movements they make as meaningful. Once the child begins to crawl, instructions and prohibitions are given. Now Samoan society is a very hierarchical one, and the child has to learn where he or she fits in on the social ladder, and where other people fit in too. When the child has a request, it will address it to the highest ranking (the most powerful) person present. But that person, precisely because of their high rank, does not reply directly or satisfy the request themselves. Instead, the high-ranking caregiver will instruct a lower-ranking caregiver as to what to do, and so it is this person who satisfies the child's request. Instead of Western alternation of speaking turns

A B A B A B A B A B, etc.

we get a 'triangular' pattern:

A B, B C, C A. A B, B C, C A, etc.

The same is true if the child does not understand what a high-ranking person says: it is a lower-ranking person who will repeat or explain or clarify what the superior person's utterance meant. And if what the child says is not clear, little help is forthcoming from adults: the child has to learn to show respect for others, which includes speaking to them in a way they can understand without effort.

Obviously, I do not wish to give the impression that 'they' (Samoans, Kaluli, Athabaskans) are exotic and that Europeans represent the norm. My purpose in using such examples is to provide a contrast so that we become critically aware of our own practices, and do not just take them for granted. Nor do I want to give the impression that there is some kind of uniform, monolithic European culture in this respect. There can be differences between two European countries that are just as big as those between Americans and Samoans, say. A quick and informal example would be *verbal violence* in the classroom. Educational systems and traditions vary considerably in the extent to which they sanction or tolerate verbal violence such as insults or sarcasm. If you compare three European countries – England, France and Finland – it is striking how they vary in this respect. In France, teachers regularly insult their pupils ('Imbécile!', 'T'es nul!') and are sarcastic at their expense. In England, or so it seems to me, direct insults are rather rare but sarcasm is common, while in Finland both insults and sarcasm are considered to be completely unacceptable in a teacher.

For the past few years, the CRAPEL (Centre de Recherches et d'Applications pédagogiques en Langues, Université de Nancy) has been carrying out an ethnographic comparison of French and English secondary school classrooms. We have an arrangement with English universities and educational authorities which allows young French and English teachers to qualify in both countries. That is, they obtain both a PGCE in England and a *Maîtrise* in French as a Foreign Language in France. Setting up a programme of this kind implies intensive negotiations concerning the syllabus and there are institutional constraints and difficulties, but it was soon realized that there were a number of problems on both sides of the Channel that could not be considered technical or institutional. They were social matters, related to attitudes and beliefs, to folk models of teaching and learning, and they resulted in trainee teachers returning from their periods of teaching practice in varying degrees of culture shock.

We have been investigating the conflicting beliefs and practices which give rise to that culture shock in a series of interviews. Differences are dealt with under four headings:

1) Time management
2) Classrooms: space and conduct
3) The teacher's role
4) The school's role

Our findings are summarized in Tables 3.4, 3.5, 3.6 and 3.7:

Table 3.4 Time management

Event	England	France
Lesson	30'–1½ hrs	1–2 hrs
Dinner break	30'–1½ hrs	1–2 hrs
(Secondary) school day	7–8 hrs	8–10 hrs
(Summer) holiday	6–8 weeks	9 weeks
Homework	30'–45' per day	2–3 hrs per day
Detention	30'	2–3 hrs

Table 3.5 Classrooms and classroom behaviour

British classrooms	French classrooms
Dirty, run-down, lively	Dull
Open: high visibility, visitors. Multi-purpose	Closed, no visitors. Specialized
Noisy, anarchic	Quieter, organized
Freedom to move and speak. Undisciplined	Disciplined
Strict dress code: uniforms, rules for length of skirts and make-up	No dress code
Focus on individual, teachers show respect	Focus on syllabus, pupils show respect
Teacher encourages	Teacher organizes
Social relationship relatively informal, physical contacts taboo	Social relationship relatively formal

Table 3.6 Role of teacher

Britain	France
Teacher's responsibilities extend beyond classroom: playground, corridor and refectory supervision	Teacher's responsibilities stop at classroom door, end of class. Supervision of corridors, meals, etc. carried out by non-teaching staff
Schooling specialist expected to carry out wide range of non-teaching duties, administration (including budget, recruitment), replace absent colleagues	Subject specialist, supported by specialists in educational psychology, social workers/administrators. Not expected to replace absent colleagues
Full '9 to 5' day	Presence only during teaching hours (16–22 per week)
Team-teaching: collective decisions on syllabus, problems, methodology, assessment	Wide degree of autonomy
Hierarchy: class teacher, head of department or year, etc., regular 'inspections' by colleagues, visits by parents	Only the inspector has right of entry (once every 3–5 yrs)

Table 3.7 Role of the school

Britain	France
Pastoral. Education: includes social and private life of whole person	Instruction: limited to academic aspects of pupils' development
Includes non-academic subjects and activites: sport, art	Seldom included
Courses on 'Personal, Social and Health Education', 'Citizenship'	Course on 'Education civique'
Communal: assembly, uniform, forms, teams	No such practices

It would not be particularly helpful to comment in detail on every point alluded to in Tables 3.4 to 3.7. They do, however, give a general idea of the social and institutional contexts in which the data were gathered. It should, though, be remembered that these are not the findings of a large-scale survey based only on measurable and objective criteria. They are the impressions of young teachers, working abroad for the first time, indeed, in many cases, teaching for the first time. They are regular in a way that is interesting to the educational anthropologist, but the main point is that for many of the young teachers concerned, these differences were a source of bewilderment, anger even, because to them they seemed so irrational and unnatural.

For the moment, let us focus on just one aspect of this study, since it seems to illustrate and confirm the points made earlier about rearing practices. In particular, if we examine Tables 3.5 and 3.6, they provide us with the following set of impressions:

- The French teachers found that English school buildings were badly maintained and dirty, but were struck by the number of exhibitions, posters and articles on display concerning topics such as the school journey. The English teachers found French classrooms uniformly dull.
- Although in both countries teachers theoretically had 'their' classrooms, the French teachers found English classrooms were in fact multi-functional, since they often doubled as the school canteen, were used for club meetings, and so on. It was also rare to find a specialized room such as an infirmary in an English school.
- French trainees were surprised to find how open their classrooms were, both physically and socially. It was frequently possible to

148

see into them from the outside, through windows in the doors or even along the length of a wall giving onto a corridor. However, it was the ease and number of interruptions which shocked them most. In France, except for the very occasional visit by a school inspector, the teacher shuts the classroom door and is left alone in charge until the end of the class, whereas the trainees had the impression that in England there was a constant flow of outsiders: the head teacher, colleagues such as the class teacher or the head of subject, administrators and pupils from other classes, many of whom did not knock before entering.

- The French trainees found that English pupils moved around the classroom much more freely. For example, if they needed something from a cupboard or desk, they did not ask for permission to fetch it. They also found English classrooms noisier, with pupils taking speaking turns more freely and initiating topics easily. All of this gave the French trainees an impression of anarchy and indiscipline. Although some found this perturbing, others attributed it to a greater respect in England for individual freedom and for cultural and individual differences. They had great difficulty reconciling this apparent lack of discipline with the extremely strict rules concerning school uniform and were particularly shocked by the fact that these rules were enforced outside the school, which several considered as an invasion of privacy.

- Almost without exception, both the French and the English teacher trainees involved in this programme over a seven-year period remarked on what they perceived as an important difference in the ways the senior colleagues they observed spoke to their pupils. This difference centres around the practice of *encouraging*. It would be difficult to exaggerate the strength of feeling expressed by these young teachers concerning the presence or absence of encouraging remarks by their opposite numbers. The English trainees are massively critical of the French, using terms such as 'cruel' and 'sadistic':

> French teachers are sarcastic ... they even go as far as to make the pupils cry ... they shout a lot ... they are cruel
>
> They criticize the pupils, rather than encouraging them ... they don't encourage them to work
>
> If something's wrong, it's wrong, so don't expect any encouragement
>
> French teachers run down pupils who are having difficulty in front of the others.

The truth of these remarks was acknowledged by many of the French trainees – but not necessarily accepted as criticisms. For them, the constant repetition by their English colleagues of expressions such as

> What a good answer.
> Very good, I knew you could do it.
> Well done.
> Thank you, OK, that's right.
> Well done, good, excellent
> What a good, detailed/accurate/thorough/reasoned answer ...
> You've got a good grasp of that ...
> It's interesting that you say that ...
> I agree with you there ...
> I like the way you supported that ...
> OK, all right.
> Quite good.
> Good, right, correct.
> Well done, good, fine.
> Super, very good.
> Great, excellent, congratulations,

was an irritant, an obstacle to communication, counter-productive in learning terms, hypocritical even, because it gave the pupils a false impression of their level of performance. Predictably, these trainees were extremely surprised when an English university teacher-trainer helpfully provided them with a long list of 'encouraging expressions'. Encouraging remarks simply do not appear in the same quantity in the repertoire of communicative practices of French teachers, perhaps even of French adults.

My colleagues Sophie Bailly and Florence Poncet have also collected written remarks by French and British teachers in their pupils' exercise books and have tried to put them in an order going from most negative to most positive (shown in Table 3.8).

A comparison of this kind is fraught with semantic and cultural difficulties, but the general impression it produces is certainly that French teachers have a register which includes considerably more negative remarks than that of their English colleagues. However, this difference can only be understood in the wider institutional and cultural context. In particular, the social identity and role of a French teacher can be seen to be based on a set of values and practices which diverge in important ways from those of a prototypical English teacher. They are more narrowly aligned on a disciplinary knowledge base, as can be seen from the absence of non-teaching duties or pastoral activities, so that contacts and relationships with pupils are highly

Table 3.8 Teachers' remarks on pupils' written work

	Page arrachée ('Page torn out')
	Nul!, Non!, Faux! ('Useless!, No!, Wrong!')
	A refaire, à recommencer, à revoir ('To be redone', 'Start again from the beginning')
Take care with ...	
Good effort	
Not finished, well done although ...	À finir ('Finish this')
Be careful with ...	Attention! ('Careful!')
Lovely effort	Des progrès! ('Better!')
Nice work	Assez bien (ab) ('Fair')
Good work	Bien (b) ('Good')
Very good	Très bien (tb) ('Very good')
Nice effort	
Excellent	

circumscribed, especially as they are free to leave the school premises when they are not actually teaching. Their teaching is aligned directly on the state *Instructions Officielles*, as can be seen from the absence of any departmental or hierarchical structure and, consequently, of any form of team-teaching. This relative degree of autonomy contrasts strongly with almost every aspect of the role of teacher in an English school.

Variation in rearing practices and discursive voices is not limited to synchronic and intercultural differences. Such variation is also a necessary concomitant of diachronic and intracultural social differences of almost any kind. If it is true that 'The past is another country, they do things differently there', this is at least partly due to the fact that 'their' rearing and communicative practices were based on different conceptions of personhood.

To illustrate this contention, I would like to look briefly at some of the ways that identities were formed in Victorian England. Although I will be referring particularly to gendered practices in the middle classes, my main point concerns the types of discourse which were addressed to and about young people between 1837 and 1914. If I were ambitious enough to suggest an overarching theory concerning the development of identities during that period, it would be that a number of institutional voices, including the church, the army, the public school system, scientific, social and philosophical associations, the novel and children's literature, were more or less consciously directed at forming a class of persons fitted and willing to expand, manage and retain the Empire. To do so, however, would be a vast and complex documentary undertaking, well beyond both the scope of this book and my competence as a historian. So I will set my sights much lower and aim simply at illustrating certain aspects of the identity formation processes.

The reign of Queen Victoria saw an exponential increase in children's literature. Two important sub-genres were the public school story and the adventure yarn. The first includes *Tom Brown's Schooldays* (1857), Thomas Hughes's fictionalized version of Dr Thomas Arnold's reform of the fundamental values, objectives and practices of institutional education. It states and illustrates the beliefs that 'character' is more important than learning and that the noblest form of character is that of the English Christian gentleman. In other words, like all philosophies of education, it is a theory of identity formation and of the ideal person. The second includes the stories by writers such as Captain Marryat, G. A. Henty and R. M. Ballantyne. Although the settings of these tales could not be more different from the ivy-covered walls of the public schools, exoticism and the absence of adult control being *de rigueur*, their ideological basis and the values they inculcate are largely the same.

In essence, these books are variants on the theme of the Young British Hero (Kitzan 2001) whose representation is strikingly uniform. He is young, often only fifteen to seventeen years old. He is brave – 'plucky' is the inevitable key-word – and he loves danger and adventure and so he needs to be stoical, tenacious, and able to endure pain and privation. He is physical and both athletic and hard-working. He is practical, 'knocking up' rafts and cabins 'in a jiffy', logical, but not too intellectual, clever or introspective. A natural leader, he is pugnacious, cool-headed and confident. His principal moral qualities are honesty, a sense of duty and sacrifice, and purity: he is unpreachily religious. Typically, he travels to exotic lands, such as Africa, Canada, Australia, New Zealand, Pacific Islands or India. He is loved and respected by all, including 'the natives', who need help, civilization, Christianity and education. He is unthinkingly racist and sexist, though this is a matter of degree. The natives are exotic, quaint, child-like, comical, illogical and lazy (except for the Chinese). Usually, he has a problem of some

152

kind at home (love, money) and sets out to make his fortune. He succeeds, but it is often a matter of luck.

I will have to limit myself to a brief quotation from each genre, but I think they will suffice to give a clear indication of the ways in which these requirements are packaged discursively. The first is from *Tom Brown's Schooldays*. Tom is dicussing cricket with one of the masters and his friend Arthur:

> (The master says) 'What a noble game it is too!'
> 'Isn't it? But it's more than a game. It's an institution,' said Tom.
> 'Yes,' said Arthur, 'the birthright of British boys, old and young, as habeas corpus and trial by jury are of British men.'
> 'The discipline and reliance on one another which it teaches is so valuable, I think,' went on the master, 'it ought to be such an unselfish game. It merges the individual in the eleven; he doesn't play that he may win, but that his side may.' (Hughes 1857, pp. 288–9)

A few lines later, the master compares the way the school is run, on gentlemanly and Christian cricketing lines, with the sorry plight of the Empire. The metaphorical transposition of cricket and its rules and values with life and ethics is a major topos of the Victorian period. More generally, team games were codified and consciously introduced for their social and moral effects. Men were needed whose sense of sacrifice and superiority would make them good team players amongst their own kind, and firm administrators of the natives. Nowhere is this more clearly expressed than in Sir Henry Newbolt's poem *Vitaï Lampada*, ('The lamps of life'), which I can only resist quoting in full by an appropriately heroic effort of the will. We are transported from a game of school cricket in the first stanza directly to a battle scene in the second:

> The sand of the desert is sodden red, –
>   Red with the wreck of a square that broke; –
> The Gatling's jammed and the Colonel dead,
>   And the regiment blind with dust and smoke.
> The river of death has brimmed his banks,
>   And England's far, and Honour a name,
> But the voice of a schoolboy rallies the ranks:
>   'Play up! Play up! And play the game!'

The third stanza draws a suitably sententious conclusion, again identifying school and cricket as the sources of manhood. This is regularly nominated as one of the nation's three or four most popular poems in BBC surveys, along with Kipling's *If* (see below).

Less moralistic, and vastly less sentimental is the letter which Henty shows Roland Graves writing to his nephew Percy in his story *Through the Sikh War* (1894), inviting him to come to India and share with him the pleasures, profits and dangers of a princely estate:

> Think it over yourself, Percy. Can you thrash most fellows your own age? Can you run as far and as fast as most of them? Can you take a caning without whimpering over it? Do you feel, in fact, that you are able to go through fully as much as any of your companions? Are you good at planning a piece of mischief, and ready to take the lead in carrying it out? For though such gifts do not recommend a boy to the favour of his schoolmaster, they are worth more out here than all the knowledge of the dead languages. It is pluck and endurance and a downright love of adventure and danger, that have made us masters of the greater part of India, and will ere long make us rulers of the whole of it; and it is no use anyone coming out here, especially to take service with one of the native princes, unless he is disposed to love danger for its own sake, and to feel that he is willing and ready to meet it from whatever quarter it may come.
> (Henty 1894, p. 18)

Nonetheless, the type of person Roland Graves is describing here – 'plucky', anti-intellectual, endowed with qualities of leadership, and so on – is clearly of the same stock as Newbolt's soldier-schoolboy and provided the model of the ideal competent adult for several generations of middle and upper-class British males as regards both attitudes and behaviour, and their position in the wider scheme of things, the Empire.

It is highly instructive to compare the passages quoted with two extracts, one verse, one prose, from Kipling. The poem *If* is essentially a list of personal requirements for the ideal adult, all of which have already been mentioned: in the first stanza alone, we find a cool head, willingness to shoulder responsibility, and self-confidence, followed by leadership, tenacity, honesty, self-control and avoidance of intellectual pretensions:

If you can keep your head when all about you	a cool head
Are losing theirs and blaming it on you	responsibility
If you can trust yourself when all men doubt you	self-confidence
But make allowance for their doubting too;	leadership
If you can wait and not be tired by waiting	tenacity
Or being lied about, don't deal in lies	honesty
Or being hated, don't give way to hating	self-control
And yet don't look too good, nor talk too wise	unpretentiousness

The list continues for a further three stanzas, to reach the conclusion that if you satisfy these requirements '– you'll be a Man, my son!'. A man, that is, as required by and of a certain class during a certain historical period. Nonetheless, the poem's enduring popularity indicates that it still speaks directly to many people's cultural model of manliness. As an adolescent schoolboy, I had a part-time job doing odd jobs and sweeping the floor in a barber's shop. Next to one of the large mirrors facing the customers' chairs, there was a large framed calligraphic copy of *If*. It was commented on by a customer from time to time, to the best of my memory always with profound respect.

Kim (1901) is a novel, Kipling's masterpiece, and its main topic is identity. Long before his work became a standing joke among anti-imperialists, he had penned this sensitive examination of hybridity and intercultural contacts. It is also a jolly good adventure yarn, set in India, where Kim, the orphaned son of an Irish soldier, lives as a vagabond, but eventually finds himself torn between Indian spiritual values and the requirements of the Empire in the form of the Great Game, working as an army spy in Afghanistan. Kipling's description of Kim's attempts, at a moment of crisis and anomie, to know himself and to find his place and role with respect to those two cultural worlds is just a moment in what is a sustained and systematic examination of the types of identity available to him:

> 'Now I am alone – all alone,' he thought. 'In all India is no-one so alone as I! If I die to-day, who shall bring the news – and to whom? If I live and God is good, there will be a price on my head, for I am a Son of the Charm – I, Kim.'

> A very few white people, but many Asiatics, can throw themselves into amazement as it were by repeating their own name over and over again to themselves, letting the mind go free upon speculation as to what is called personal identity ...

> 'Who is Kim – Kim – Kim?'

> He squatted in a corner of the clanging waiting-room, rapt from all other thoughts; hands folded in lap, and pupils contracted to pinpoints. In a minute – in another half-second – he felt he would arrive at the solution of the tremendous puzzle; but here, as always happens, his mind dropped away from those heights with the rush of a wounded bird ... (Kipling 1901, p. 185)

Every aspect of Kim's identity is unstable: he is not a boy or a man, not Indian or British, Catholic or Hindu or Buddhist; he is multilingual, of the army yet not in it, has no family, class or caste, yet his experience and talent allow him to move freely between and in a wide range of social groups. For the Imperial Intelligence Service, this makes him the

155

perfect spy, for the Tibetan lama he chooses to follow, the ideal seeker of selfhood.

The final voice I wish to introduce in this brief examination of the formation of Victorian identities is that of John Ruskin (1819–1900). In his aesthetic and social criticism, he articulated with outstanding clarity and great intelligence a detailed theory of gendered identities which perfectly caught the ideology of his class and time. The specific social identity we have been looking at so far – call it male empire-builder for the sake of brevity – is determined, as a term in a system, on the basis of the oppositions it enters into with other terms, other identities. In this case, the primary opposition must be with (middle-class) women. Ruskin's aim was to explain and justify the nature and repercussions of that opposition and he did so on the basis of a doctrine of 'separate spheres', with men and women seen as equal but different, playing complementary roles, possessing complementary qualities, rights and duties. As in all other forms of apartheid, the notion of equality is totally subverted in the interest of the dominant group, but I shall leave readers to judge that for themselves from the quotation which closes this chapter, though perhaps it should come with a health warning attached for even the mildest of feminists or simply for readers of a logical disposition. For the moment, let me just summarize the main points underpinning Victorian gender ideology in Table 3.9.

Table 3.9 'Male and female spheres': Gendered roles in nineteenth-century England

MALE SPHERE	FEMALE SPHERE
Public, social	Private, domestic
Marketplace, agora, battlefield	Home, house
Government, institutions, power	Family, children
Parliament, club, library, office	Kitchen, parlour, nursery
Discipline, command, dominance	Obedience, submission, care
Leadership, physical strength, courage	Support, timidity, passiveness
Capitalism, individualism	Christianity, self-sacrifice
Reason, science, logic, intellect	Emotions
Creativity, literature, self-expression	Motherhood, reproduction, imitation, decoration
Health, sports	Sickness

With these points in mind, let us turn to look at extracts from Ruskin's text *Queen's Garden* (1865). He begins with an affirmation of equality and complementarity:

> We are foolish, and without excuse foolish, in speaking of the 'superiority' of one sex to the other, as if they could be compared in similar things. Each has what the other has not: each completes the other, and is completed by the other: they are in nothing alike, and the happiness and perfection of both depends on each asking and receiving from the other what the other only can give. (p. 1)

He then proceeds to enumerate the main differences of character:

> Now their separate characters are briefly these: The man's power is active, progressive, defensive. He is eminently the doer, the creator, the discoverer, the defender. His intellect is for speculation and invention; his energy for adventure, for war, and for conquest, wherever war is just, wherever conquest necessary. But the woman's power is for rule, not for battle, – and her intellect is not for invention or creation, but for sweet ordering, arrangement, and decision. She sees the qualities of things, their claims, and their places. Her great function is Praise: she enters into no contest, but infallibly judges the crown of contest. By her office, and place, she is protected from all danger and temptation. The man, in his rough work in the open world, must encounter all peril and trial: to him, therefore, must be the failure, the offence, and the inevitable error: often he must be wounded, or subdued; often misled; and always hardened. But he guards the woman from all this; within his house, as ruled by her, unless she herself has sought it, need enter no danger, no temptation, no cause of error or offence. This is the true nature of home – it is the place of Peace; the shelter, not only from all injury, but from all terror, doubt, and division. (p. 6)

After a long disquisition on home, sweet home, he touches on education and the forms of knowledge which should be made available to members of each sex. His views may be less than politically correct, but as I have been trying to show throughout this book, he is entirely right to see differences in social identity as directly dependent on differences in knowledge and on recognition by dominant others:

> I believe, then ... that a girl's education should be nearly, in its course and material of study, the same as a boy's; but quite differently directed. A woman, in any rank of life, ought to know whatever her husband is likely to know, but to know it in a different way. His command of it should be foundational and progressive; hers, general and accomplished for daily and helpful use ... speaking broadly, a man ought to know any language or science he learns, thoroughly – while a woman ought to know the same

language, or science, only so far as may enable her to sympathize in
her husband's pleasures, and in those of his best friends ...
A woman may always help her husband by what she knows,
however little; by what she half-knows, or mis-knows, she will only
tease him. (pp. 8, 9)

I have quoted Ruskin at length because his text is such a clear example
of the main points I have been trying to make in this chapter.
Concerning the use of power-backed discourse, and specific types of
communicative practices to distribute or withhold knowledge in the
interest of the speaker's own group. Not many readers, I suspect, would
subscribe to his views, but his identification of access to knowledge, his
refusal to recognize women's competence on certain epistemic and
social domains, provides a perspicacious analysis of the role of
knowledge in delineating discursive positions and constraining identities.

Notes

1 Marina Warner, in her wonder-full study *Fantastic Metamorphoses, Other
  Worlds: Ways of Telling the Self* (2002), a study of relevant literature from the
  Greeks to Philip Pullman, suggests and illustrates four processes to account
  for 'shape-shifting': Mutating, Hatching, Splitting and Doubling, each of
  which threatens conventional ideas of identity and consistency in thought-
  provoking ways.
2 I understand that 'Burmese' does not in fact have any pronouns strictly
  speaking, using instead conventional nominalized expressions such as
  'honoured guest' or 'your servant' as terms of address.
3 *Sic.* 'Group' would be a more likely reading.
4 The pedagogical implications of this analysis have not been considered here,
  but I believe that they are immediate and important. They can be
  summarized as follows.
     Most language-teaching activities and materials are based on models
  where participants who become aware of an imbalance of knowledge are
  willing, and able, to resort to appropriate collaborative discourse strategies to
  restore the equilibrium. This is not really surprising, as classroom discourse
  itself tends strongly to fall into this category; teachers are there to explain,
  reveal and share various kinds of knowledge. The result, though, is a
  pedagogical world where everyone is on the sunny side of the street: native
  speakers who have time to give long, clear explanations and shop-assistants
  who are unfalteringly polite; a world where everyone is friendly, interested,
  honest, generous and helpful – and never is heard a discouraging word; an
  anarchistic society in Kropotkin's sense (1899) founded on the ideals of
  'mutual aid', 'supporting institutions' and 'rhetorical transparency', but
  which does not always correspond to social reality, since discourse can also
  be used to obtain or confirm an advantage, to dominate and to dissimulate.

5   'De la part des autorités, je vous souhaite sincèrement la bienvenue. En conduisant sa voiture dans un endroit inconnu, il arrive même au conducteur le plus prudent d'enfreindre sans le vouloir les règles de la circulation. Vous venez vous-même de contrevenir aux règles de stationnement. Je vous prie de vous assurer, avant de vous arrêter la prochaine fois, qu'il est permis de se stationner ou de s'arrêter. Dans la plupart des cas, un panneau vous indiquera la règle actuellement en vigueur. S'il y a un automate, je vous prie de veiller à ce qu'il y a dans l'automate une somme suffisante pour le temps que vous voulez réserver. Si vous voulez, venez donc au bureau du surveillant de stationnement ou à quelque poste de police pour de plus amples informations.
En cas de contraventions répétées, vous risquez d'être mis à l'amende. Je suis pourtant persuadé que cette contravention fut involontaire et je vous souhaite un bon séjour dans notre pays.
            Le surveillant de stationnement
                Helsinki.

6 Obviously, varying configurations of voices may specify other aspects of social identity, roles, power, etc., besides those which impinge on 'the learner', but for the sake of clarity of exposition, this will not be followed up here.

7 This is a topic which has come under intense scrutiny in recent years. See Ray Gibbs *The Poetics of Mind* (1994) for an excellent survey. Nonetheless, much remains to be done on discursive and interactive aspects of the child's acquisition of the skills necessary to interpret figurative speech: for example, I know of no work on *joking, teasing* or *riddles* from this point of view.

4 The Stranger

4.1 The Stranger: a social type

In the Museum of Modern Art in Brussels, there is a painting by the Flemish expressionist Constant Permeke. It depicts the interior of an inn or popular restaurant. The onlooker is in the centre of the dining room, facing into one corner, where there is a table. Simple wooden chairs occupy the centre of the picture which is crowded with a number of solid-but-shadowy figures, including two women attending to children, a waiter bearing a dish of food and clad in a long white apron, and, in the foreground, a plump, bald figure with a tea-towel thrown across one shoulder who must surely be the *patron*. He stands impassively facing the doorway which occupies the top right-hand corner of the picture. In the doorway, which is the scene's main source of light, is a man who is built rather like the *patron*, but bigger and more formally dressed. He is wearing a black coat and his right hand rests on the handle of an unopened umbrella. With his left hand, he is doffing his hat and strangely, given the animation of the scene, it is this movement, this act of greeting, which is the focal point of the picture. Yet at the same time this gesture also serves to hide his face, leaving him an anonymous, awkward bulk, blocking the light and the doorway.

The picture is called 'L'étranger'/'De vreemdeling' – the foreigner or stranger – and, for me at least, captures powerfully, both figuratively and metaphorically, all the ambiguity and potential of meeting and being a foreigner. Despite the ordinariness of the setting, despite the fact that the *patron* seems to be the only one to take any notice of the new arrival, there is a degree of expectancy, urgency and uncertainty which comes from a great artist's identifying and expressing something of the essence of our social nature. Anything could happen.

This situation is both literally and metaphorically *liminal* (the stranger is standing on the threshold, between the world outside and the world inside), *adumbrating* (the stranger's shadow is cast before him, foreshadowing some immediate yet unknown events) and *epiphanic* (like the Magi in the Gospels, prototypical foreigners come from afar to witness the godhead of Christ shining through the form of a human baby and a new covenant no longer limited to the chosen people: there is literally a shining through of the light behind him).

You will have recognized, perhaps, that the vocabulary I am using (liminal, adumbrating, epiphanic) is in fact the terminology used by anthropologists (in particular those who are interested in rites of passage, for example Van Gennep 1909) to discuss inter-group interaction. My choice is deliberate, because what I hope to do here is precisely to explore the notion of 'The Stranger', or 'The Foreigner', not with brush, paint and canvas but with instruments taken from anthropology and sociology.

On the whole, linguists and applied linguists have been content to leave foreignness and foreigners to the realm of common sense. For example, if we look at the expression 'foreign language learning' (or 'teaching', for that matter), we are immediately struck by the fact that whereas two of its constitutive elements – 'language' and 'learning' – have been the objects of intense scrutiny and the subjects of vast numbers of publications over the years, the third, 'foreign', has remained relatively unexamined. There are exceptions, in particular some of the work being done in the field of intercultural communication, for example (Scollon and Scollon 1995; Byram 1997; Zarate 1994), and a small number of publications problematizing the concept of the 'Native Speaker' and its adoption as the unique model for foreign language learners (Adami *et al.* 2003).

Now this is rather surprising for at least two reasons. The first is that linguists, above all, are in a position to challenge this particular piece of common sense, simply by comparing the expression 'the stranger' with its translation equivalents across languages and cultures. The English language, for example, draws a distinction between 'foreigner' and 'stranger' which is notoriously difficult to express in French, with its single expression 'l'étranger'[1]: German, on the other hand, has both 'Ausländer' and 'Fremde', roughly corresponding to the English distinction. Finnish has 'vieras', which, according to the context, can be translated into English as 'foreigner', 'stranger' or 'guest': Mika Waltari has a short story, 'Vieras tuli taloon', a title which is extremely difficult to translate: did a guest come home, or a stranger come to the house? From language to language, from culture to culture, there are fundamental differences in the ways in which this semantic field is segmented, differences which can penetrate every nook and cranny of the legal code, social attitudes and interaction.

One of the best-documented cases is Ancient Greece. The Greeks had *'barbaros'* for non-Greeks (and which, interestingly, was a contemptuous onomatopoeia for the way all foreigners were supposed to talk), *'xenos'*, for a Greek from another city-state who, though not a citizen, had recognized civil rights which were defended by the *proxenetes*, a sort of ombudsman, and '*metoikos*', for someone who had 'changed house', usually an artisan or merchant living in a Greek town without rights of citizenship, the object both of admiration and fear. Interestingly, though rather depressingly, both *proxenetes* and *metoikos* have survived into modern French, though it should be noted that *proxénète* means 'pimp' and *métèque* is your general, all-purpose term of abuse for 'dirty foreigners'. And of course much has already been made of the fact that the Latin word for foreigner, *hostis*, means both 'enemy' and 'guest' (cf. 'host' and 'hostile'). How is the unknown figure in the doorway going to be treated? Is he a threat or not? *Is he friend or foe?*

The second reason why this lack of interest in the foreigner is surprising is the fact that the foreigner ('stranger', 'marginal man', etc.) is regarded as a highly problematical category in the social sciences – anthropology, social psychology, sociolinguistics and sociology in particular – which is virtually defined by the notion of outgroup member. The problems in question concern two main and related issues: the first is identity and the second is the ways in which identity impinges on forms of interaction. In other words, how do speakers go about categorizing their interlocutors as 'foreigners' and how does that perception influence interaction?

One of the clearest illustrations of the slipperiness of the social category foreigner is to be found in a situation which I have known at first-hand for many years and which has been studied in detail by Finnish sociolinguists such as Marika Tandefeldt (1990, 1996, 1997). In the vast archipelago that stretches along the Finnish coast and out into the Gulf of Bothnia across to Åland and Sweden, you have not only part of one of the great dialect continua of the world, beginning as it does in Austria, sweeping up through Germany (and Switzerland, Alsace, Luxembourg, Belgium and Holland, Denmark, Northern Scandinavia, Sweden, Finland and petering out in Russia and the Baltic states) but you also have, in the Finnish language, a highly vital variety which is expanding into Sweden (leapfrogging across the archipelago, as well as through economic immigration of Finns into Sweden). It is comparable to the effect you get when you throw two stones into a pool, setting up two sets of ripples which meet and mesh. The result is a pattern of bilingualism so complex that it makes nonsense of the official statistics which say quite simply that 94 per cent of the Finnish population is Finnish-speaking, 6 per cent Swedish-speaking. In other words, as in almost all such national censuses, no allowance is made for bilinguals.

However, understanding this situation is not just a matter of introducing a third category – 'bilinguals' – into the statistics. Partly, of course, this is because degrees of bilingual competence vary enormously so that you have speakers who are, say, Swedish-dominant with just a touch of Finnish and others who are Finnish dominant with a smidgin of Swedish and between the two you have a continuum where every possible degree is represented. And then there are the monolinguals and the ambilinguals and the functional bilinguals – and they have surprising difficulty in accurately recognizing one another as members of their own speech communities or as foreigners.

Tandefeldt was able to show that speakers were not always able to identify even monolingual speakers belonging to their own monolingual or dominant speech community. That is, she found cases where a monolingual speaker of Finnish, listening to a recording made by another monolingual speaker of Finnish, would declare him or her to be a Swedish speaker. She also found cases where an individual, self-identified as a mother-tongue speaker of Swedish, was declared to be a native speaker of Finnish by Finnish speakers. I shall resist the temptation to be ironic at length about terms like 'native speaker' in the light of these findings, but it is clear that they call into question any approach to linguistics which is based on 'the intuitions of the native speaker'. Moreover, the two categories 'foreigner' and 'non-native speaker', which are often used even in the technical literature as if they are synonyms, are simply not so. They are two separate complicating factors in identity.

Three sources of help in disentangling these questions are available: first, the sociological literature on the Stranger which has developed since the beginning of the last century provides a rich typology of types of foreigner and stranger. Second, one of the central questions of ethnography and ethnolinguistics is 'What does it mean to be a member of a specific group and how is this sense of identity manifested and maintained in daily life?'. Research on the notion of ethnicity has proved particularly useful for conceptualizing and delineating certain major forms of identity. And third, work in the field of discourse analysis and, more generally, in the social psychology of language, on such topics as compensation strategies, exolinguistic discourse and membershipping, provides conceptual and methodological tools for investigating the communicative and interactional dimensions of inter-group relationships. Let us look at each of these areas in turn.

It is not difficult to understand why 'the stranger' should be a central focus in sociological theory. Any approach to the description and analysis of society which sets out to identify the rules for membership of social groups will also necessarily be a model of the member's competence in identifying non-members. A 'team' – or, for that matter, an army, family, gang, profession or church – that cannot differentiate members from non-members is a contradiction in terms. Mrs Thatcher said famously – and fatuously – that 'There is no such thing as society'. But apparently she was also in the habit of asking 'Is he one of us?' which is, of course, based on totally opposite premises. Moreover, the modalities and practices of inter-group relations are the very stuff of which social functions are made.

So at the very beginning of this century, the founding fathers of sociology, Durkheim, Weber and Simmel, all had something to say about this matter. The fact that they were all themselves outsiders is an irony which will not be missed by historians interested in the social conditioning of ideas, nor will the relevance of what they had to say to the social construction of German nationhood and their own position as Jews, in many ways the prototypical outsiders.

There can be no doubt, though, that the seminal work is Simmel's 'The Stranger', published in 1908. It was also the most influential; pick up any work on the topic and you will find his name. What is surprising, particularly when you know that Simmel was also the author of a 1,000-page work entitled 'The Philosophy of Money', is that 'The Stranger' is only six pages long. Yet in those few pages he set the terms and the agenda for all subsequent debate: even those sociologists who rejected his sociology as being too qualitative and introspective, and insufficiently data-based (and for most of the twentieth century they were in the majority) recognized his work as foundational.

For Simmel (1950, p. 10), '*Society* is merely the name for a number of individuals, connected by interaction'. Larger social structures and institutions are the product of interaction and although he accepted that it is legitimate to investigate them, he believed that priority should be given to the processes through which they are formed and maintained, including the ways in which they are objectified and naturalized so that they seem to possess a life of their own, one which might even function in a way which is inimical to the individual's interests. His interest in the minutiae of interaction went against the current of institutional sociology. To his contemporaries and for decades after his death, his work seemed fascinating (he was by all accounts a brilliantly entertaining lecturer) but trivial, since he deliberately avoided studying or theorizing macro-level issues and structures, preferring to analyse the nitty-gritty of social interaction. (Coser (1971) includes a full account of Simmel's life and career, the development of his thought and the waning and waxing of his reputation.)

In very broad outline, Simmel's sociology was based on two concepts: social forms and social types. Social forms I shall take as being approximately synonymous with the modern sociologist's 'structures'. Social types are categories of person defined according to their relationships with others, which I interpret as categories or parameters of social identity. These relationships can be specified in terms of the expectations of and reactions to the type's behaviour. These behaviours fix the individual's position within the social matrix. Simmel's theorization of the stranger is deceptively simple. He suggests that the category can be characterized or situated along four parameters: position in space, position in time, social position and relational position. In a remarkable anticipation of postmodern theory and discourse analysis, he argues that these positions are instantiated by specific forms of interaction and discourse. This is not a world-weary, nothing-new-under-the-sun claim: Simmel is the man who developed some of the major ideas in the modern social sciences, as can be seen from what seem to have been his terminological innovations (– to take just three: interaction, dyad and intersubjectivity). For Simmel, a typical example of the Stranger is the European Jewish trader, who is no 'owner of soil'.

The Stranger, then, is characterized by:

1) *Position in space*: the Stranger is both wandering and fixed: spatial relations 'are the condition ... and the symbol ... of human relations'.
2) *Position in time*: 'The person who comes today and stays tomorrow ... a person without a history.'
3) *Social position:* for Simmel, the Stranger, paradoxically, 'like the poor and sundry "inner enemies" is an element of the group itself while not being part of it ... To be a stranger is naturally a very positive relation: it is a specific form of interaction.'
4) *Relational position:* '... is determined, essentially, by the fact that he[2] has not belonged to it from the beginning, that he imports qualities into it, which do not and cannot stem from the group itself.' (*ibid.*, pp. 402–8)

Simmel also observed that the stranger, by virtue of his position, can possess a level of objectivity regarding the host society that is unattainable by members of the group since he is not radically committed to the unique ingredients and peculiar tendencies of the group.

Again, this lack of commitment to the group's values and customs can mean that the stranger may be called in as a confidant, since people will share thoughts with him that they would withhold from closer acquaintances, precisely because there is less likelihood of their confidences having any consequences. In other matters, he may be called on as judge or mediator, since he is not beholden or related to the contenders, again because he is

> ... not bound by commitments which could prejudice his perception, understanding, and evaluation of the given.

These remarks show, as Harman (1988, p. 18) points out, that:

> Simmel's Stranger is culturally competent: that is he is a member in linguistic terms and able to communicate ... while social variables exclude him from being regarded as one of their 'own'.

Every one of these points was subsequently taken up and developed on the basis of social typology by later sociologists. Indeed, almost every important twentieth-century sociologist has at some time or another addressed the problem of the Stranger, the majority of them basing their approach on the notion of social type. For some – in the USA in particular – it was the focal point of their work. Even the most summary outline of the literature in question would have to include reference to at least the following authors and concepts (a detailed historical and sociological study of the development of the field will be found in Harman's 'The Modern Stranger' 1988).

Park's concept of 'The Marginal Man' (1928) was taken up by numerous sociologists and used as a book title by Stonequist (1937). Wood labelled her categorization as 'The Newcomer' (1934), since she wished to emphasize the importance of pre-established relationships with members of the community as a major factor in determining the Stranger's position. The particularity of her approach is that it involves examining the Stranger's intentions, which were almost completely neglected by other writers. Following Simmel, these writers present the Stranger as a cultural hybrid, a highly cosmopolitan character. It was already clear, though, that this type did not correspond particularly well with American reality, and a number of variants were suggested, including Hughes's 'Unequal Man' (1949) who is the representative of marginalized and minority group members in their attempts to become recognized as equal social members, not by sacrificing their own identity, but by broadening the membership criteria of the dominant group. This approach to the marginal man as one who has definitely left one culture with the aim of becoming a member of another had the considerable merit of not foregrounding issues of race or lifestyle.

Siu's 'Sojourner' (1952),

> ... is defined as a stranger who spends many years of his lifetime in a foreign country without being assimilated by it. The sojourner is par excellence an ethnocentrist. This is the case of a large number

of immigrants in America and also Americans who live abroad. (Siu 1952, p. 34)

Sojourners have neither the desire nor the possibility to acquire membership and, consequently, they form ghettoized ethnic communities.

However, as the Stranger made his journey from Europe to the USA, he underwent a transformation. For Simmel and the other Germans, including Schütz (see below), the focus was on the experience of being a foreigner: they tried to develop an insider's perspective on how individuals come to terms with being a stranger, how, in interactive behaviour, do you 'do' being a stranger. Their analysis, that is, is based on the idea of linguistic and social negotiation (– and consequently is rich in its implications for foreign language pedagogy). For the American pragmatists of the Chicago school, however, the focus is a very different one indeed. Writing from the perspective of the host community, they ask questions like: what impact will these strangers have on our community? How should we receive and deal with them? How can we make them more like us?

It is not, of course, difficult to understand how this transformation came about in a society whose very survival depended on the peaceful coexistence of vast incoming numbers from literally dozens of different ethnic groups. But a high price had to be paid (by the foreigners) in that this approach means neglecting or denying the basis of the identities of the people concerned. In Harman's words:

> ... the Stranger's origins in German Idealism have undergone a rather unpleasant assimilation into a different world without much heed being paid to the traces of 'home' that by all rights belong to and are buried in any stranger. (*ibid.*, p. 14)

Numerous criticisms have been made of the shift in American social policy from 'Melting Pot' to 'Salad Bowl', many of them cogent. But in the programmes of bilingual education and multicultural syllabuses there is a renewed respect for the most fundamental right of all, the right to identity, which should be applauded. Otherwise, Simmel's observation that the Stranger is 'un homme sans histoire' takes on a new and frightful meaning: he can only be accepted, tolerated, if he is willing to undergo voluntary amnesia.

A recent addition to the typology of the Stranger is presented and examined in Elizabeth Murphy-Lejeune's (2002) work on 'the new Strangers' who are the student travellers financed by the European Commission within the framework of the Erasmus and Socrates programmes. The situation and type in question are different enough from the conditions obtaining in the USA to generate interesting

168

questions about the nature of 'strangeness' and she combines rich empirical data with deep knowledge of the literature on the Stranger. In fact, her work represents a return to the phenomenological perspective of Simmel and Schütz and her methodology is consequently largely ethnographic and discourse-analytic. Her central focus is on the experience of the stay abroad and its effects on the students in question in terms of their attitudes and representations. Complementary works by her associates include Michael Byram's publications on intercultural communicative competence and on language-and-culture (1997, 1998) and on educational exchanges (Byram *et al.* 1997), and Geneviève Zarate's study of the image and stereotypes of the Stranger in relationship to foreign language didactics (1994). Taken together, their work forms a coherent and opportune application of the Simmel–Schütz tradition to a contemporary phenomenon.

Although all of these publications remain of real value and interest, it would be impossible to enter into a detailed examination of each of them here. However, in the context of our discussion of the relationship between identity and the sociology of knowledge, there is one which forces itself upon our attention: Alfred Schütz (1899–1959) 'The Stranger: an essay in social psychology', which he published in 1944, four years after his arrival in New York.

In this work, Schütz's aim is both clear and ambitious: to establish 'a general theory of interpretation' which will account for the ways in which members of a group understand, construct and explain the reality of their daily lives. In order to do so he analyses in detail the situation of a particular social type, the stranger. He inherited the notion of 'social typification' from, amongst others, Weber and Simmel and, as can be seen from the list of titles given above, it had become one of the preferred methods for sociological inquiry during the twentieth century. Simmel had written on types such as 'The Miser and the Spendthrift', 'The mediator', 'the poor', and 'the renegade' and Schütz also published studies of 'The Homecomer' and 'The Well-informed Citizen'.

A 'social type' is *not* a case study: it is an idealized or generalized model of a certain number of characteristic features, an abstraction which Schütz uses to test and develop his own theory of interpretation and to critique other approaches. Although probably motivated by his own recent experience, his choice of the Stranger is most appropriate in the light of his overall aim, as the Stranger's situation is one in which matters of interpretation are foregrounded, often in an acute and topicalized way. These reasons also largely explain why he limits his study to the experience of a recently arrived immigrant who has just moved from one Western culture to another, and who is in the first phase of adaptation. Unlike the members of the Chicago School, whose perspectives he otherwise largely shares, Schütz is not interested in the long-term processes of assimilation, integration or acculturation.

Since his aim is to develop a general theory, Schütz naturally wishes to compare the situation of the Stranger with those of similar social types. He mentions six, pointing out that they also exemplify different points of *mobility*:

1) the candidate wishing to become a member of an exclusive club (social mobility)
2) the new fiancé who wishes to be accepted by his in-laws (family mobility)
3) the son of the farmer who goes to college (educational mobility)
4) the town-dweller who moves to the countryside (geographical mobility)
5) the new recruit joining the army (national mobility)
6) the members of a family of impoverished workers moving to a town where an economic boom is in progress (economic mobility)

In each of these cases, the individuals concerned may go through a period of 'crisis' or 'shock' to greater or lesser degrees, a topic that has received considerable attention from social psychologists, the *locus classicus* being Kalevi Öberg's article on 'culture shock' (1960).

Still with his aim of producing a generalized paradigmatic model in mind, Schütz is also careful to mention explicitly certain cases which he excludes from the social category of the Stranger:

1) the short-term visitor
2) children and 'primitives'[3]
3) members of non-European or 'distant' cultures

Schütz next proceeds to compare, first, scientific knowledge with everyday knowledge and thought and, second, the native or member's knowledge and thought with that of the Stranger.

His discussion of the differences between the sociologist's scientific modes of thought and everyday thought owes much to Max Weber. Despite the interpretative nature of his agenda, he does not accept a fully-fledged ethnographic, actor's perspective approach, because everyday thought does not function in ways which satisfy the scientific criteria of coherence, consistency and analytic rigour. Instead, everyday thought is characterized by:

1) a lack of coherence resulting from an absence of organization and hierarchy and to the ephemerality of much of its content;
2) a lack of clarity or explicitness; an immense amount of knowledge is taken for granted. Moreover, the 'quest for certainty' which is fundamental to the scientific mode is largely absent, with approximations and previously established beliefs being preferred;
3) internal inconsistency: individuals are capable of accepting as equally true two statements which are logically incompatible.

Schütz's point is that the natural logic of social interaction and discourse, miraculously economic and nuanced though it may be, is not the logic of the logicians who from Leibniz to Dewey have studied scientific logic. There is no use in studying interaction and conversation as if they were based on 'logical' principles, since their usefulness results largely from ignoring those very principles. On the other hand, if we want a scientific understanding of the operation of interaction and conversation, there is no use using a language and logic which is not explicit, rigorous and consistent: scientific terminology and methods will have to be adopted.

In their different ways, several of the most important lines of development in the modern Social Sciences, and particularly in sociology and linguistics, can be seen as reactions to Schütz's line of argument and to pressures emanating from the sociology of knowledge: speech-act theory and the analogies of non-truth-value statements (Austin 1962; Searle 1969), enunciation (Ducrot 1985; Benveniste 1974) and of course ethnomethodology (Leiter 1980; Benson and Hughes 1983; Sacks 1992) and the more recent forms of conversation analysis (ten Have 1999; Hutchby and Woofit 2002).

What is striking, Schütz points out, is that this incoherent, inexplicit and inconsistent system is considered to be coherent, clear and consistent by the members of the group in question, perfectly adequate for understanding and making oneself understood, and a reliable guide to action and thought. Only when confronted by another cultural model, other recipes or interpretative schemas, other forms of 'thinking as usual', other 'of courses', 'etceteras' and assumptions, does it reveal its largely arbitrary, unsystematic and selective nature. And this is exactly what happens when the stranger appears.

That this risks producing some form of misunderstanding or communicative breakdown goes almost without saying. But it does more than that. Cultural models and the knowledge they propose provide reassurance and comfort to the members of the groups concerned in the forms of conventions and schemas, solutions to problems, strategies for avoiding conflict and unpleasantness. Once acquired, their application requires little thought or effort, merely conformity. The local becomes universal, the arbitrary natural, and subjective social reality is objectified. In our everyday conversations, we spend an immense amount of time reassuring ourselves and one another that things are just as we thought they were and that we are just who we think we are (see Section 3.4 on phatic communion). For this reason, the Stranger represents a challenge not just to local conventions but to nature, to the universe, to life. His truth is not true because it is not our truth: he's a liar. His good is my bad: he is evil. His reality is not real: he is stupid or insane. Little wonder foreigners are so often seen as a 'threat to the social order by right-thinking people'.

In the situation which Schütz is analysing – immigration to a new country – members of the host community are inevitably in the majority and it is the Stranger who is expected to make an effort to adapt, since the natives have a monopoly on the power to exclude. The specificity of this situation is only really brought out when we think of other situations, such as those involving missionaries or colonial administrators who often most definitely expect the natives to change. The personal and collective memories, the past of the Stranger are no longer relevant, nor, to a greater or lesser degree, are language, cuisine and religious and other practices. In some cases anonymity and the loss of certain aspects of social identity may be welcome, a chance to make a fresh start. In others, the lack of relevant schemas and knowledge results in *anomie*, a sense of meaninglessness (see Section 4.2, below). And in all cases there is a change in identity, if only because the Stranger's original nationality or ethnicity, which was not salient at home, because it was shared by everybody, now takes on far greater classificatory importance, acting as a vehicle of stereotypes and attitudes, positive or negative. Moreover, until such time as experience of the host culture and contact with natives has allowed the Stranger to acquire knowledge of and competence in their mental schemes, culture and language, he will necessarily continue to perceive and interpret his interactions with them on bases of his own cultural filter, including heterostereotypes that may have been acquired during childhood or well before arrival in the new country.

Although the Simmel–Schütz approach to the Stranger was and is extremely influential, it can no longer be considered a completely satisfactory model even for the specific social type Schütz had in mind, the European immigrant to the USA. Times have changed. Globalization, modernization and the new technologies of communication have combined to produce many situations where the rules for identifying members and Strangers have become blurred. Urbanization and immigration in particular have produced societies where members are strangers to one another. It has been estimated that until the coming of the railways in Great Britain in the 1830s, the great majority of the population passed the whole of their lives within a 10-mile radius of their place of birth, which in turn implies a highly restricted social circle. Most of us nowadays meet people every day whom we have never met before and yet are regularly in contact with others (by telephone or email) whom we never actually meet. The search for identity and membership is a constant preoccupation of all members of such societies, not just the new arrivals. This has necessitated new forms of social interaction, or at least it has greatly increased the frequency and importance of those involving the negotiation of identities and more generally the management of relations with people we do not know. Competence in this 'language of membership' is often more important to being recognized as a member than specific details of, say, pronunciation and syntax. Many years ago when I made my first visit to the USA, I was naively puzzled by the fact that speakers with (to me) strong foreign accents were fully accepted as 'Americans' and New Yorkers, whereas I was immediately spotted as a foreigner: 'You talk *pretty*,' said a waitress. Only much later did it dawn on me that the same kind of thing happened in London. 'Strangeness' has replaced 'familiarity' as the default setting for encounters in such societies. Indeed, non-verbal signals and symbols – one thinks of the logos of certain world-wide brands in particular – are the most effective ways of saying 'I have arrived'.

4.2 Anomie, recognition and citizenship

This constant negotiation and renegotiation of memberships and identities which is so characteristic of modern urban and industrial societies is the strongest possible indication that at any given point there are groups and individuals who are bidding for recognition of one kind or another. Several terms and explanations have been given for their situation, the most recent variation being that of 'social exclusion', but unquestionably the most fruitful historically has been the concept of 'anomie'. Moreover, this term provides us with a useful starting-point for discussing a number of other concepts which regularly crop up in both popular and technical discussions of identity: these include 'recognition', 'citizenship', 'community', 'multicultural-ism', 'a sense of belonging' and 'otherness'. Obviously, a fully detailed examination of all of these terms is out of the question but I hope to show that they are related in ways which are interesting and helpful in mapping the landscape of identity.

The term 'anomie' was coined by Jean-Marie Guyjean in 1885 from Greek roots meaning 'an absence of any fixed law' as part of his riposte to Kant, entitled *Esquisse d'une morale sans obligation ni sanction*. In Guyjean's ethics, 'anomie' is a desirable state of affairs, the only one in which the individual is truly free to make authentic moral judgements. However, in the context of much nineteenth-century thought and the attrition of belief in the teleology of revealed religion, 'anomie' was stripped of any positive connotations to become synonymous with the bleakest of outlooks, one in which life was completely pointless. The sudden apprehension of meaninglessness, the 'Doubts' expressed by so many Victorian writers, and the need felt by sociologists to conceptualize this psychological change and in particular the sense of moral and social disorientation, came to find expression in the term. So for Durkheim, famously, anomie is a pathological form of the division of labour, characteristic of modern production techniques, the very opposite of an 'organic' society (Durkheim 1893). The absence of any kinds of general rules and structures means that there is no epistemic or social matrix within which individuals can find their place. Since, as we have seen, social identity is constructed on the basis of such positions, their absence can only result in, first at the societal level, a lack of recognition and cooperation between workers and employers, giving rise to a permanent state of conflict and, second, at the individual level, a lack of a sense of identity, of existence even, leading, in extreme but not necessarily uncommon cases, to suicide (Durkheim 1897).

Berger glosses the Durkheimian approach to anomie as follows:

> Society orders experience. Only in a world of social order can there develop a 'collective consciousness' that permits the individuals to have a subjectively meaningful life and protects them from the devastating effects of *anomie*, that is, from a condition in which the individual is deprived of the social ordering processes and thereby deprived of meaning itself.
>
> It is language which provides us with the coordinates necessary to position ourselves in the social order. The first step in establishing our sense of social order is to claim meaning for ourselves which if recognized by others is the very essence of social identity. (1970, p. 376)

Although Durkheim dropped the term shortly after the turn of the century, it was resuscitated by members of the Harvard School in the 1930s, in particular R. K. Merton. Merton's use of the term, however, involves a considerable shift of semantic focus: where Durkheim conceives of anomie as the effect on the individual of an absence of aims or meaning in life, a personal pointlessness negating the sense of self and social identity, Merton (1938) uses the term to describe a situation where individuals lack the means for attaining their objectives or are prevented from doing so by some element in the surrounding culture or society. Such situations can only give rise to what is, or is perceived to be, deviant or criminal behaviour by members of the host culture, as these individuals strive to resolve the tensions and contradictions between their own aims and local sociocultural norms. The parallel with the semantic development of 'The Stranger' is striking. In both cases, American sociologists adopted the perspective of the host culture, asking questions about the impact the Stranger would have on that community. How, in the context of a complex and unstable social order, can Strangers be granted the recognition by those around them which is the essential foundation of social identity? How could that new identity be shaped in a way that was unthreatening and acceptable, so that 'they' would come to resemble 'us'?

I have already used the term 'recognition' on several occasions to emphasize the importance of the part played by social processes in the construction – or more precisely, the co-construction – of social identities. As we have seen, no form of identity can be truly described as social unless it is in some sense recognized by others. The expression 'in some sense' is not mere semantic pussyfooting, since the processes in question are varied and complex, as can be seen by the number of alternatives available: 'attribution', 'ascription', 'imposition', 'ratification' and so on: 'Some are born great, some achieve greatness, some have greatness thrust upon them'. In this discussion I will concentrate on recognition as a quasi-synonym of what the moral philosophers such as David Hume, Emmanuel Kant and Adam Smith have called 'mutual respect'. However, it is important to note that, far from being an academic archaism, this notion has become a nodal point in popular discourse concerning social relations in general and those concerning attitudes to inter-group identity claims in particular. For example, the most recent political party to emerge in Great Britain is called simply 'Respect', and the term was central to many of the complaints and demands formulated by the disaffected young manning the barricades in the *banlieue* in France during the widespread riots at the end of 2005.

'Recognition' is central to the ethical philosophical system developed by Hegel (1770–1831). However, his idealism and his Christian teleology, not to mention the use and exegesis of his ideas by writers as different as Marx, Dilthey and the existentialists, have tended to obscure the very great originality of his contribution to modern understandings of the nature and emergence of personal identity. I will

175

avail myself of the non-specialist's privilege of making simplifications, both historical and philosophical, with the blunt statement that Hegel was the first to investigate and formulate systematically the inter-subjective conditions which are necessary for the emergence of self. Individuals, says Hegel, wish to be recognized as such, that is in their individuality, their specificity. Self-awareness, knowledge of who and what one is, depends on the experience of social recognition. As we are singular expressions of a universal human nature, otherness is fundamental to our being. It is otherness which makes interaction both possible and necessary. I can only exist as an individual if other individuals exist and if we know it. A human community is a community of recognition: it can only exist to the extent that the individuals concerned recognize the existence of one another. Hegel set out, therefore, to enumerate and explore the ethical and social conditions in which a modern identity is constructed in interaction, intersubjective couplings. In his analysis, there are three kinds of recognition: affective, ethical and social.

- *Affective recognition* results from other meaning-makers being well-disposed to the individual. Their attention, love and kindness is essential to the acquisition of self-confidence, a belief in the fact and value of our own existence. If affective recognition is withheld or withdrawn, personal identity is reduced, damaged or destroyed.
- *Ethical recognition* implies that the individual is worthy of respect, both legally – he or she is an agentive subject having rights (the first of which is, of course, to be recognized as such) – and morally – he or she is credited with the capacity to make moral distinctions.
- *Social recognition* is the expression of the loyalty and solidarity which members of the group display to one another through their mutual inclusion in group activities.

In ethical and political terms, Hegel has shifted the discussion of social relationships based on justice and a fair distribution of resources to one based on the institutional recognition of the individual's identity. A just society is one which guarantees the integrity of the individual and, by extension, the cultural groups he or she is a member of. It is not unreasonable to see Hegel's approach as an attempt to chronicle and theorize the major social developments taking place during his lifetime, as aristocracies were transformed abruptly or gradually into democra-cies, shifting their value systems from ones based on honour and hierarchy to ones based on dignity and equality. The social and interactive repercussions had been heralded in the conversational etiquette of the eighteenth-century coffee-house (as opposed to the aristocratic salon) (Coser 1970, pp. 19–25).

> First gentry, tradesmen, all are welcome hither, and may without affront sit down together.
> Pre-eminence of place none here should mind, but take the next fit seat that he can find:
> Nor need any, if finer persons come, rise up for to assign to them his room.
> (*ibid.*, p. 20)

As Coser comments:

> The coffee-house thus levelled rank, but it led at the same time to new forms of integration. It helped to replace a solidarity based on common styles of life or common descent by one based on like opinion ... Individuals learned in contact with others to value their own opinions, and they also learned to be guided by standards that slowly emerged from reciprocal interaction and discussion. Heteronomous standards of tradition were thus replaced by autonomously evolved standards of mutuality. (*ibid.*, pp. 20–1)

The emergence and development of coffee-houses as they evolved into the preferred meeting-places of specific interest groups (Whigs to Button's, Tories to White's, Child's for clergymen and so on), in some cases to become highly exclusive clubs, is an exceptionally clear example of the tight fit between domains of cultural knowledge, forms of interaction and group identities, and our understanding the mechanisms of such a social change greatly benefits from being seen as an extension or realignment of patterns of Hegelian recognition.

The relevance of recognition as an explanatory concept for the formation of individual and group identities is by no means limited to historical instances. As the title of one of his most important publications shows, recognition plays a pivotal role in Charles Taylor's reflections on the subject of multiculturalism, *Multiculturalism and the Politics of Recognition* (1992).

Taylor's analysis of the theoretical and practical problems posed by multiculturalism is carefully balanced and nuanced. Any kind of identity politics – social, linguistic, regional, religious or whatever – expresses a claim to be recognized as different. But since that difference is itself an expression of human nature – a specific variant somewhere along the spectrum of variability – such claims are always at the same time demands to be fully recognized as 'human beings', 'citizens', members of society'. Claims to be recognized as different are never claims to be recognized as inferior, after all: they are invariably based on the perception that recognition will improve the lot of the claimants in some relevant way.

The refusal or negation of the demands formulated by identity politics movements, when not due to downright hostility, is usually based on an assimilationist rationale. However, both assimilationist and multicultural policies present disadvantages and dangers. On the one hand, policies aiming at assimilation will, intentionally or otherwise, always produce some form or degree of discrimination, since they require unilateral sacrifices of the domains of difference (sacrifices which are often made on the basis of promises which are not kept). On the other hand, multiculturalism based on the universal principle that all individuals are fully human and deserve to be recognized as citizens with full rights entails the logical necessity to refuse recognition of practices based on a rejection of that universal principle: honour killings, caste, racial discrimination and infanticide, for example.

The problem is an age-old one: all liberal societies contain the seeds of their own destruction, since they may allow groups opposed to their values to use their freedom to negate liberalism. Democracies have been stifled this way. Universal principles, Taylor argues, should not be waived in the interest of local cultural specificities. He is, in fact, cautious about recommending an unlimited or untrammelled multiculturalism which might get out of hand and result in the destruction in the name of local standards and practices of the very universal principles which protect and legitimate the rights in question. In schematic terms, the choice is not between 'multi-culturalism' and 'mono-culturalism', but between civilization and barbarity. So-called monocultural societies are often portrayed as 'repressive', 'colourless' or whatever but they – like all human societies – are very, very fragile and not to be carelessly endangered. Whether we talk in terms of monoculturalism and assimilation or of multiculturalism and recognition, we need to ask the question 'What exactly is being assimilated? or 'What is being recognized?'

As we have seen, one of the most important forms of recognition is the attribution to the individual of the quality of or right to citizenship. The citizen is fully human and fully social and as such has dignity, rights and duties. Citizenship is not only a quality, however: like other attributes of social identity, it is something one does, the performance of political actions. It is a defining principle of modern democratic practice that all members of a society are entitled to be citizens unless they have forfeited that right through anti-social behaviour or are considered too young. Even these slight restrictions, however, show that there are limits as to what we might mean by 'fully human' and that they have repercussions on recognition and social identity. And as

Marcel Mauss showed in his classic essay (1938), other forms of society, predicated on different views of human nature, different beliefs and value systems, will necessarily produce different social and legal representations of 'a person' and of identity. Looking at the types of person who are granted citizenship is therefore an excellent way of examining the identities or types of personhood available in the society in question, the hierarchical relations between them and the criteria for their attribution.

In Ancient Greece, citizenship was acquired by birth and all those who participated in the life of the city were citizens, whatever their differences of class and status, age, occupation. All, that is, except foreigners (including those who had been granted residence), women and slaves. The Greeks devoted much thought to the concept of citizenship and the nature of community and this has led some observers (Castoriadis 1986) to see citizenship as dominating all other forms of identity as far as they were concerned. Their most funda-mental opposition of all – Greek/Barbarian – was established on the basis of 'isonomia', the equal participation in the exercise of power and law-making by citizens who owed obedience to the law and not to a man or ruler. For the Romans, from the time of the Edict of Caracalla (212 BC) onwards, foreign freemen could become citizens and like all citizens they then acquired the right to perform certain legal acts such as marrying, entering into a contract or bringing a case to justice. This right was not extended to non-citizens, another example of identity as the primary felicity condition for the performance of acts. And as Mauss (*ibid.*) also points out, in other societies individuals may not be considered as complete persons until they have children, own property or die.

Modern thinking on citizenship is seen by many commentators as being essentially a belated interpretation of Greek and Roman repub-licanism (Walzer 1997). In some cases, there has been a clearly discernible line of development from a 'Greek' model, based on ethnicity or biological relationships, which is then conditioned by considerations of a political and material nature until finally the 'Roman' model of citizenship as an abstract right emerges. For others, however, this account is just too neat: many countries, perhaps the majority, muddle along with definitions of citizenship (and nationality) which are attempts to square the circle by reconciling ethnicity with universality. Another objection is that such an account looks suspi-ciously like an embarrassed Whig historian's version of the reasons why the right to vote was slowly dissociated from property in nineteenth-century Britain. The horror of French Revolutionary ideas and of democracy itself expressed so frequently and forcefully by intelligent and responsible writers was not just a matter of selfishness or mindless snobbery. It was an expression of the belief that the lower orders were, in the fullest sense, 'a different class of person', not fully human. Time and again they are referred to as 'animals', 'beasts'. As such they lacked feelings and were largely insensible to pain. Their lower position on the Chain of Creation justified the appalling treatment that was meted out to them in mines and factories.

Citizenship, in the sense of enjoying and exercising full legal and social rights in a community, is obviously a vital ingredient of social life and as a concept it goes some way to explaining what we might mean by 'a sense of belonging', an expression which occurs sooner rather than later in almost any discussion of identity. However, and perhaps just as obviously, it is certainly not a full explanation of the individual's relationship to society. In the approach to social identity adopted here this is to be expected. Citizenship is just one of the group identities possessed by an individual and they may well be in competition with one another: religious, ethnic, linguistic or professional considerations, for example, may be given priority over the public interest, not to mention motivations of a strictly material kind, globalization or sheer indifference.[4]

To account more fully for 'a sense of belonging', recourse may be had to the notion of 'community' which is probably the most important concept in sociology and social psychology. Community represents an attempt to grasp social relations in terms of their affective and moral characteristics rather than their utilitarian and material constraints and contingencies. People have feelings about one another, they enter into close and lasting relationships whose psychological and emotional dimensions are important to them. The simplest transaction – buying a loaf or a pint of beer, say – can become the symbolic expression of the affective ties, the mutual recognition and shared memories and experiences that we refer to as 'a sense of belonging'. A customer becomes 'a good customer', 'a regular'; the family that moves in next door become neighbours or friends.

Whereas the Greek Socratic philosophers saw community as aiming at the social good and providing the norms which would ensure free and equal participation in a stable and satisfactory way of life, modern philosophers, Hobbes and Kant in particular, tended to see it as a basis for establishing the contractual arrangements such as those seen in political representation or delegation which are always necessary to protect the citizen's rights. For the conservative Edmund Burke (1729–1797), especially from the time of the French Revolution onwards, 'community' and, indeed, any kind of overarching concept or structure such as 'the State', 'Government' or 'Society', was to be viewed with the deepest suspicion, since it represented depersonalized power and a threat to individual rights and responsibilities, to traditional religion and hierarchy and, if allied with commercialization and democracy, could only result in the disempowerment of the individual and the destruction of the social fabric. The aims of government should not be universal abstractions such as 'liberty' and 'equality', but the provision of the conditions in which individuals could lead rational and moral lives with as little interference as possible, a task for which a hereditary aristocracy was better suited than unbridled democracy. Burke's *Reflections on the Revolution in France* (1790) and Tom Paine's rejoinder *The Rights of Man* (1791) together form a debate about human nature and types of personhood and their implications for the ways in which individuals are to be adequately and justly integrated as members of society, the positions and identities, the roles and rights which are to be made available to them.

It was the German sociologist Ferdinand Tönnies (1855–1936) who gave the term community its contemporary definition and socio-psychological sense with his distinction between *Gemeinschaft* and *Gesellschaft*, community and society (1887). Community, largely asso-ciated with a traditional agricultural way of life whose members live in small towns or villages, is held together and functions on the basis of historical and affective ties with as its foci, the family, the church and the neighbours. Members of a community share the same values, beliefs and customary practices, which are mostly implicit or uncon-scious, and mutual support rather than personal profit is the basis of the economy. Society, on the other hand, is a product of urbanization and is characterized by individualism and competition. Social relations are based on explicit contracts rather than trust and custom (just one instance of a general tendency towards abstraction) and the economy is that of the market whose values are efficiency and profit.

Shorn of its romantic nostalgia, Tönnies's distinction has proved extremely fruitful and has been debated and developed by Durkheim, Weber and Simmel amongst others, partly at least because it draws attention to issues of subjectivity and affectivity, culture and inter-action, precisely those areas which, as we have seen, impinge on the construction and negotiation of identities. Urbanization and the transition to modernism created new social spaces and relations and new identities had to emerge to occupy them, new forms of negotiation and knowledge transaction that did not depend on everybody knowing everybody but instead provided the norms for living as and interacting with a stranger. This original insight should not be forgotten even though the term has been usefully extended to more specific forms of social figuration such as professions (Sainsaulieu 1988), knowledge-

181

based or epistemic communities of practice (Kuhn 1970; Holzner and Marx 1979; Riley 2002), communities of practice (Wenger 1998) and participants in specific forms of public debate (Habermas 1981).

Along with community, one of the most powerful sources of 'a sense of belonging' is the ethnic group or nation-state. Much ink and blood has been spilt trying to distinguish between the two terms, which is extraordinarily difficult both semantically and politically, since they share a number of common features, in particular the idealized belief of the people involved that they share a common history and a common line of descent, a common language and a common culture. This difficulty is further exacerbated by the fact that modernism and globalization challenge and reconfigure not just the customs and institutions but the very forms of interaction on which both ethnic groups and nations are based: urbanization brings into daily contact individuals and groups with different linguistic and cultural backgrounds: for example, it is estimated that over three hundred languages are spoken in the Paris region; the mobile telephone has cut the last link between speakers and places; participation in an Internet forum may be world-wide – and if it is it will probably be in English. Moreover, trans-national movements and institutions of all kinds from Greenpeace to Islam, the European Union to Microsoft increasingly propose forms of allegiance which are not focused on the nation-state (Castells 1997). At the same time, minority movements, and not just ethnic and linguistic ones, challenge the hegemony of the nation-state and its most powerful contingent characteristics such as patriarchalism.

For those who live in them, nation-states provide contexts of personhood which differ from other forms of social organization in the processes, values and criteria used to shape notions such as identity, self, individuality and personality. A nation-state is a socio-political structure, a form of government, in which power, in the form of a number of functions and domains, is centralized with respect to a given population and territory, giving rise to a real and perceived unity of praxis and purpose. The most important of these functions and domains include: the armed forces, foreign policy, fiscal policy (in particular, taxation), law, education and religion. This centralization is the driving force behind national unity and is usually manifested in formalized institutions – a capital city, with courts and ministries – and in social roles and positions – a monarch or president. Historically, most nation-states such as the countries of Europe began as monarchies, under individuals who are seen retrospectively as 'uniting the country for the first time', such as Alfred the Great or Henry VII.

A number of extremely powerful symbols express both the sense of national unity and the individual's sense of belonging to an entity whose dimensions are more than merely local. These symbols include the crown and the flag, the currency and, above all, the language. The emergence of a nation-state always includes the emergence of a national language, which is increasingly standardized and becomes the sole variety to be used in state institutions and functions. Non-standard varieties are invariably seen as threats to national unity and identity and may be actively repressed or left to wither as the result of neglect. Together with circumstances of birth (parents' nationality, place of birth – the word natio is Latin for 'to be born'), the ability to speak the national language 'like a native' is the major requirement for recognition as a 'national'.

Historically, the printing press has played a major role in the standardization of languages, since it requires and allows the formal codification and normalization which is their defining characteristic (i.e. they are languages which 'have rules' in the shape of dictionaries and grammar books). Inasmuch as books were the first items of mass production, they can be seen as harbingers of capitalism and the industrial revolution which, in the early modern period at least, both contributed greatly to the development of the nation-state. In almost all European countries, one of the first books to be widely available was, of course, the Bible, in the national language, a direct challenge to Latin and to the supra-national power of the Papacy (Christendom, the Holy Roman Empire) which it represented. By making it possible for individuals to read the Bible for themselves, printing brought about a major shift in the relationship of the individual to the state and to knowledge, that is, a shift in the nature of identity. Nationalism, capitalism, Protestantism and reading emphasize in their different ways privacy and individualism, providing a new configuration for identity.

In both the official and popular versions of their histories, nation-states are represented as the inevitable result of the destiny of 'a people' or 'race' which has gone through great ordeals in order to attain its liberty. By and large such versions are highly romanticized retrospective justifications of the final result, history written by the winners. It is difficult to think of any modern nation-state which is, as it were, a single 'pure' ethnic group which has made good, becoming a 'nation' with no cultural or linguistic admixture from other groups. Nonetheless, a number of the criteria used in the process of (self-) identification of national or ethnic groups are relevant, not because of 'racial purity', but precisely because 'identity' is a construct which is subject to a number of social and psychological imperatives whose parameters are set by sociocultural factors. Significantly, almost all of these features have linguistic correlates, and it is to these that we will now turn by examining briefly those criteria which delineate and constitute ethnic and, *mutatis mutandis*, national groups (Anderson 1983).

1) The group has a name and other symbols
It is invariably the case that when you have a social configuration of any kind (family, teenage gang, rugby team, commercial enterprise, political party), you name it. This seems to be a social and cognitive imperative: groups need names to think and talk about themselves (Zonabend 1977). Rather touchingly, the names ethnic groups tend to choose for themselves often translate as 'The People' or some similarly generalized bit of ethnocentricity: Lévi-Strauss (1977) quotes several examples including 'The Men', 'The Excellent Ones', 'The Good', 'The Complete'. The obverse of this coin is that all others are lumped together as non-human 'monkeys', 'lice eggs', 'the wicked' – barbarians, who begin at the territorial border and get worse the further you go. This, as numerous anthropological anecdotes show, can result in a situation where the traveller who sets out to meet the barbarians can never find them: they are always just over the hill or on the other side of the river. A further complicating factor is the fact that the various other groups with which a given group comes into contact may each have their own name for it.

Subordinate groups may have considerable difficulty in imposing the use of their chosen name. A case in point is that of the Hmong of Vietnam, long oppressed by their own and the Chinese national authorities and known by them as the Miao or 'savages'. Forced into exile as a result of their support for the USA in the Vietnam War, they were in a position to use their own choice of name, which means 'The Men' (Chô Ly 2004).

Of course, amongst the symbols of the group is language, but not necessarily a language as Europeans tend to use the term (see 4, below). It is significant that in the case of nation-states the name of the nationality usually coincides with that of the language.

2) The group's main aim is survival (as a social group)
To do so, it transmits knowledge (culture, language, culture coded in language). The process of transmission implies rearing and educative practices (see 3 below, and Section 3.5) to ensure the survival of its identity, one of the most common being, of course, 'Don't talk to strangers'. The group also punishes and defends its members, in cases of transgression or aggression.

184

3) The group has its distinctive practices
These will include the group's maintenance systems, that is, its arrangements for providing food, clothing, shelter and medical care. Although such matters will always depend to a very great extent on the local physical environment, they are invariably encoded symbolically and accumulate rich meanings and values, becoming the subject of behavioural norms within the group. Groups also have their distinctive communicative and rearing practices (see Sections 3.3 and 3.5), as well as rituals and ceremonies. All coordinated symbolic activity is expressive of the group's identity: it is being the group. Of particular interest are the rites of passage, whose function is to recognize or perform changes in individuals' membership of specific social figurations, roles and statuses. Rites of this type are basically repeated and codified closed sets of acts, whether verbal or non-verbal, and are often solemn affirmations of the group's or the individual's relationship to the supernatural and to one another. Births, marriages and deaths are universally recognized, but during the twentieth century the expression was increasingly extended, especially by sociologists such as Goffman (1967) and Maisonneuve (1988), to include daily, less formal, sub-group interactions including hen or stag parties, initiation ceremonies (the army, a gang), examinations to obtain driving licences or the right to practise a particular profession, as well as a variety of relatively fixed interactions and exchanges. In all cases, the functions of rites of passage are membership- and, therefore, role- and identity-related. It is true, however, that the symbolic value of the rite can seem to be only very partially related to its nature and object: in the French town where I live there are fraternities for the local quiche, plums, two kinds of pâtés, a cheese and no doubt other comestibles, the membership of which is not limited to producers and retailers by any means. Yet they all have elaborate robes and regular meetings and public processions. On the one hand, wider regional and political values are being expressed and, on the other, becoming a member of the group is seen as desirable in itself.

4) The group recognizes a set of language varieties and (linguistic) values
In a world where (i) the majority of the population is at least bilingual, (ii) dialect continua are a common phenomenon and where geography is only one of a multitude of parameters of sociolinguistic variation, (iii) independent national languages may display a considerable number of commonalities and a considerable degree of intercomprehension (Italian/Spanish/French; Swedish/Danish/Norwegian, for example) but where dialects of the 'same language' might be mutually incom-

prehensible ('Chinese', 'Arabic', 'English', for example) and (iv) the majority of language varieties have never been standardized – in these circumstances, to speak of individuals having 'a language' which 'symbolizes their identity' is an inadequate account. To take the very simplest of examples, it does not explain how Scottish, Australian and American speakers of English might simultaneously consider themselves as members or as outsiders with respect to particular groupings.

'Values' in this context refers to the parameters of ethnolinguistic vitality along which particular varieties are situated by particular groups. The high prestige rating of RP/Standard English by many non-standard speakers would be a case in point, or the respect for classical Arabic shown by speakers of national or regional varieties. Similarly, questions of register, aesthetic judgements, perceptions of varieties as being 'modern' or 'old-fashioned' or as being the vehicles of specific areas of culture, knowledge, attitudes or beliefs are distributed differentially on the basis of (clusters of) varieties, rather than 'languages'.

5) The group shares a commonsense world of social reality
A group's social reality includes its collective representations, values, beliefs, roles and norms, which are encoded in language and maintained through interactive discourse. (See, in particular, Sections 2.2–5.)

6) The group has internal structure
Social stratification and the specifics of family structure and formation will necessarily be encoded in the language, and to the extent that they differ from those of contact groups will be more or less salient as identifying traits. The distribution of power and the egalitarian or hierarchical nature of internal relations is encoded linguistically in the address system, pronouns and other indices of social deixis.

7) The group may have a territory and bioethnic traits
The facts that you are here and that you look and talk like one of us will inevitably result in my perceiving and categorizing you as a member of my group. (Indeed, if that turns out not to be the case, I am likely to get angry, to blame you for shaking the foundations of my world, a reaction familiar to many bilinguals or to, say, the children of Pakistani immigrants to Norway.) The notion of territory needs to be distinguished from Western concepts of property and legal ownership in order to take into account the relationship of nomadic peoples such as the Peuls (West Africa) or the Same (Northern Scandinavia and Finland) to the land.

186

8) The group can identify strangers and has specific forms for interaction with them
Again, although all kinds of indexical features (uniforms, hair-style, NVC, culinary or religious practices) may help us identify strangers, one of the main vectors for membershipping is language, and, in particular, strategies for membershipping, for carrying out the process of social classification, both intra- and inter-group (see Section 3.4.1).

9) The group has a history
Members of both ethnic groups and nations usually see themselves as descending from some common ancestry. This belief is transmitted through myths and legends. (Hobsbawm 1990; Anderson 1991; Colley 2005). These invariably include stock heroic figures who are responsible for territorial unification, expelling foreigners and winning independence (e.g. Robin Hood, William Tell, Joan of Arc).

10) Members are conscious of membership
The combined effect of the factors listed above is a sense of belonging, a strong and conscious orientation towards other members and group values and norms.

These are primarily criteria for self-identification, although they can be used by knowledgeable outsiders as well. It is possible to adopt a more general approach to ethnic identity by taking into account other sociological variables.

In an important study entitled *Language in Ethnicity: A View of Basic Ecological Relations* (1986), Harald Haarman discusses language ecology (a term he has borrowed from Einar Haugen) in relation to ethnicity and aims to provide a framework that will serve as an empirical tool for the analysis of linguistic variation within the wider network of social relations. This means taking into consideration all the factors and fields involved in the sociology of language, and then relating them to the concept of ethnicity, a theoretically valid but practically daunting ambition.[5] His framework of functions and variables is, at the very least, a valuable check-list, and one which is all the more useful because it is richly exemplified. Among the variables which he identifies, three in particular have implications for the formation of identities:

1) Ethnodemographic variables
This is conceptualized as a polarity between focused and dispersed populations, with population density seen as a feature of settlement, which will in turn generate interactions within or between the ethnic groups present in the area. Ethnic homogeneity or heterogeneity will

result in specific forms of social continuities and discontinuities, forming the boundaries between group identities. Other factors will include the degree of urbanization and whether the group is settled, migrant or nomadic.

2) Ethnosociological variables

These variables concern relative population sizes when compared to contact groups or, where applicable, to a national majority, and whether they are stable, increasing or diminishing. Birthrates, the sex balance in the population, age structure, social stratification and the organization of family relations (for example endogamy versus exogamy, patriarchy versus matriarchy, or the number of spouses allowed) all contribute to the specificity of the group in question and its culture.

3) Ethnopolitical variables

What are the forms and functions of the relationship between the ethnic group and the state: is there some degree of autonomy for the territory and its settled inhabitants, as in Åland, Val d'Aosta, Wales or Hong Kong, or does the ethnic group have no special rights to maintain its language and culture as in the case of Kurds in Turkey? What is the institutional status of a community's language: does it have any form of recognition and, if so, how is it categorized in terms such as 'regional', 'official', or 'language for administrative usage'? What is the language's reproduction potential, above all, its status as a medium of instruction in schools? How does the division of labour pattern with respect to other ethnic groups in a state: are members of the group represented in all social groups or classes, or only in lower classes, as in the case of Moroccan guest-workers in Germany?

A final important point remains to be made concerning the relationship between ethnicity and culture. As Fredrik Barth has been arguing for many years (1969), the two are not co-terminous. Nor are cultures isolates, like pieces of a mosaic, fitting together neatly, one beginning where another ends. Unlike social groups (but, significantly, like languages), cultures exist as continua and they do not respect either political, demographic or linguistic boundaries. Elements of a culture can be shared by numerous cultures. This is perfectly in keeping with the approach to culture-as-knowledge developed in Chapter Two, where it was emphasized that culture is distributed differentially and it is a phenomenon that existed long before the specific forms of cultural diffusion we call globalization.

Cultural differences exist, of course, and some of them may be severely restricted with respect to population or territory. Nonetheless, commonalities exist, too, and in great quantities. It is precisely the emphasis on differences which characterizes the contemporary approach to identity and, as leaders of minority movements know, differences can be claimed and emphasized, invented even, for political purposes. Moreover, since there is also a tendency for those who emphasize differences to be those who have the least contact with other groups or the host society, and who spend the most time with members of their own ethnic group, it is from their ranks that the activists and leaders will be drawn, and their version of the group's identity which will be publicized as authentic. This may well be perceived and reported by outsiders as 'unrepresentative radicals taking control' of the movement in question, with 'moderates' being 'sidelined', but in fact it is by no means necessarily the result of a conspiracy, but simply the reflection of patterns of inter-group contact and interaction.

4.3 Pragmatic failure

Although I am British, I have lived and worked for much of my professional life in Nancy, in north-east France. For most of that time, my family and I lived in a residential suburb on the fringes of town, not far from where one of the main roads into the centre of town, the Avenue de Boufflers, joins up with the A31 motorway to Paris. Every working day, I would descend the Avenue de Boufflers on foot on my way to the University. Surprisingly often, lorry drivers who had just left the motorway would ask me for directions, presuming quite reasonably that someone walking along a main road at eight in the morning and carrying a briefcase must be a local on his way to work, someone who would have the information they needed.

Winding down the window, the *routier* would say 'S'il vous plaît, monsieur – pour aller à Vandoeuvre?' (or whatever happened to be his destination). Now, as I say, his reasoning was flawless and I did indeed possess the local knowledge he wished to obtain. But as soon as I opened my mouth, something happened. As I began to speak – 'Oui, monsieur, continuez tout droit et puis à gauche au deuxième feu ...' – the lorry-driver's expression would change from one of friendly inquiry to one of puzzled frustration.

'Blast!' he would say to himself (or some suitably Gallic equivalent thereof). 'Just my luck! There must be three hundred thousand people in Nancy and I have to choose a foreigner. And a foreigner, by definition, cannot possibly know something more about France than a French *routier*.' And so, with a muttered 'Merci quand-même' ('Thanks anyway') he would wind up his window again and drive off in the middle of my perfectly correct instructions.

My accent had betrayed me. Or rather, it had betrayed him, since it led him to attribute to me an identity which he assumed was not compatible with possession of the sociocultural knowledge he needed.

In this section, we will be examining dysfunctional communication of this kind: *pragmatic failure* (or *crosstalk*), a label which is attached to a wide range of gaffes, clangers, *faux pas*, dropped bricks and misunderstandings. In very general terms, these dysfunctions result from an interactant's applying inappropriate social rules or knowledge to the production and interpretation of discourse and related communicative behaviours.

In the light of our earlier discussion of the relationship between knowledge, communicative practices and the individual, then, it could be argued that all cases of pragmatic failure are related to identity in one way or another. But this will clearly be very much a matter of degree: in some cases, such as the example I have just given, (mis-) identification will lie at the very heart of the problem; in others, other situational and communicative factors will be far more important in determining the nature of the problem, but there will still be a faint uncertainty, perhaps little more than a fleeting impression, about our interlocutor's identity or ethos, or about 'where they are coming from'.

Although pragmatic failure can occur in interaction between any pair of individuals, including native speakers of the same language, it has attracted most attention as a salient feature of exolinguistic discourse, discourse where at least one of the interactants does not have full mastery of the language being used. This specific focus was largely due to the fact that applied linguists interested in a variety of topics, including the communicative approach, error analysis and interlanguage, became progressively aware that there were numerous cases of 'transfer' and 'interference' which could not be accounted for on the basis of contrastive models limited to formal issues related to phonological, lexical and morphosyntactic structures. Encouraged by the studies being carried out by sociolinguists and ethnographers of communication (Hymes's 'Speaking' model was especially influential), they attempted to extend the paradigm of contrastive linguistics to include the sociolinguistic factors involved in communicative interference (Loveday 1982a, b).

In this didactic perspective, the prototypical case of exolinguistic discourse is 'Foreigner'/'Native' or 'Non-native Speaker'/'Native Speaker' interaction, the very situation for which language teachers are preparing their learners, and as the unconscious result of traditional pedagogical discourse instances of pragmatic failure came

190

to be seen as 'errors', but errors due to differences in 'culture' rather than 'grammar'. We will return to this highly unsatisfactory simplification later, but it is important to note that from the outset pragmatic failure was a concept that was clearly framed in terms of identity, even if the full implications of this postulate have only surfaced very slowly indeed, starting with the problematization of the model of the 'Native Speaker'.

Thomas (1983, p. 99) defined and distinguished pragmalinguistic and sociopragmatic failures as follows:

Pragmalinguistic failure ... occurs when the pragmatic force mapped by S(peaker) onto a given utterance is systematically different from the force most frequently assigned to it by native speakers of the target language, or when speech act strategies are inappropriately transferred from L1 to L2.

Sociopragmatic failure ... refers to the social conditions placed on language in use ... while pragmalinguistic failure is basically a *linguistic* problem, caused by differences in the linguistic encoding of pragmatic force, sociopragmatic failure stems from cross-culturally different perceptions of what constitutes appropriate linguistic behaviour.

This is an important and insightful distinction, and one which reflects an opposition between those rules and norms which are *language*-specific and those which are *culture*-specific. However, as we have seen, language is itself part of culture, so that in practice the distinction often becomes extremely fuzzy. It is obviously best, as Thomas points out, to see these two terms as poles of a cline, rather than as discrete categories. At the pragmalinguistic end, we are dealing with (mistaken) beliefs about the language and at the sociopragmatic end we are dealing with (mistaken) beliefs about the society. Pragmalinguistic failure results from a failure to identify or express *meanings* correctly, sociopragmatic failure results from a failure to identify some aspect of the *situation* correctly. Pragmalinguistic failure refers, therefore, to a dysfunction in discourse processing and production; sociopragmatic failure refers to a failure to perceive, categorize and evaluate social reality in accordance with a particular set of norms. Both result in inappropriate language use or misinterpretation.

However, in the context of a discussion of the relationship between language and identity, it is important to keep in mind the fact that pragmatic failure of any kind, whatever its technical cause, always has repercussions on the interactants' perceptions and categorizations of one another. Since the major modality for the expression of group identity is the group's communicative practices, any deviation from those practices will immediately be regarded as strange or – depending on the degree of 'error' – inexplicable, stupid, crazy, and so on. And since these judgements may well be reciprocal, there is always the risk of further or extended failure, or even of the whole interaction spinning out of control into total mutual rejection and repugnance.

With this in mind, let us look at some attested cases of pragmatic failure:

1) *Englishman*: Can I give you a hand?
   Japanese lady traveller (burdened with two suitcases, baby, etc.): So sorry, so sorry, you are very kind.

The Englishman could not tell whether the Japanese lady was accepting or refusing his offer, as what he took to be an act of apologizing does not have that illocutionary force in his standard variety of English.

2) English-speaking learners of German ... are likely to produce an unconventionally high degree of indirectness in their foreign language speech. This was illustrated during one of my own early visits to Germany. When the time came to pay the bill in a restaurant, I used the German structural equivalent of 'Can I pay, please?' (that is, 'Darf ich bitte zahlen?'). The waiter informed me that I should not sound as if I were asking him a favour but should be firmer and more authoritative, by saying 'Zahlen, bitte!' (Littlewood 1983, p. 201)

In the light of examples of this kind, it is interesting to speculate on the emergence of national stereotypes and the formation of negative impressions – both of which are closely related to perception of ethos and identity (See Section 5.1, below) – with bossy, impolite Germans giving orders and hypocritical, effete Englishmen always beating around the bush.

3) Po moemu' (in my opinion) and 'kazetsja' (it seems to me) are often used in Russian, much as we use 'I think' in English. Normally, these expressions are used to deliver considered judgements ('St. Sophia's is, in my opinion, the finest example of Byzantine architecture in the Soviet Union.', 'It seems to me you have misunderstood the situation.'). Russian speakers of English tend to use them for rather less weighty opinions ('It seems to me there's someone at the door.', 'In my opinion, the film begins at eight.'). (Thomas 1983, p. 102)

4) *French hotel receptionist* (handing back her passport to a British visitor): Your passport, please.

This usage is now so widespread that it should perhaps simply be considered as characteristic of Global English. But it still continues to surprise or even shock many native speakers and for them at least it is a clear marker of 'foreign' identity.

5) *French host*: Vous prendrez un petit cognac?
   Irish guest: Merci.

The Irishman wanted a cognac, but tragically he never got it as 'merci' functions as a refusal rather than an acceptance in many cases unless disambiguated by non-verbal communication such as a nod of the head or a smile, or by further verbal negotiation – 'Merci oui, ou merci non?'

6) *Hostess* (to a foreign visitor who has just given her a small present): Oh, you really shouldn't have!
   Visitor (anxious and puzzled): But I ... why not?

The foreigner gave his hostess the impression that he was socially inept, because she had lost sight of the highly idiomatic nature of her ritual expression, whose literal or propositional meaning – 'It is wrong/forbidden to give presents' – is the complete opposite of its illocutionary force: 'Thank you, that is exactly what is expected of you'. Liminal interactions of this kind – the foreign guest has literally just crossed his hosts' threshold, at the same time the two groups he and his host represent are brought into contact – are a pragmatic minefield, precisely because identities and practices are sharply foregrounded and juxtaposed in such situations. The nature of the gift being offered is usually selected from a limited list in any given society – flowers, chocolates or wine, say – so that any deviation will call attention to itself. This may have positive effects, as when a small souvenir from the guest's culture is found to be unusual or interesting or to correspond in a reassuring way with the hosts' stereotypes. But it can also be a source of puzzlement: my wife and I were once the recipients of a carefully-wrapped packet from an African doctoral student that turned out to contain a framed photograph of himself, a form of self-presentation that left the pair of us completely perplexed. Then there is the gift which has high value for the giver which is not appreciated by the receiver: that punnet of slightly rotten raspberries with wooden pips is in fact a generous portion of cloudberries direct from the giver's native Lapland. And finally, there is the age-old question, to unwrap or not to unwrap, which can also involve highly face-threatening acts for the giver and other guests.

7) A Frenchman invited a Dutchman for dinner. The Dutchman arrived nearly three hours earlier than the Frenchman expected him.

A prime example of *faux amis*: because they were using the same word, 'dinner', the two men thought they were talking about the same thing. But in fact they had different referents in mind, different aspects of social reality: people eat 'dinner' much earlier in Holland than in France. This is related, though, to cultural chronemics, the symbolic appropriation and social use of time. What does it mean to be punctual or late in a given society? In Finland, guests will do everything possible to arrive at exactly the time for which they are invited, sometimes arriving early and then walking round the block or standing on the landing until it is the moment to ring the bell. In France, such punctuality might seem slightly crass: one is expected to appear approximately ten to twenty minutes 'late'. The length of time a particular category of speech event such as a sermon, a meeting, greetings or a lesson, can take also varies considerably. This might explain why it is so common for cultural groups to categorize contact groups as 'fast' or 'slow'. The French, for example, stereotypically perceive the Swiss as slow in both words and deeds, the Italians as hectically rapid.

8) A lady comes to a bus stop, where a foreigner is quietly waiting.
   Lady: Excuse me, but have you been here long?
   Foreigner: Why yes, over twenty years!

Obviously, the lady wanted to work out how long she was likely to have to wait for the next bus. But because of his identity, and because of the expectations he has developed over the years by being asked the same question in bus-stop-free contexts, the foreigner hears a request for very different information.

9) In both French and Swedish, there are attention-getters such as 'écoutez' or 'hör du' which are used frequently. The English translation is 'listen', which can be used in the same way, but which if used as often as in French or Swedish gives the impression that the speaker is annoyed, or has a complaint to make, or is accusing the interlocutor of failing to pay due attention.

Foreigners watching debates on French television often comment on how rudely participants keep interrupting one another. Discounting for the moment differences in the synchronization of turn-taking proced-ures, this impression can be seen as at least partly due to cultural variation in the rhetorical values attributed to the 'same' communicative practice, resulting in divergent assessments of a speaker's ethos or image. (See Section 5.2.)

10) *American*: ... we must have lunch some time.
    Foreigner: When? Tuesday?

Since Art Buchwald's articles on the topic, this example has been the *locus classicus* for intercultural communicative failure. As in example 6 above, the source of the misunderstanding lies in the high degree of idiomaticity of the expression, together with the fact that constitutive elements of the act of inviting are missing: as far as the American is concerned, this is simply a politeness formula along the same lines as 'Nice to have met you' or 'See you'. Again, though, as in example 2, it is interesting to speculate on the communicative sources of negative heterostereotypes, with US Americans being accused of superficial friendliness and 'foreigners' of being too pushy socially speaking.

11) *Danish Chairman* of an international conference, in his welcoming speech to the delegates:
    We meant to give you all a meal this evening ...

Luckily, he then pulled a curtain to reveal a magnificent smorgåsbord. Buried somewhere in the deep structure of this utterance, there must be a lexico-pragmatic feature specifying the rule that if you state a past-tense intention relevant to an about-to-be-announced present state of affairs, it is because you have been unable to realize the intention. However, as with most speech acts, there are strings attached in the form of a felicity condition: does the speaker possess the competence (power, status, etc.) necessary for the effective performance of the act in question? It is the speaker's role as Chairman that (in)validates the act in question.

Examples of sociopragmatic failure:

1) A fourteen-year-old British boy who had lived almost all his life in France went to army cadet camp in England. He wrote the following postcard to his 81-year-old aunt, a nun, in that country:
   'Dear Aunty, Thank you for the £5. Camp is fine but very hard. The food is disgusting and I am knackered. Love, Finn.'

'Camp seems to have widened his vocabulary,' observed the aunt. True, but much obviously remained to be learnt in terms of register: 'knackered' was clearly inappropriate here, but not in camp, because of the sociolinguistic norms related to age and status governing discourse between the categories of identity represented by the individuals in question.

2) A group of Swedish teachers visiting a French university addressed all their French colleagues as 'tu'.

Together with greetings (see Section 3.4.2), terms of address, including pronouns, form one of the most direct and powerful identifying strategies. The choice of pronoun is not merely grammatical – singular versus plural, for example – as it is invariably a marker for some of the most important parameters of social relationships (sex, power and solidarity, etc.). Although Swedish also has a second-person singular/plural opposition (Du/Ni), its functional contours clearly do not coincide with French Tu/Vous. Interestingly, there have been attempts in the relatively recent past to introduce a 'Du reform' in Sweden, with 'Ni' being banished in the interests of social equality and harmony, a striking example of verbal hygiene and political correctness, and one which was doomed to failure. But Swedish teachers and pupils continue to use 'Du', whereas it is almost unheard of for French teachers and pupils to 'tutoyer' one another (Brown and Gilman 1972; Mühlhäusler and Harré 1990).

3) A foreigner who was learning Finnish tried using swearwords. It was soon made clear to him by his workmates (who all swore regularly) that he should not do so. 'Foreigners don't swear.'

One of the functions of swearing – and of code-switching, which it resembles in many ways – is affirmation of group membership. As part of the repertoire of 'tough' talk characteristics it is the verbal equivalent of spitting on the pavement, a proclamation of masculinity above all, but also to some extent of class and age. But as anthropologists have remarked, the primary identity 'foreigner' is often so powerful that it neutralizes all other aspects of the individual's identity, even gender. Swearing therefore comes to be seen as oxymoronic, a contradiction in social terms, a denial of the self-evident fact that one is a foreigner.

4) *Young nurse*: This is your room, Lina.
   My mother: I'm called Mrs Riley.

This kind of problem has been the subject of often quite heated discussion on the BBC in recent years and it throws into relief all the main topics of this book. On the one hand, we have a person playing the highly distinctive role of nurse and for whom the notion of 'caring' extends beyond the provision of certain medical services and into the domain of personal empathy, justifying in her eyes the use of the forename. Her elderly patient, on the other hand, keenly aware that she has become just that, a patient, tries to reassert her full identity and, thereby, to redefine and to retain some control over the situation. 'Caring' has come into conflict with 'respect' due to different definitions of the role relationship and of the divergent forms of agency they entail. Often trivialized as simply 'the younger generation's lack of formality', an instance of diachronic sociolinguistic change, this is in fact evidence of the ongoing nature of the reconfiguration of selves and identities, the redefinition of roles, and the redistribution of power.

5) *German tourist* to a Lapp (after a twenty-minute conversation): How many reindeer do you have?
   The Lapp immediately stumped off, furious.

A taboo topic, akin to asking the average European how his or her bank account stands. But as soon as we start asking *why* it should be taboo, the typical replies we receive – because it's private, personal, not your business, and so on – make us realize that in some cases at least possessions are perceived as constitutive elements of identity, starting probably with clothes, but extending variously to commodities such as cars or to property such as the family home or farm.[6]

6) *A*: Would you like to come round for a meal on Saturday?
   B (colleague of Pakistani descent): I'll think about it.

In most European cultures, the norms governing the response in an invitation/invitation response exchange include alacrity of reaction, an expression of thanks with indications of enthusiasm and/or pleasure, explicit acceptance. When obliged to defer their reply, speakers should provide a socially acceptable reason 'Sorry, I don't know if John's free on Thursday ...') with a promise to give a definite answer as soon as possible ('... but I'll give you a ring the second I get home'). When obliged to decline, speakers should provide socially acceptable reasons accompanied by expressions of regret. It appears, however, that these norms are not universal and that in some societies it is customary for the invitee simply to acknowledge the invitation, deferring the reply for, say, a week or so, as a decision of such importance should not be taken hastily. This provides fertile ground for misunderstanding, as the absence of enthusiastic response (etcetera) may be perceived as a socially inept strategy for declining an unwanted invitation, that is, as a denunciation of a personal relationship with the inviter.

7) *Female Asian student*: Bonjour, Monsieur Riley.
   PR: Bonjour Mademoiselle X.
   Student: Vous êtes marié, monsieur?

What aspects of social identity are relevant to a given situation? I would not have been surprised if my bank manager or tax inspector had asked me this question. The student later explained that she felt that this information was essential to situate me as a person within her system of social deixis, so that she could select and use appropriate terms of address, honorifics, greetings, politeness strategies, and so on. Since 'being married' has almost no such linguistic fall-out in either English or French – notoriously there is no masculine equivalent for the minimal Miss/Mrs or Mademoiselle/Madame opposition – I looked for another interpretation. And blushed.

There are at least two other categories of pragmatic failure. Though both have received a certain amount of attention from anthropological linguists, to the best of my knowledge they have not been attributed technical descriptive labels. The first of these we might tentatively call *inchoative failure,* since it refers to the incipient stage of discourse, the interface between speech and silence, when an individual makes the choice to speak or not. Failure to appreciate the 'true' value of discourse, the relative status of silence and speech in a given situation, in both quantitative and qualitative terms, varies from one culture to another, although obviously there are marked intra-cultural variations, too: 'strong silent men' may well find themselves married to 'gossips', and differences in role and personality also influence how much we say, and how much attention is paid to it.

Nonetheless, the ethnolinguists are categorical: the quantity of discourse and the value which is placed on it are by no means uniform. For example, Gardener (1966) reports that 'Men in Pulija [India] almost stop talking around middle age'. Kernan (1977) points out that in Belize [British Honduras] the individual's social status is largely dependent on their verbal ability, with people being categorized on the basis of a sophisticated speech-act taxonomy and an advanced metalanguage. Coulthard compares the upbringing of children in different cultures from this point of view:

> ... the Anang value speech highly and the young are trained in the arts of speech, while for the Wolof, speech, especially in quantity, is dangerous and demeaning. French children are encouraged to be silent when visitors are present at dinner; Russian children are encouraged to talk. Among the Arucanian there are different expectations of men and women, men being encouraged to talk on all occasions, women to be silent – a new wife is not permitted to speak for several months. (1977, p. 49)

Scollon and Scollon (1981) studied the social and communicative relationships between English-speaking Americans and Athabaskan

Indians. They drew the conclusion that the reciprocal negative evaluations were in large part due to rhetorical differences: the English speakers 'talk to strangers to get to know them', whereas the Athabaskans 'get to know someone in order to be able to speak'. The French find a lively exchange of different points of view stimulating and enjoyable, whilst for people as different as the Finns and the Japanese (Kunihiro 1975) 'language as an instrument of debate and argument is considered disagreeable and is accordingly avoided'. In most European countries, fluency and precision of expression are signs of intelligence and high status, but in countries such as Morocco and China the sage says very little: 'A mouth is for eating with'. Then there are those societies where a meal is an occasion for conversation and those, including much of Asia, where it is not: a small group of Korean visitors in France, asked for their opinion of French cuisine, replied that they enjoyed the food but that 'too much talking gave them indigestion'. Calame-Griaule (1965) reports that amongst the Dogon a speaker's physical posture is related to the degree of importance attributed to their utterances, with things said lying down or sitting, for example, being taken less seriously than those said standing. When I first met my Finnish in-laws, I was obviously keen to make a good impression. It took me some years to realize that my constant stream of interested questions and comments must have seemed very tiresome and even impertinent to them at times.

In brief, it will be seen that the inchoative differences mentioned here provide fertile ground for pragmatic failure and consequently for misunderstandings and negative impression formation. I could go further, and argue that, in communicative terms – as opposed, say, to sociopolitical or geographical ones – there is never a case where we have a native speaker and a non-native speaker: in communicative terms, both are foreigners with respect to one another. Only by appealing to non-communicative criteria can individuals label others as 'foreigners':

> It's my country.
> Whose language is it anyway?
> Why don't you go back where you came from?
> Let's see your passport/identity card.

Then there is the fact that most linguistic analysis is carried out by (white, male, middle-aged, middle-class) academics on their own variety, which is invariably dominant and standardized. Like history, linguistics is written by the winners. And the winners are always 'native speakers'. What we need is a variationist or anthropological linguistics, or, if you prefer, a 'bilinguistics' or an 'exolinguistics', a dyadic linguistics, that is, a linguistics which takes into account formal variations, and relates them not just to social classes but to the conditions of production which constitute the social knowledge system, where access to knowledge and power depends directly on the individual's linguistic, communicative and discursive competence. Far from being merely theoretical, this touches on contemporary problems (racism, the role of the mother tongue in education, etc.) which we ignore at our peril.

4.4 Compensation strategies

In the previous section, we looked at causes and cases of communicative breakdown or dysfunction. Although the examples discussed are all authentic, it is important to remember that individual participants in such interactions (in any interactions) are not simply the passive objects of sociolinguistic or cultural pressures, benign or malign. To the extent that they are aware of communicative problems, they may have recourse to a wide range of tools for dealing with them. In so doing, they demonstrate a degree of autonomy and resistance and thereby affirm their own identities. Precisely because the range of means to which they may have recourse is so wide, including as it does various forms for the negotiation of meaning, dialogical and dialectic discourse and non-verbal communication, it is difficult to find a single, satisfactory term that covers all of them. I will be using the term 'compensation strategy'.

A strategy is defined as a conscious, goal-directed plan of action which can be modified in real time to take into account events occurring in the environment, thereby maximizing the actor's chances of obtaining a successful outcome. Put more simply, it is a flexible plan, one which includes options: 'If A, then 1. But if B, then 2. Or if C, then 3 . . .'

Although the word strategy is Greek in origin, meaning 'general', 'someone with the capacity or art of directing large bodies of men', it was not introduced into other European languages until the early nineteenth century, when Carl von Clausewitz (1780–1831), Director of the Berlin Military Academy, used it as a major theoretical and analytic tool in his philosophy of war and, more particularly, to describe and explain the nature of Napoleon's genius (Clausewitz 1832). Trainee officers in the Prussian army were introduced to the concept through a methodology based on war games (Wilson 1968). It was clearly an idea whose time had come, because it spread rapidly through the other disciplines taught in the Academy, mathematics first and foremost, and then meteorology and economics. Over the following two centuries, it went on to become one of the key terms in the social sciences, providing an intellectual bridge between intention and action in one direction, and observed behaviour and cognition in the other. This was particularly true from the 1950s onwards, for two very different reasons: the first was the scramble to develop non-Clausewitzean (i.e. non-zero-sum) models to deal with new realities resulting from the invention of nuclear weapons, such as 'mutually assured destruction' and 'deterrence'. The second was the surge of interest in individual cognition and in sociolinguistics.

I have no uncontested first date of use for 'strategy' in linguistics or applied linguistics publications, but it is quite clear that by the end of the 1970s the term was firmly established (Berrendonner 1977; Corder 1980; Faerch and Kasper 1983). This list of references is highly selective, but a glance at the titles in question suffices to show that 'strategy' had become, if not a buzz-word, a popular way of conceptualizing a number of rhetorical and psychological issues: illocutionary strategies; politeness strategies; argumentative strategies; narrative strategies ... and compensation strategies.

Compensation strategies are plans of action to which speakers or hearers may have recourse when they are aware that their linguistic or communicative resources are for some reason inadequate to deal with the matter in hand, in other words, when they have a problem expressing themselves or understanding their interlocutors. The lack of knowledge or competence needs to be compensated for by other means if the problem is to be avoided or solved and a successful outcome achieved.

Since it may not be entirely obvious as to how compensation strategies are related to identity, we need to step back a little to see them in their wider discursive context. As we saw earlier, speakers will select and formulate their utterances on the basis of who they think they are talking to, in both social and situational terms, and, it has been argued, in terms of the kinds of knowledge that have consequently been attributed to them. We sort our interlocutors into situationally salient categories (bus conductor, old friend, child, lawyer, neighbour, Irishman, etc.) and we 'choose our words' accordingly. There is clearly a real danger of social stereotyping here, but at the same time speakers retain the right to suspend or further refine their judgements through further negotiation of meanings or identities. Let it be clear, though, stereotypes are as essential as they are dangerous. Without them, we simply would not know where to start: if every time we wanted to say something, we had to say everything, we would be unable to say anything. The most banal remark imaginable would need to be prefaced by encyclopaedic contextualization, a complete world of discourse, which would in fact prevent the speaker from ever getting to the point.

In this book, we have already looked at some of the ways we go about classifying or identifying our interlocutors (see Section 3.4, Membershipping strategies). In the case of compensation strategies, one particular form of indexical information – accent – often plays a major role in orienting our perception of their identity and our attribution to them of certain kinds of knowledge, beliefs and attitudes, or their absence. The term indexical information, as used here, refers to those signs and behaviours which communicate messages about individuals, especially their social identity and personality. So anything which tells us about, say, the individual's sex, age, occupation, religion, ethnicity, marital status, socioeconomic class, state of health or mood, level of education and so on is included under this heading. A great deal of this information is non-verbal: we make judgements about people according to the clothes they wear (uniforms, Hermès scarves, jeans), hair-styles (coloured, long, shaven, bald), jewellery (crucifix, wedding ring, Rolex watch), skin colour and texture, posture and gesture, muscular tonicity – the list is an extremely lengthy one.

Both personal experience and scientific observation have shown accent to be one of the most sensitive indicators of speaker identity, as William Labov and Peter Trudgill have so convincingly demonstrated (Labov 1972; Trudgill 1974), despite the fact – or is it because of the fact? – that such judgements are often out-of-consciousness. Indeed, this identifying function of accent seems well-nigh universal, with variation in accent delineating iconically and in a profoundly nuanced way the contours of the identities, social structures and relationships available in the society and situation in question. One of the best-known cases (though by no means the best understood) is the relationship between accent and class in Great Britain. When George Bernard Shaw's Professor Higgins teaches the cockney flower-seller Eliza Dolittle 'to speak like a lady', she *becomes* a lady, a new person: her 'posh' accent triggers off perceptions, behaviours and expectations in the people she meets which place Eliza in a new set of discursive positions which can only be economically referred to with reference to the construct 'class'.

On 1 April 1958, at the age of seventeen, I started work as a clerk in the head offices of an insurance company in the City of London, along with five other young men of the same age and with the same qualifications. We were ushered into the manager's office one by one for brisk interviews, after which we were divided into two groups of three: those who would continue to work under the direct supervision of the manager, trainee managers, and the rest of us, who were promptly banished to the outer office, trainee clerks. The only objective difference between the two groups was accent: despite all the efforts of my grammar school – which included elocution lessons – I still spoke with a strong cockney accent. It was an epiphanic experience for me and I was furiously indignant, but not just because I felt humiliated: more to the point was the fact that 'they' were to be paid a salary of £612 per annum, whilst 'we' would receive £306.

Less anecdotally, consider the three following exchanges:

1) *Two Londoners*
   A1: Where are you from?
   B: Lambeth
2) *Two Englishmen*
   A2: Where are you from?
   B: London
3) *Frenchman and Englishman*
   A3: Where are you from?
   B: England

In these exchanges, B is the same individual throughout, but he selects and formulates his information according to his perception of his interlocutor (i.e. the three different As). This perception is based on his interpretation of the indexical information available to him from their different accents. In exchange 1) B recognizes that A1 is, like himself, a cockney: he concludes that A1 therefore possesses a detailed knowledge of London and selects his answer accordingly. In exchange 2) B recognises that A2 is English but not a Londoner, so he provides A2 with an answer requiring a different level of information. In exchange 3) B meets A3 in France and consequently selects the most general form possible.

In all three cases, then, B formulated his utterance according to what he thought his interlocutor could understand. If, as the conversation continued, it became apparent to B that he had 'underestimated' A in some way, he might well refine or negotiate further. For example, let us imagine that the Frenchman in exchange 3) turns out to know London far better than B thought (i.e. than his stereotype had led him to expect), the conversation might proceed as follows:

    A: Where are you from?
    B: England.
    A: Really, what part?
    B: London. Do you know London?
    A: Of course I do! I worked in the City for five years.
    B: Oh, right – then you'll know Lambeth, that's where I come from.

This process – the selection and formulation of utterances according to the situationally determined perception of identity – is fundamental to any account of communication as the establishment of a state of intersubjectivity. As the social anthropologist Evans-Pritchard observed:

> What does a Nuer mean when he says 'I am a man of such-and-such a *cieng*'? *Cieng* means 'home', but its precise significance varies with the situation in which it is spoken. If one meets an Englishman in Germany and asks him where his home is, he may reply that it is in England. If one meets the same man in London and asks him the same question he will tell one that his home is in Oxfordshire, whereas if one meets him in that county he will tell one the name of the town or village in which he lives. If questioned in his town or village he will mention his particular street, and if questioned in his street he will indicate his house. So it is with the Nuer. A Nuer met outside Nuerland says that his home is *cieng Nath*, Nuerland ... If one asks him in his tribe what is his *cieng*, he will name his village or tribal section according to the context ... If asked in his village he will mention the name of his hamlet or indicate his homestead or the end of the village in which his homestead is situated ... The variations in the meaning of the word *cieng* are not due to the inconsistencies of language, but to the relativity of the group values to which it refers. (1940, p. 136)

When Evans-Pritchard talks of 'the relativity of group values' he is referring essentially, though not exclusively, to the discursive positions available to and adopted by individuals, the positions in which 'they find themselves', which constitute their identities at a given moment in time, space and social reality.

When speakers have recourse to compensation strategies, they reveal 'gaps' in their knowledge or competence. These gaps can be just as important in determining (perceptions of) their identity as knowledge they actually possess, especially in dyadic encounters whose contours and procedures are based on an assumed asymmetry of knowledge, such as service encounters, specialist/non-specialist or teacher/pupil discourse and so on. Of course, compensation strategies can occur in interactions between 'native speakers', but when they co-occur with a 'foreign accent', the repercussions on the perception and negotiation of identities are particularly marked.

The above examples all concerned the formulation of place. The closeness of the connection between identity and place needs no further emphasis here, but it is worth reminding ourselves both that the expression 'local knowledge' is much more than a metaphor and that the names we give to places identify the givers as much as the places: New York or Wapawamough? Leningrad or St Petersburg?

However, it is important to remember, too, that that participants in interactive events can and do negotiate any piece of information or reference which they realize is not initially shared, and that in so doing they are necessarily realigning their identities, albeit in minute (though by no means necessarily trivial) ways. This can occur in exchanges between native speakers:

A: I saw your Mum the other day.
B: Oh yeah?
A: Not to talk to like. Just through the car window.
B: Through the what?
A: The car window.
B: What car window?
A: My car window.
B: You got a car?
A: I haven't just got the window!
   (From *The Likely Lads*, BBC 1974)

A and B are old friends who have not seen one another for some time. While B has been in the army, A has gone up in the world and his social identity has changed in a number of ways: he has joined the local tennis club, become engaged to be married, and he has bought a house – and a car. He wrongly assumes that B knows all this. B, however, has some difficulty adjusting his perception of A to accord with this new information, and in this specific passage, to re-classify him as a car-owner (rich, middle-class, settled family man, and so on). So he has to adopt a strategy of requesting more and more information on which to base his recategorization of A's identity.

Here are two examples taken from the second language classroom:

1) *Learner:* She's my ... she's in my family.
   Teacher: Your aunt?
   Learner: No. She's married with my brother.
   Teacher: Oh, your sister-in-law.
   Learner: Yeah.
2) *Teacher:* Russian eggs, prawn cocktail, honeydew melon ...
   Learner: What's that – 'prawn'?
   Teacher: What? Oh prawn it's ... they're a sort of sea-food.
   Learner: Fish.
   Teacher: No, not fish. Like very small lobsters or *homard*.
   Learner: Very small (laugh) *crevette. Crevette?*
   Teacher: Yeah. *Crevette* – prawn.

2nd Learner: Honeydew?

Teacher: You know melon?

2nd Learner: Melon?

Teacher: Yes, well it's just a sort of melon.

2nd Learner: With honey?

Teacher: Yes. No No No. Honeydew is just a name, it's just kind of melon. I think it's green. The skin is green and inside it's yellow.

2nd Learner: Is *pastèque*?

Teacher: I don't know, maybe.

2nd Learner: A sort of melon.

Teacher: Yeah, a sort of melon.

In exchange 1) the learner does not know the English term 'sister-in-law'. He therefore adopts, first, a strategy of semantic over-generalization. But this misfires, as the teacher identifies a wrong referent ('your aunt?'). The learner then switches strategy, providing more information in the form of a circumlocution or description: 'She's married with my brother'. The teacher is now able to proceed to a correct identification, which the learner confirms.

In exchange 2) the teacher is going through a menu in English. The learner has a comprehension problem this time, not one of expression. His strategy is to appeal for help. The teacher tries to provide the requisite information, first by giving a general classification ('seafood') then by analogy ('like very small lobsters') followed by a translation (*homard*). At this point the learner correctly thinks he understands (*crevette*) but he still wants his hypothesis confirmed (*crevette?*). The teacher provides the confirmation that mutual agreement on this meaning structure has now been reached ('Yeah. *Crevette* – Prawn').

The second learner now weighs in with a similar problem. What is a 'honeydew'? The teacher first checks that the learner does in fact know what a melon is, since he wants to adopt the strategy of approximation ('it's just a sort of melon'). However, this does not satisfy the learner, who has recognized 'honey' and taken it literally. The teacher is now forced into a description of this particular kind of melon in terms of its significant features. The learner asks for confirmation of the hypothesis by producing a translation ('Is *pastèque?*'). Unfortunately, the teacher is unable to confirm or disprove this hypothesis. However, this does show that it is not, in the teacher's view at least, terribly important to know what particular kind of melon this is. It suffices to know, they agree, that it is just 'a sort of melon'.

In these extracts, we have seen a number of different communication strategies. In classifying such strategies, we need to ask whether we are dealing with a problem of expression or a problem of comprehension:

this leads to difficulties of description and observation because, since we cannot tell exactly what is going on in people's heads, we can only deduce that comprehension strategies are being applied from clues in the learner's discourse, i.e. via expression. Another important point to take into consideration is whether or not the strategy in question involves the cooperation of both participants in the discourse. Finally, it is important to note who initiates the strategy in question and whether there is an appeal for help.

Remember, though, that we are still dealing with the negotiation of meaning: communication strategies are those plans we follow when, in interactive discourse, we come up against a conscious problem of some kind. They are cognitive mechanisms for dealing with an imbalance of knowledge. The different strategies represent different ways of trying to restore a balance of knowledge and, therefore, to establish common ground.

Some Compensation Strategies:

1)   Topic avoidance
The speaker decides not to attempt to say or talk about X, because he does not feel competent to do so. This may be marked explicitly by such expressions as 'Let's talk about Y instead'.
2)   Message abandonment
Having started an attempt to communicate a message, the speaker gives up because it is too difficult. This may be marked explicitly by such expressions as 'I can't say it in English'.

To some observers 1) and 2) are not really strategies, since they do not involve solving the problem in question. They do get rid of the problem, though, and so can be included here for the sake of completeness. There are two other main categories:

3)   Self-repair strategies
–   where the speaker tries to solve the problem on his or her own.
4)   Collaborative strategies
–   where the speaker tries to recruit the help of his interlocutor.

Note that the speaker may be either the native speaker/teacher or the foreigner/learner, though any particular strategy may be more commonly used by one rather than the other.

Self-repair Stategies

For the sake of simplicity, we shall exclude from this category

a) False starts: where speakers immediately correct themselves, e.g. 'I give gave him the book'
b) New starts: where speakers correct themselves at the next possible completion point, e.g. 'I give him a book. I gave him a book'
c) Rehearsed productions: where the speaker prepares his discourse in advance – by learning it by heart, for example.

a) and b) are excluded for purely practical reasons. (c) is excluded because it is not really a strategy, since no negotiation is possible.

The self-repair strategies themselves include:

d) Borrowing or transfer from another language, usually but not necessarily the speaker's mother-tongue, e.g.:
'There was a lot of circulation' (for 'traffic', French *circulation*)
If no attempt is made to make the item conform to the target-language norms of pronunciation etc., we are dealing with language switch.
e) Literal translation where the speaker takes a term from one language and translates it literally (or 'word for word') into another, e.g.:
'... it was in a handkerchief'.
The equivalent expression in English for *dans un mouchoir* is 'neck and neck'.
f) Word coinage where the speaker invents a word, either on the basis of his own language, e.g. saying 'inonded' for 'flooded' (French *inondé*), or on the basis of his knowledge of the target language, by making a noun from a verb, for instance, or vice-versa. Taking the noun *embuscade* he forms the verb *embuscader* which though not correct is perfectly comprehensible.
g) 'Smurfing': the speaker uses 'empty' or meaningless words to fill gaps in his knowledge, relying on his interlocutor's guessing their meaning from the context. 'Thing' or 'true' are typical examples, but there are many others:
'Whatsit', 'thingummy', 'machine' and so on.
h) Approximation: the use of a word which the speaker knows not to be correct, but which he hopes will nonetheless convey his message. This may involve:
– under-generalization: where a low-coverage word is used instead of a high-coverage one, e.g. 'rose' is used instead of

'flower', or 'construction' for 'building'.
- over-generalization: where a high-coverage word is used instead of a low-coverage one, e.g. 'bag' for 'handbag'.
- inappropriate words of the same level of generalization e.g. 'lorry' for 'van'

i) Circumlocution: the speaker uses more words than are necessary to convey his message, e.g.:
   'There was some land between the houses that nobody used' (for 'wasteground')

j) Description: the speaker describes some aspect of the item to which he wishes to refer (appearance, function, etc.):
   'The thing you use when you want to take the cork out of a bottle of wine' (for 'corkscrew')

k) Non-verbal communication: the use of mime, gestures, facial expressions, noises, etc. as well as expressive interjections and intonation.

Collaborative Strategies

Here we are dealing with attempts to influence the interlocutor's behaviour in such a way as to solve a problem:

l) Establishing identity as a foreigner, as someone who has had or will have problems in expression, e.g.:
   'I'm sorry, I'm a foreigner. I only speak a little English. I don't understand.'

m) Appeals:
   - to speak more slowly, articulate clearly e.g.:
     'Could you speak more slowly, please'.
   - to repeat:
     'Sorry, could you say that again, please'
   - to explain or clarify:
     'Sorry, but what does X mean?'
     'I'm sorry, but I don't understand what you mean.'

n) Requests for assistance:
   - for translation, e.g.:
     'How do you say *gentil* in English?'
   - for adjudication, evaluation and correction, e.g.:
     'Is that right?' 'Can you say that in English?' 'Which is correct, X or Y?'
   - gambits: where the speaker asks his interlocutor to provide a missing item, e.g.:
     'It's one of those ... you know... I can't find the right word ... what's it called?'

o) Checks:

Having formulated a hypothesis about whether messages have been understood, speakers can test them or check on them by:

– feedback: speakers provide or request feedback as to whether their own or their interlocutor's messages have been understood:

'I know', 'I understand'/'Do you understand?' 'Know what I mean?'

– confirmation: speakers make explicit their interpretations of their interlocutor's meaning or intention, e.g.:

'You mean you want me to …?'

– Additional information: speakers provide or request further information in order to test their hypotheses about their interlocutor's meaning or understanding, e.g.:

'Spain – you know?' 'Where they fight bulls?'
'Yeah – Spain.'

In the context of a discussion of the relationship between knowledge and identity, compensation strategies are important because they manifest the ways in which individuals attempt to come to terms with gaps in their or their interlocutors' knowledge. They foreground knowledge distribution at the most fundamental level of social interaction, dyadic communication. At the same time, by providing indications of the nature and extent of limitations on cultural knowledge, they enable them to situate the individual with respect to relevant categories of social identity.

Notes

1 In fact, French also has the noun 'un inconnu', but this word means that the person in question is unknown to the speaker and carries no implication that they have come from elsewhere or that they are not familiar with the locality.

2 Simmel and his translator consistently refer to the stranger as 'he' and I see no point in distorting the record.

3 It is not clear what Schütz means by 'primitives'. The whole thrust of his work argues against any kind of derogatory meaning. 'Economically underdeveloped' or 'pre-industrial', perhaps?

4 Sometimes, several of these factors may come together: in 2005, the French government launched a campaign to improve the country's extremely poor road safety record. Measures included increased surveillance, stiff penalties and an end to the tradition whereby administrators could make the traffic tickets of friends and relatives 'disappear'. The result was an appreciable drop in the number of road deaths and accidents – so the association representing garage mechanics angrily demanded compensation for the drop in business.

210

5 Other approaches covering at least part of the same ground include Giles (1977) on ethnolinguistic vitality and Fishman (2001) on reversing language shift.

6 The 'commodification' of identity and the recasting of the individual as consumer ('I shop, therefore I am') are commonplaces of modern social theory, but the emergence and shaping of this form of personhood, which I hardly touch here, are probably most clearly discussed by the historian Asa Briggs in his book *Victorian Things* (2000). Obviously, advertisements provide inexhaustible material for such discussion: take the case of the text reading 'Who would you like to be for the next twenty-four hours?' showing a glamorous woman hesitating over her choice of wristwatch. The title of Lunt and Livingstone's fascinating *Mass Consumption and Personal Identity in Everyday Economic Experience* (1992) speaks for itself.

5 Reconfiguring identities

5.1 Ethos and the communicative virtues

5.1.1 Ethos

The approach to discourse analysis which I have adopted in this book is neo-Aristotelian, partly in the very general sense that it is postulated on the presence of a hearer, but more specifically because I find the Aristotelian concept of *ethos* as developed by Ruth Amossy and others (1999) particularly helpful and insightful.

Ethos, you may remember, is one of the three pillars of Aristotelian rhetoric, along with *logos* (argument) and *pathos* (emotion). Ethos is communicative identity. It is an amalgam of speaker identity (who I am and who I want to be taken for) and perceived identity (who you think I am and who you take me for). It is being used by discourse analysts to refer to the self-image projected by a speaker in and through his or her discourse, but also as it is filtered through the hearer's perceptions, expectations and values, especially as constrained by social roles and genres: it is interpreted self-expression, the rhetorical and socio-psychological product of mutually influencing communicative behaviours and judgements.

It is usually glossed as the *credibility, reliability* or *trustworthiness* of character that speakers or writers adopt or project towards their audience. Arguments and information, speech acts and declarations of moral and emotional engagement only have value for hearers to the extent that they can trust the person expounding them. This leads directly to the conclusion that the *sine qua non* of illocution and, indeed, of all interpretation, is appropriate identity. As Aristotle pointed out, to win trust, it is necessary to demonstrate three principal characteristics: intelligence, virtue and goodwill. The terminology may be old-fashioned and moralistic ('ethical') but the requirements for being taken seriously, of being listened to with respect, are still much the same as they were in Aristotle's time. Speakers naturally wish to make a good impression on their hearers, to be seen as reliable and of good character.[1] Hearers, in order to arrive at a valid interpretation of the speaker's utterances, need to relate those utterances to the context. And the most fundamental question in any situation is, who is speaking to me? And can they be relied on? Ethos is the product of this ongoing assessment of performance. It is at the heart of all expressive behaviours and is the essential and necessary starting-point for all interpretation.

We are now in a position to develop further the approach to the architecture of identity that was outlined in Chapter Three, by introducing the notion of ethos into the equation. See the diagram in Figure 5.1.

In this socioconstructionist approach to identity (Mead 1934; Vygotsky 1978), the architecture of personhood and the individual psyche is seen as the product of an intrapersonal dialogue between the Self and the Me, the forms of which are determined and learned by the communicative practices acquired in and through interpersonal dialogue, intersubjective couplings. In this perspective, the Me is seen as the individual's personal perception of his or her social identity. Membership of these groups forms a bundle of roles and discursive positions which the Self may occupy, though with varying degrees of choice and awareness. Public perceptions of the Me and of a person's social identity form *ethos*.

The Self, Ethos and the Person have different temporal or existential orientations: the Self is fundamentally diachronic, as the locus of the individual's memories, providing the sense of continuity and a historical site for ongoing experience. The Person is a fundamentally

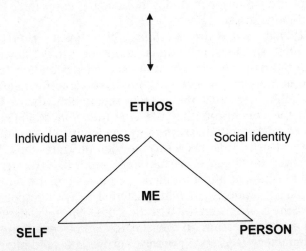

Other-directed communicative behaviour/Others' perception of the person

ETHOS

Individual awareness   Social identity

ME

SELF   **PERSON**

Figure 5.1 Personal identity

synchronic (though often highly repetitive) account of successive discursive positions or roles. And between them, as it were, we have Ethos, the-past-in-the-present, judgements as to and of present performance in the light of previous knowledge and contacts, including public reputation and stereotypes.

I have tried to summarize and systematize these ideas and relationships in Table 5.1, though obviously a static visual convention risks grossly oversimplifying their dynamic and highly interdependent nature.

Table 5.1 Ethos in the architecture of identity

SELF	ETHOS	PERSON
– which individual? Singular or numerical identity: private, subjective	– rhetorical identity. Projected self plus perceived self	– what sort of individual? Social identity: public, intersubjective
That entity whose reactions we report by using 'I', which has a proper name	Interpreted self-expression. The 'Me' I perceive in others' reflected behaviours and judgements	The 'You' that others address, construct, observe
The agent of my actions, separately embodied in a numerically and physically distinct organism	The product of a mutually influencing set of behaviours, judgements	A set of discursive positions, rights and duties. The sum of all the social figurations of which I/You is a recognized and competent member
Diachronic locus. The continuing site of my memories and thoughts, emotions, ongoing experience	The past-in-the present: 'reputation', including earlier contacts and stereotypes in the light of present performance	Synchronic locus. Dynamic performer of social roles

5.1.2 The communicative virtues

As I mentioned above, for Aristotle, speakers need to demonstrate the characteristics of intelligence, virtue and goodwill if they are to establish a trustworthy and convincing ethos. This idea has been taken up and developed by discourse analysts and social psychologists interested in the relationship between discourse performance and various aspects of the construction of social identity, such as social categorization, membershipping, the formation of attitudes, impressions, stereotyping and accommodation. Amongst the most important characteristics of performance are what have become known as the *communicative virtues*. This term has been proposed by Marui *et al.* (1996), who argue that since notions such as English *politeness*, German *Höflichkeit* and Japanese *teinei* do not have exactly the same coverage in sociocultural and interactive terms, it is necessary to develop a higher-order notion which we call 'concepts of communicative virtues' ... which are historically developed and continually transformed in ongoing social interactions. As they explain:

> It is futile to try and describe social interaction as determined by an internalised system of rules and norms; interactants sometimes feel themselves compelled to act according to rules while at other times they are expected to violate them. What actors refer to when deciding whether to apply a given rule or not is in effect the concept of communicative virtues, and this is true as well in their evaluation of those many cases where there is no specific rule available for application.

Anticipating an objection which has no doubt already occurred to many readers (– what is the negative of a communicative virtue? A communicative vice?), they continue:

> Although we call them communicative virtues, concepts of communicative virtues are employed to produce a vast range of social realities, some of which have their darker sides. (1996, pp. 385–6)

As I read them, Marui *et al.* are making a point which is considerably more important than the observation that the application of one and the same 'rule' can result in opposite evaluations of the quality of different encounters. The broader point is that the evaluation may be carried out on the basis of criteria (communicative virtues) other than those on which the 'rule' is predicated. How else can we account for the facts that, for example, politeness can be judged as 'cold', or that speakers are continually juxtaposing or qualifying politeness with other qualities: 'He was polite, but unfriendly', 'She was polite, but unhelpful', and so on. Unless we recognize the existence of other, competing values we can never hope to extricate ourselves from increasingly complex rules of politeness. If, like pre-Copernican astronomers, we continue to insist that politeness is the earth at the centre of the social universe, we will be forced to develop more and more rules to 'save appearances' as other observational data are obtained. Only by recognizing that politeness is not the only and not even necessarily the most important communicative virtue can we hope to produce a more coherent, and possibly a more economic and elegant, model of social interaction.

The communicative virtues, then, are socially valued characteristics of discourse, commonly bearing labels such as 'clarity', 'competence', 'pleasantness', 'helpfulness' or 'niceness' (see the list in Table 5.2). The presence of these characteristics contributes to a positive perception of ethos by hearers and to a successful negotiation of identities and outcomes.

Table 5.2 Communicative virtues

Socially valued characteristics of communicative behaviour

Attentiveness	Enthusiasm	Persuasiveness
Authoritativeness	Friendliness	Perspicacity
Charm	Fluency	Politeness
Cheerfulness	Funniness	Relevance
Clarity	Frankness	Respectfulness
Coherence	Helpfulness	Sensuality
Competence	Honesty	Seriousness
Confidence	Integrity	Simplicity
Consistency	Intelligence	Sincerity
Conviction	Kindness	Straightforwardness
Courteousness	Liveliness	Sweetness
Diplomacy	Modesty	Sympathy
Discretion	Niceness	Tactfulness
Eloquence	Open-mindedness	Tolerance
Energy	Originality	Wittiness

This list is at present largely intuitive, rather than corpus-based: near-synonyms and further suggestions have been added to be used as stimuli in the next stage of the project to probe our respondents' interpretative repertoire further. Our problem is that we do not as yet have any kind of systematic basis for constructing a taxonomy of communicative virtues. *Mutatis mutandis*, I would say that we are now in the position concerning the communicative virtues that we were in vis-à-vis speech acts thirty or forty years ago: we know that they exist and that they are important, in that they have psychological reality for speakers as part of common sense, but an enormous amount remains to be done, much of it theoretical, in the way of defining or categorizing them, establishing hierarchies or linking forms to functions.

As social constructs, the communicative virtues vary according to the values, beliefs and practices of whoever is doing the constructing. They are culture-specific criteria for the assessment of performance, sensitive to institutional, situational and interpersonal constraints such as setting, role, genre, power relations and degree of familiarity. The communicative virtues form part of the individual's interpretative repertoire as defined by Potter and Wetherell:

> ... broadly discernible clusters of terms, descriptions and figures of speech often assembled around metaphors or vivid images ... [used] for making evaluations, constructing factual versions and performing particular acts. (1995, p. 89)

This explains, to some extent at least, why it is so easy to find counter-examples to the Gricean maxims: far from being universals of natural logic, terms such as 'brevity', 'relevance', 'perspicacity' and 'sincerity' are in fact labels for the local communicative virtues of a particular community.

At first sight such labels seem extraordinarily naive and unscientific, but they are the criteria which ordinary speakers use to assess the quality of communication in the widest possible sense. From an objective, outsider's point of view, they may not be *the truth*, but they are *their* truth from the speaker's perspective. They have psychological reality and describing them is therefore fundamental to any ethnographic account of social interaction.

Moreover, much of modern sociolinguistics and discourse analysis is predicated on the notion of 'appropriateness', but investigation of that notion – trying to find just what it is that makes a given utterance or exchange 'appropriate' – has been surprisingly limited: certain categories of speech acts, topic selection and politeness have been studied in detail, but there are numerous aspects of discourse which remain untouched: friendliness, interest or trustworthiness, for example. What seems to have happened in many cases is that these terms have all been lumped together under politeness. Work on politeness has been an enormously rich source of insights into interpersonal behaviour and relationships over the last generation (Brown and Gilman 1960; Goffman 1959, 1972; Brown and Levinson 1987), but if it is to progress beyond the somewhat mechanistic and monocausal models of face-work, it needs to be both refined and extended along the lines of the communicative virtues.

These two terms, then, ethos and communicative virtues, are intimately connected. Speakers behave in ways which they hope will maximize their chances of communicative success: hearers judge speakers' performances and react accordingly. When I am giving a lecture, I hope that my words are producing effects on members of the audience that they would label as, say, 'witty', 'wise', 'knowledgeable', 'clear' and 'convincing'. Unfortunately for me, however, ethos is not just a matter of the unilateral imposition of such impressions and, for all I know, they may in fact be searching the antonymic parts of the lexicon for items such as 'boring', 'irrelevant', 'confused' or 'uninformed'. It may be just as well that our species is not telepathic.

It is this bilateral approach to the speaker's self-presentation which explains why some analysts prefer the term ethos to the social psychologists' 'self-image'. For largely historical reasons related to the emergence of inquiries into identity from theological considerations of the nature of the soul, there has always been a strong tendency to take the self as the starting-point and as the point of reference for all other aspects of identity. Even writers whose avowed preoccupation is social identity spend much of their time pondering over the internal relationships between the many – the individual's repertoire of roles – and the one, the self. This is an important and interesting question, but by giving it priority the focus of attention is removed from the external factors which condition those roles and the ways in which others perceive that individual's identity. The notion of ethos shifts the focus back to those external factors whilst at the same time forming part of a coherent approach to the overall architecture of personal identity.

5.2 Negotiating identities in intercultural service encounters

To illustrate the ways in which the notions of ethos and the communicative virtues can be usefully implemented in the study of identities in interaction, I am going to describe an ongoing research project being carried out by myself and a group of colleagues at the CRAPEL.[2]

Three main factors motivated this research. First, there was the CRAPEL's long-standing interest in intercultural communication and in the communicative approach to language teaching and learning, together with a relatively more recent focus on the notions of identity and self-expression. In this perspective, learning a foreign language is seen as an extension of self and personhood, an extension of the range of meanings of which the individual is capable. Everyone – researchers, teachers and learners alike – agrees that 'you learn a foreign language to express yourself', but just what is this thing that is being expressed, the self? And how does it relate to communication in general and to foreign-language communication in particular? How is the individual perceived by others and on what criteria do they base their judgements?

Second, the choice of this particular topic-area, service encounters, was simply a practical response to the professional needs formulated by certain of our groups of language learners, particularly in adult education: telephone operators in a forestry research centre, hospital or hotel staff, for example. This topic was lent a degree of urgency by the increasing awareness (heightened by government-funded surveys) that an alarmingly high proportion of foreigners involved in encounters with French service providers in the context of business or tourism were dissatisfied with the experience in some way. I say 'alarmingly high' because France's biggest industry is tourism and given the ferocious competition cannot afford to let things slip. At a more anecdotal level, I must confess that my personal interest in the specific topic of service encounters in France was spurred on by my experience when I was on sabbatical leave recently. I visited colleagues in several countries and was struck by the frequency with which I encountered remarks of the type: 'Oh, you live in France, aren't you lucky! A wonderful country – but aren't the shop assistants rude!' For 'shop assistants', you can substitute civil servants, hotel receptionists, travel agents, and so on. And for 'rude', you can substitute unhelpful, aggressive or unpleasant. Always the same category of social inter-action, service encounters, the same socio-professional categories and the same kinds of adjectives. So I thought to myself, well, this is very strange, the French don't find one another rude, in fact they think of themselves as being politer than many other nationalities.

Third, there were also more immediate, local pressures being felt within our university, which has seen its intake of foreign students shoot up in the past ten years, so that one student in eight is now a foreigner, or 6,000 individuals taking all the tertiary institutions of Nancy together. Unfortunately, it had become a matter of daily observation that our university services and structures were not prepared in any sense – numerically, linguistically or attitudinally – to deal with this influx, giving rise to innumerable problems, miscommunications and occasionally more serious conflicts. So we decided that it was high time we took a look at exolinguistic service encounters on our own doorstep.

The service encounter is a praxiological class of social interaction during which one participant provides another with a service of some kind: goods or knowledge in the form of expertise, rights, information, decisions. (Goffman 1959, 1972; Weller 1998). Since the work of the Pixi group in Bologna (Aston 1988) the prototypical case of service encounter has been that occurring between a customer and a bookshop assistant, but the concept owes its power to its generalizability to many other kinds of situation: buying a ticket at a railway station, booking a hotel room, consulting a doctor, opening a bank account, registering for a university course.

The term exolinguistic means that there is an asymmetry in the levels of communicative competence of speaker and hearer, and so the prototypical case of exolinguistic discourse is usually taken to be so-called 'foreigner talk', or 'Native/Non-native conversation', where one of the participants does not have the same degree of mastery over the language as the other. There is, of course, justification for this, but if we limit our definition to the Native/Non-native speaker dyad alone, we will miss out on some very important issues and insights, for example the fact that many of the characteristics of Native/Non-native speaker discourse are also to be seen in Specialist/Non-specialist, Insider/Outsider and Adult/Child discourse between native speakers. The asymmetry of Native/Non-native speaker discourse is just one instance of a wider category of epistemic asymmetry and variations in access to and the distribution of knowledge, and the discourse characteristics common to these different kinds of interaction are illustrative of the communicative practices of simplification and the negotiation of meaning, which may be culturally specific.

The two principal aims of this project are, first, to arrive at a better understanding of what makes for a successful or satisfying service encounter and, second, to examine pedagogical applications and implications. Ideally, we would like to produce materials and activities for training participants with a view to increasing levels of satisfaction. Anticipating one of our findings, it is worthy of note that, contrary to what one might expect, there is no simple relationship between the purely instrumental or transactional outcome (the service is or is not efficiently provided, 'I got what I came for') and feelings of what one might call social or communicative satisfaction. Time after time, participants distinguish between the two, as can be seen from the following utterances:

1) She was kind and helpful, but it didn't work out.
2) He wasn't exactly polite, but I managed to get the forms I wanted out of him.

Examples such as these also clearly illustrate the importance participants give to the communicative virtues in their perception and assessment of encounters.

The research methodology we adopted was a reasonably standard exercise in the collection and analysis of authentic spoken discourse, preceded by a literature search on identity. The recordings fall into three main classes:

1) interviews with a range of French service providers. These include librarians, shop assistants, members of the university administration, hairdressers, government employees and employees in the public utilities such as gas, electricity and telecommunications;

2) interviews with their clients. These include a majority of foreign teachers and students;

3) video-recordings of service encounters. At the time of writing, we have nearly thirty hours of recordings made in the reception area of an organization providing language and literacy training for both immigrants and native speakers. Obviously, our focus is on the encounters involving immigrant clients, but those involving native speakers provide an extremely useful basis for comparison.

The interviews were semi-structured, that is, they were based on questionnaires, but the interviewers were free to follow up any further line of inquiry if they thought it might be relevant. They also asked respondents to recount any instances of pragmatic failure, that is, misunderstandings leading to dissatisfaction or conflict, or, occasionally, to great hilarity. The questionnaires were first tried out in a small-scale pilot study which revealed gaps and necessary amendments, and different versions were produced for the service providers and the foreign students. In particular, interviewers were under instructions to follow up and seek more detail on expressions which seemed to them to be related to the communicative virtues. For example, if, as regularly happened, the interviewee said something along the lines of 'the service provider was (un)friendly, (un)helpful or (im)polite', the interviewer asked 'What gave you that impression?' or 'What did they do or say to make you feel that?' In this way, we were able to establish a first, short list of communicative virtues, constructs which form that part of the individual's overall interpretative repertoire used in the categorization of ethos. We were also able to formulate some first, rudimentary hypotheses about the contextual and communicative factors triggering the ways in which some of the communicative virtues operate: what it is that makes me feel that such-and-such a behaviour is pleasant, helpful, aggressive, supercilious, and so on.

Our first, unsurprising observation, is that it is very easy to find communicative virtues (or at least expressions for communicative virtues) in one language for which there is no adequate translation equivalent in another. This is, of course, the inevitable result of cultural variation in communicative and rhetorical practices. What is surprising, though, is that, far from being a matter of relatively fine shades of meaning, these differences can concern the most frequently-occurring items in our corpus. Striking examples from our interviews with English-speaking students are *friendly, helpful, nice* and *kind*. Not one of these words has a consistent, non-context-sensitive translation equivalent in French. Even where seemingly satisfactory translations are found, that is, they tend not to have the same semantic cover, frequency or register.

Even such a simple lexical-level observation can be related, we believe, to far wider issues, such as role. For example, many French service providers often see themselves as competent professionals, acting as resources for their clients. As such, they tend not to initiate exchanges, proactively make suggestions or ask questions, preferring to react to a client-led agenda. However, clients from other communicative cultures, perhaps including most of the English-speaking world, may have very different expectations and, when these are not fulfilled, will pass judgements on what they see as passivity or unwillingness to do their jobs in terms such as 'unhelpful' or 'not service-minded'.

This impression may be reinforced by the absence of a smile, one of the most frequently-mentioned themes in our corpus and often cited as self-evident justification for the use of terms such as 'unfriendly' or 'unpleasant'. However, our interviews with French service providers indicate a very different point of view. As competent professionals, they take both themselves and their clients seriously, and that implies a serious expression: 'I don't go in for smiles *à l'américaine*', as one of them put it. In a rather convoluted way, this analysis of the ethos they aim to project is confirmed by the fact that the French word 'sérieux' is far from being a translation equivalent of English 'serious'. In the context of service encounters, it usually means something like 'competent', 'conscientious', doing things properly or professionally or, one might even say, 'being service-minded'.

Among the sources of dissatisfaction most commonly referred to by our non-native respondents was the feeling that they were being membershipped as foreigners first and clients or customers second. The lack of a greeting or eye-contact, explicit remarks about their accent or linguistic incompetence, being kept waiting and lack of interest were amongst the most frequently-cited reasons for this impression. However, our corpus so far reveals little objective difference in respect of these factors between the treatment meted out to native and non-native clients, even including the remarks about accents, with informants from the Midi and Belgium also expressing varying degrees of irritation about service providers' reactions to their native but non-local varieties. It should also be remembered that in some situations, such as banks, the *préfecture* or the university, there may well be different rules and procedures for native and non-native clients, so that it is actually necessary for the service providers to foreground this aspect of client identity.[3] (Cabrol Bastos 2002).

To avoid conflict or misunderstanding, both service providers and their clients will often carry out *identity checks* to establish or confirm their understandings of salient aspects of identities and roles:

> *Student to clerk in University Registrations office:*
> C'est vous qui faites les validations d'acquis?
> (Is it you that does the course exemptions?)
> *Job Centre clerk to applicant:*
> Vous avez votre carte de demandeur d'emploi?
> (Have you got your job-seeker's card?)

As we saw earlier, foregrounding a specific aspect of one's social identity in order to orient one's interlocutors' expectations and perceptions is a major aspect of the construction of ethos: by laying claims to membership of a particular social category, speakers aim to establish their competence (knowledge, experience) in the relevant domain, thereby confirming their credibility. We also saw that when speakers do not expect to be challenged, they tend to have recourse to 'bald, on-record' realizations. Observation of service encounters in France shows such strategies to be common, possibly because they have a dual function: as well as being identity claims, they are compensation strategies, preparing the ground for possible communicative, cultural or administrative problems.

> I'm an Erasmus from Denmark.

> En tant qu'étudiant roumain en deuxième année d'études doctorales, il me faut une attestation d'inscription pour avoir ma carte de séjour.
> (As a Romanian PhD student in my second year, I need a certificate saying I'm registered at the university in order to obtain my resident's card.)

> Nous autres étudiants en psychologie sociale ...
> (We students of social psychology ...)

With the possible exception of accent, nothing could demonstrate more powerfully the iconic relationship between language variation and social structure than the close and systematic correlations to be found between technical terms, slang, passwords, localisms, etc. and categories of social identity. Although this is a strikingly prominent characteristic of professional discourses, it is certainly not limited to them. Using domain-specific terms (which is not the same as simply knowing or recognizing them) constitutes in itself a claim to a specific body of knowledge and experience. By definition, such terms can also be used to exclude from the social group or category in question individuals who fail to establish their credentials, and outsiders trying to use insider terms are usually swiftly rebuffed by being forced to abandon the discursive position concerned and are very often subject to derision. Here is an example:

> *Student to clerk in University Registrations office:*
> A: Bonjour c'est pour un imprimé EPR12 s'il vous plaît.
> B: Pourquoi?
> A: C'est la dame de la CAF qui l'a dit EPR12.
> B: Oui je veux bien mais pourquoi – je distribue pas les imprimés comme ça.
> A: C'est pour montrer que je suis inscrite à la Fac parce que je demande une aide une allocation.
> B: Ben voilà fallait le dire.
> (A: I've come for an EPR12 form please.
> B: Why?
> A: It's the lady at the CAF (Caisse d'allocations familiales) who told me EPR12.
> B: That's as may be but why? I don't give out forms just like that.
> A: It's to show I'm registered at the Faculty because I'm asking for an allowance.
> B: There you are, you just had to say so.)

Since power is seldom distributed perfectly symmetrically in service encounters, negotiating identities is rarely the be-all and end-all of such strategies. In this case, by denying the student's right to use the technical term, the service provider is not merely excluding her from the category of people having that right, she is also asserting and demonstrating her institutional authority.

Earlier (Section 3.4), we looked at strategies for negotiating language choice. In service encounters in France, an officially and often effectively monolingual country, most such strategies are simply not an option. Basically, the client has the choice of requesting the use of a foreign language, or of initiating the exchange in the foreign language in the hope of provider compliance:

- *Request*
  Hi. You speak English, please?
  A little.
- *L2 Initiation*

> I'm an Erasmus from Denmark.
> Ici on parle français, monsieur.
> (We speak French here, sir.)

As the second example shows, compliance is not always forthcoming. Indeed, it is worth mentioning that one of our informants said that she habitually refused to comply in the absence of a request.

Oral anecdotes are passages of monologistic narrative of varying length embedded in stretches of interactive discourse. It is convenient to distinguish between first-order anecdotes and second-order anecdotes. In first order anecdotes the speaker relates events in which he or she participated or was present. Second-order anecdotes are accounts of events in which the speaker was not directly involved. Anecdotes present a number of interesting characteristics as discourse. For example, as my use of the term monologistic indicates, the speaker who begins an anecdote claims immunity from interruption for a certain time. However, this dispensation is only given and maintained if the performance and content of the anecdote satisfy a number of criteria – originality, credibility and relevance above all. So turn-taking and topic nomination in the vicinity of anecdotes are often highly atypical when compared with the discourse in which the anecdote is embedded.

Now, as many readers of this book will no doubt recognize, anecdotes tend to be extremely thick on the ground in social science interviews of almost any kind, because they have a very broad functional spectrum indeed, including the exemplification, argumentation, explanation, and justification of knowledge, beliefs, values and attitudes. In more spontaneous, multi-participant forms of social interaction, such as a group of friends having a drink or a meal together, anecdotes can also play an important role in the reaffirmation of social values. This phatic bonding is clearly part of the ritual of constructing or maintaining group identity, and as such presents a number of specific discourse characteristics, such as high levels of co-construction and appeals to shared memories.

Taken together, then, it can be seen that anecdotes are vehicles for the encapsulation of remembered experience and as such are the fundamental materials from which selves are constituted and self-expression is made. It is not surprising, then, to find that they are very often instruments for self-presentation and the construction of ethos.

Geneviève, in her early twenties, has just arrived from Gabon to take up a university place in France. She is describing her dealings with the CROUS, a body responsible for student board and lodgings, and the MGEN, which handles health and insurance matters.

Je me rappelle j'avais fait un tour quand je constituais mon dossier pour le CROUS on m'avait demandé d'assurer ma chambre et l'assurance il fallait la prendre au MGEN j'arrive là-bas et je présente mes papiers je dis je viens assurer ma chambre + la dame me dit carrément 'ici on ne travaille pas de connivence avec le CROUS' j'ai rigolé j'ai dit 'mais la dame du CROUS m'a demandé de venir ici pour assurer ma chambre' elle me dit 'non vous vous êtes trompée de bureau' ah bon je suis repartie au CROUS j'ai dit ça à la dame elle me dit 'mais c'est pas possible ou bien c'est vous qui vous êtes exprimée mal' j'ai dit 'en tout cas j'ai tenté c'est quand même le même français que nous parlons' elle a dit 'd'accord je vais appeler' elle a formé le numéro elle a appelé à la MGEN ( ) elle explique et les dames qui ont pris la communication m'ont demandé de repartir (rire) je repars cette fois-ci je suis pas allée vers la même dame j'ai changé de personne je suis allée ailleurs ( ) à l'hôpital par contre il y a une semaine je suis en train de faire un bilan de santé je suis tombé sur un médecin qui m'a mise vraiment à l'aise pas de problème.

(I remember they gave me the runaround when I was putting together my application for the CROUS they'd asked me to insure my room and I had to get the insurance from the MGEN I get there and I show them my forms and I say I've come to insure my room + all the lady says to me is 'here we don't work together with the CROUS' I laughed I said 'but the lady at the CROUS told me to come here to insure my room' she says 'no you've come to the wrong office' oh right I went back to the CROUS and I told the lady there all that and she tells me 'that's impossible or it's you that expressed yourself badly' I said anyway I tried after all it's the same French as we are speaking she said 'right I'll call' she dialled the number she called the MGEN ( ) she explains and the ladies who took her call asked me to go back (laugh) back I go this time I didn't go up to the same lady I changed I went to a different person ( ) on the other hand when I was having a medical check-up at the hospital a week ago I got a doctor who really put me at ease no problem.)

The protagonist of this narrative presents herself as someone who has a sense of humour ('j'ai rigolé') and who is also persistent – she laughs ('rire') as she recounts how she was sent backwards and forwards. She can stand up for herself and make a good point in an argument ('j'ai dit ... c'est quand-même le même français que nous parlons'). She demonstrates that she's not a difficult customer ('à l'hôpital ... pas de problème'). She compares the MGEN lady's blunt way of speaking with the doctor's ability to put her at ease, which reflects favourably on her capacity and right to make such judgements.

These various aspects of her discourse form a clear and consistent pattern of Geneviève's self-presentation and provide her listeners with the materials which form the basis for their judgements and perception of her ethos. More generally, when we 'tell a story' we need not only to provide our listeners with a context for the story, we also need to contextualize the telling. This will be done through competent use of the linguistic resources available to us – tense, aspect, deictics, anaphora and genre conventions in particular – but also by anchoring our narrative with respect to our own and our interlocutors' horizon of experience. To do this, we need to agree as to the meanings of earlier utterances, but we also need to agree to why the story is being told and who is telling it to whom. This is why we so often have recourse when initiating anecdotes to expressions such as

> I always remember ...
> That reminds me of ...
> I was once ...

where we position ourselves as narrators in relation to ourselves as the continuing locus of our memories. This is exactly what Geneviève does with 'Je me rappelle' (I recall) before entering on her self-presentation in narrative.

Intercultural and exolinguistic service encounters are very vulnerable to pragmatic failure, both for communicative reasons and for reasons related to balance of power and recognition of rights:

- Almost without exception, our Chinese informants complained about the proliferation of mechanical greetings to which they were subject in service relations in France, including both shops and offices, and in the kitchens of their halls of residence. And almost without exception, French service providers and students emphasized the importance they attribute to greetings in establishing the conditions for satisfactory outcomes:

  French service provider:
  Je ne supporte pas les gens qui n'ont même pas le temps pour saluer. Un petit 'bonjour', c'est la moindre des choses.
  (I can't stand people who haven't even got the time for a greeting. Just saying 'hallo' is the least one can do.)

- Smiling can be perceived both positively and negatively, according to the individual's cultural background and, we would claim, their repertoire of communicative virtues. The 'failure' of many service providers to smile was never commented on by Chinese informants, for example, but was a regular cause of complaint for North Americans and British interviewees. Moreover, when questioned on this point, French service providers readily admitted to not smiling very much (indeed, one remarked that it was an American habit), explaining that they were professionals who took their clients seriously and that only a serious demeanour was therefore appropriate.

- A foreign tourist sits down at a table on the terrace of a Parisian café, orders a beer and pays for it with a high-denomination banknote. The waiter disappears into the inside of the establishment and when he reappears makes no attempt to give the tourist his change.

    Tourist: Hey, I gave you €20.

    Waiter: (Slapping forehead with the open palm of his hand) C'est pas vrai!

    The tourist rises ominously to his feet, but the waiter is already assiduously counting out his change.

    The literal meaning of the waiter's utterance is 'It's not true!', which the tourist interprets as a refusal to give him the money he is owed. But the expression usually functions as an all-purpose exclamation that something is amiss, in this case that the speaker has forgotten something important due to hectic working conditions. It is as close to an apology as the tourist is likely to get, but so far from what he expects that he completely misinterprets it, partly due to the expression's highly idiomatic nature, partly to his own inability to attribute an appropriate communicative virtue to the waiter's performance.

From a didactic perspective, 'Foreigner' or 'Non-native Speaker'/ 'Native Speaker' interaction, the prototypical case of exolinguistic discourse, is the very situation for which language teachers are preparing their learners, and as the unconscious result of traditional pedagogical discourse, instances of pragmatic failure came to be seen as 'errors', but errors due to differences in 'culture' rather than 'grammar'. This is a highly unsatisfactory simplification, but it is important to note that from the outset pragmatic failure was a concept that was clearly framed in terms of identity, even if the full implications of this postulate have only surfaced very slowly indeed, as the implications of the problematization of the model of the 'Native Speaker' were gradually taken on board.

5.2.1 Forging identities

The lively interest in service encounters which was so evident in the 1970s and 1980s seemed for a while to have considerably abated, but was given fresh impetus by growing concerns about globalization, verbal hygiene (Cameron 1995) and their implications for identity. Equally important was the liberalization and privatization of large-scale public services (railways, utilities such as gas, electricity and water, post and telecommunications) which entailed a major shift in the status and roles of the personnel concerned, who were required to metamorphose from functionaries working for state monopolies into service providers working in competitive markets (Borzeix *et al.* 1992; Borzeix 2001; Weller 1998).

To carry out this transformation, vast professional programmes were set in motion and recourse was had to the services of experts and consultants in training service staff and in intercultural communication. In a number of cases, the model of expected behaviour, the ethos, on which these programmes were based was imported lock, stock and barrel from the United States, seen as the world leader in 'service-mindedness'. Naively, this model was promulgated as 'best practice', rather than as the expression of a set of local values and communicative virtues. (The analogy with attempts to impose Gricean maxims onto culturally divergent communicative economies comes irresistibly to mind.) A variant of this model which is now widespread in France is a behavioural algorithm known by the mnemonic 'BRASMA' (André 2003):

Bonjour	(Hallo)
Regard	(Eye contact)
Attention	(Attention)
Sourire	(Smile)
Merci	(Thank you)
Au revoir	(Goodbye)

Visit any French supermarket and you will have the experience of seeing twenty or thirty cashiers simultaneously going through this routine, time and again, day in, day out. Personally I find this rather chilling, but more to the point is the fact that many members of the French public find this behaviour ludicrously inappropriate, commenting on it negatively in and out of the cashiers' presence. Indeed, these extremely hard-working people have become figures of fun, stereotypes of empty-mindedness. Since French society is highly verbal, and egalitarian as regards striking up conversations, it is most unlikely that customers are objecting to simply being addressed and, indeed, observation shows considerable quantities of phatic and conversation. It is the communicative cloning of the company image at the expense of self-image, an inappropriate ethos framed in terms of inappropriate communicative practices, which we judge to be the source of the problem. I can cite two other examples of ethnocentricity masquerading as self-evident, universally valid 'best practice':

1) In a factory in France owned and managed by foreigners, a poster was displayed and used in training sessions in which the French were described as 'Cartesian', 'Abstract', 'Individualistic', 'Rethorical' (*sic*) and 'Preferring words to actions', whilst people of the employers' nationality were stated to be 'Practical', 'Pragmatic', 'Team players' who 'preferred actions to words'. When I was subsequently (and very belatedly) invited in to try to pour some oil on what had become very troubled waters, each side described the other as 'inefficient' and 'impolite'.

The closure of the factory the following year with the loss of over 600 jobs, after only eighteen months' full and highly profitable operation, was part of the world-wide slump in the telecommunications market and to a take-over by a rival firm that simply wished to eliminate a competitor, but it is certainly not too far-fetched to see these ethos-related negative impressions and communicative misunderstandings as a contributory factor. They were largely due to the fact that the international company had decreed English as the sole working language for the enterprise. As far as any reflection had gone into this decision, it seemed to be based on the ideas that, first, English is the language of business and international communication so that there was no need for management and workforce to learn one another's languages and, second, that using a 'neutral' language like English would create a level playing-field for management–workforce relations. Nothing could have been further from the truth: the managers spoke fluent English, the workforce, almost without exception, very little. Some of them admitted that they had 'enhanced' their curriculum vitaes in this respect because they needed the work.

An additional problem was the fact that each side spoke an English which was rooted in their own cultural values and communicative practices. For example, French falling affirmative intonation patterns were perceived by the management as aggressive and impolite and the management's own intonation patterns were perceived by the workforce as 'surly', 'unfriendly' – and impolite.

Again, a system of management based on regular 'work-meetings' was implemented, but without any thought being given as to how this English expression might be interpreted by each side. In brief, the management saw work meetings as an occasion for reporting on work that had been done, decisions and plans that had been made, and projects that had been carried out. Work-meetings, they believed, should last no longer than thirty to forty minutes and should consist of

231

a series of reports from both sides, with little or no discussion. For the French, however, a work-meeting was seen as a meeting where the work would actually be done, the plans made, the decisions taken. It would, therefore, involve full discussion of policy and detail, and could be expected to last two to three hours. The management saw the French attitude as 'coming to the meeting with empty hands', 'laziness' and 'inefficiency', wasting in time lengthy and pointless discussions of 'things they should have thought about earlier'. The workforce saw the management as a group of authoritarian control-freaks who did not respect their expertise and whose old-fashioned methods were hasty and inefficient.[4]

2) Foreign consultants hired to train management-level staff in the Nordic travel industry attributed 'defects' in their communicative performance in meetings which are in fact related to turn-taking procedures, speed of delivery and argumentative strategies to 'poor presentation skills', rather than seeing them as different communicative norms aiming at the projection of an ethos in many ways distinct from their own. They also requested their trainees to simulate greeting and parting routines to show that they were 'warm' and 'friendly', which even those who accepted (some flatly refused) found unnecessary and excruciatingly embarrassing. ('Hugging!' said one in a tone of real disgust.)

One can only conclude that we need to take a hard look at the models underpinning so-called intercultural training (Scollon and Scollon (1992), is an especially powerful critique). Far from being culturally sensitive, they can be unconsciously naive attempts to transpose the trainer's communicative practices and values to the learner's behaviour, in which case they are ethnocentric, unethical and counterproductive. Any morally or pedagogically valid approach to intercultural training must be based on respect for and knowledge of the learner's culture and communicative economy and will take the form of observation, sensitization and the negotiation of identities and 'mini-cultures', with the aim of participating in encounters where no participant is forced unwillingly to sacrifice their own ethos, culture or identity by being modelled in the image of another (Adami *et al.* 2003).

In the *Times Literary Supplement* of 13 July 2003, Susan Sontag discussed the Schleiermachian concept of authenticity. Schleiermacher (1768–1834) was led by his ideas about national and personal identity to believe that the height of inauthenticity would be to speak two languages equally well. In that article, Sontag continues to examine 'a perfect Schleiermachian scenario of inauthenticity', telephone call centres, with particular reference to those in India. Although there have been numerous publications on the topic in recent years (Cameron 2001; Boutet 2001), Sontag's, though not particularly technical, is certainly one of the most thought-provoking and elicited diametrically opposed reactions from and amongst Indian commentators.

Sontag begins by situating the phenomenon clearly and simply in the context of globalization:

> The young people, all of whom already speak English, who compete successfully for the coveted jobs in the call centres, and have completed the arduous course designed to erase all traces of their Indian accent in English (many fail) are being paid what is a munificent salary for office work in India, though of course far less than what IBM, American Express, GE, Delta Airlines, and chains of hotels and restaurants would have to pay to Americans to do the job – reason enough for more and more such tasks to be 'outsourced'. It also seems that Indians perform the tasks better, with fewer errors, which is not surprising, since virtually all of them have college degrees.

She then focuses on the implications of this situation for the workers' identities (and in particular, I would say, their ethos):

> Nancy or Mary Lou, Betty, Sally Jane, Megan, Bill, Jim, Wally, Frank – these cheerful voices had first to be trained for months, by instructors and by tapes, to acquire a pleasant middle American (not educated American) accent and to learn basic American slang, informal idioms (including regional ones) and elementary mass culture references (television personalities and the plots and protagonists of the main sitcoms, the latest blockbuster in the multiplex, fresh baseball and basketball scores, and so on), so that if the exchange with the client in the United States becomes prolonged, they will not falter with the small talk, and have the means to continue to pass for Americans.

> To pull this off, they have to be plausibly American to themselves. They have been assigned American names and little biographies of their American identities: place and date of birth, parents' occupation, number of siblings, religious denomination (almost always Protestant), high school, favourite sport, favourite kind of music, marital status, and the like. If asked, they can say where they are ... letting on that they are in Bangalore, India, would get pretend-Nancy or pretend-Bill instantly fired. (All the calls are routinely and undetectably monitored by supervisors.) And, of course, virtually none of these young people has ever left home. Would 'Nancy' and 'Bill' prefer to be a real Nancy and a real Bill? Almost all – there have been interviews – say that they would. (Sontag 2003)

233

5.3 Standardization and scaffolding

In this section, we are going to look at two topics which might be regarded as poles apart, since the first, standardization, is situated at the macro level of sociolinguistic structure, the patterns of distribution of language varieties, and the second, scaffolding, is situated at the micro level of social interaction. Nonetheless, the point I wish to make is that both these phenomena participate in the identity formation processes and that this can only be properly understood in terms of the functioning of the social knowledge system. On the one hand, standard languages are privileged with respect to the conservation, distribution and legitimation of much institutional knowledge and its related activities and discourses, consequently playing a hegemonic role with respect to the discursive positions and identities available in those epistemic and social domains. On the other hand, scaffolding is an interactive process whereby individuals establish and share meanings – learn – in intersubjective couplings.

5.3.1 Standardization

Of all the linguistic factors contributing to the formation and expression of social identities probably the most pervasive is the complex social and historical process of standardization whereby one or more language variety is codified and for that and a number of other reasons which will be mentioned later, is considered as superior in many ways to non-standard varieties. Standard languages are related to identity in a number of important ways. First, they are seen as symbolic of the nation (indeed, they are sometimes called 'national languages', which is often but not necessarily the case). Second, they are used, often exclusively, as the medium of communication by most important institutions including the legal and educational systems; the armed forces, the administration and the church, each of which plays a role in defining, providing and distributing the positions, roles and identities available in the society in question. Third, a standard language results in the creation and acceptance of attitudes towards language use and its users, on the basis of which crucial local, communal, aesthetic and moral judgements and social categorizations will be made.

Fourth, standard languages entertain socially meaningful relations with related non-standard varieties, so that stylistic variation or code-switching reflects speakers' choices and changes of positions and allegiances. The principal characteristics of a standard language are codification, prestige and symbolism, and functional elaboration (a more detailed discussion and one which situates standardization within the wider context of sociolinguistic variation will be found in Downes 1998).

The terms codification and correction refer to the establishment of norms (of grammar, spelling, style, etc.) and their propagation through such publications as manuals of grammar, dictionaries and books of rhetoric. Standardization is largely dependent on the existence and systematization of a system of writing and writing practices. These, of course, have to be learnt, so from the start, degree of mastery of the standard variety tends to be equated with an individual's level of education as well as perceived social correlates such as class, intelligence, authoritativeness and conformity with the 'official' views and values taught at school. It is important to remember that for a variety of reasons (sex, socioeconomic class, ethnicity, distance) not all children have access to schooling, an important though not unusual example of the roles of institutional structures in the identity formation processes and of their consequences in terms of the individual's repertoire of communicative competences. This applies, *mutatis mutandis*, to teachers, pupils and to those who are excluded from this area of the social knowledge system. It also explains why most modern states consider mass education in the standard language to be essential for ensuring social and national unity. Enforcing prescribed norms is not limited to the education system: institutions such as the BBC or the French Academy play an active part and publishing houses invariably have extraordinarily detailed style-sheets or handbooks and the publication of pedagogical guides to good speech and writing continues unabated.

The development of a standard language depends almost entirely on social and historical contingencies. In Europe, at least, linguistic standardization has invariably accompanied the wider processes of political and economic centralization leading to the emergence of nation-states (see Section 4.2). It is generally accepted that modern standard English, for example, is largely based on the 'East Midlands dialect' of the thirteenth and fourteenth centuries. The selection of this variety was not due to any intrinsic qualities, but to a combination of geo-demographic and social factors: the land in this part of the country was particularly suited to sheep-farming, a major source of national income, and attracted and supported a high proportion of the overall population. Part of the region's wealth was used to found the Universities of Oxford and Cambridge, and London, on its way to becoming one of the biggest cities in Europe, became a major trading centre and the seat of government as the court and the administrative services necessary to centralization became entrenched there. English was, of course, in competition with both French and Latin. The

Anglicization of the aristocracy, through intermarriage and the loss of their continental possessions, and of the clerisy, largely as the consequence of the advent of Protestantism, slowly brought to the language the prestige that its use by the elite and its primacy in an ever-increasing number of functional domains bestowed upon it.

The importance of Protestantism in the construction of British national identities, long acknowledged, has been insistently underlined in recent years by a number of historians (in particular, Colley 2005; Schama 2000). The resurgence of public interest in history and the extraordinary success of their publications and television programmes is in itself symptomatic of the quest for identity so characteristic of British society at the turn of the century, as is the suggestion that there should be a test of Britishness for applicants for citizenship. A powerful expression of this interest occurred in January 2002, when the Public Records Office opened up online access to the details of the 1901 National Census. In the first four days, there were some 115 million hits, a colossal rate which threatened the whole British telephone network with collapse.

The rejection of the supra-national power of the Papacy in the sixteenth century led inevitably to a rejection of the practices through which that power was exercised and expressed. Speaking English became more and more closely related to being English, a symbolic and affective relationship that was progressively reinforced until, by the end of the nineteenth century competence in any other living language was looked on askance by certain parts of the population.

A striking example of the conscious use of a standard language to form identities – in this case, citizens of the French Republic – is the French *dictée*. Dictation, that is an exercise where pupils transcribe a text read aloud to them by a teacher as a test of their mastery of orthographic, phonomorphemic and morphosyntactic rules ('spelling' and 'grammar'), is still a standard activity in French schools. I use the word 'standard' in its fullest sense: this is one of the ways in which the norms of standard French are transmitted and the process of standardization maintained. It should never be forgotten, though, that the result of that process is the creation of a set of attitudes towards language which directly influences peoples' behaviour, and in the case of the French this can be clearly seen from the special role and importance they attribute to the *dictée*.

There is general agreement that France is one of the most centralized states in the world, both linguistically and politically, and that the written code is the major form of selection in French society. All French children between the ages of approximately seven and fourteen do from two to three *dictées* per week. Marks achieved in these exercises play an important role in calculating the individual child's overall grade (*la moyenne*) and in deciding whether or not he or she is doing well enough to go up a class at the end of the year.

What is remarkable to the outside observer is that the *dictée* has become a national sport. Again, I feel that I have to emphasize the point that the word 'national' is being used here in its fullest sense: the French language is seen as symbolic of the French nation-state, along with the flag and the *Marseillaise*: to be good at dictation is, therefore, not merely a matter of marks, it is to be a good French citizen, to show that you have a proper sense of values. Every year, Bernard Pivot, a French TV personality who has made his reputation as the host of serious literary and cultural discussion programmes, organizes a nation-wide dictation competition. In fact, one should say competitions, because there are so many entrants (in 2005 there were nearly 212,000) that there have to be various eliminatory stages. First, there is a local round, then a regional round, an interregional round and the final in Paris: there are also special age-groups, special conditions for people who have got as far as the final in previous years, and a special category for foreign entrants. Security arrangements are far stricter than for ordinary school or university examinations. The prize-giving ceremony is attended by members of the government and famous people from all walks of life. Newspapers publish full details of the progress of the competition, as well as the text used in the final.

Au diable la varice! s'écriait cette très vieille Athalie qui grimaçait sous la douleur. Elle devait tous ses grands rôles, prétendait-elle, à de curieuses tisanes de plantes porte-bonheur: l'aigremoine, la sarriette, la cynoglosse et la joubarbe utilisées inconsidérément, ou à des genêts, des gaulthéries et des hyacinthes pendus dans sa loge. Enfin, aux questions sur son oeil demeuré de braise, elle avançait toujours la raiponce. Quoiqu'elle aimât la chlorophylle, elle fuyait le vert. Elle alla même jusqu'à crânement exiger de blancs-becs qui prétendaient à l'empyrée où se sont installés Maeterlinck, Genet et Beckett que fussent retirés de leurs oeuvres des mots comme vertugadin, verroterie, vermée ou vertu. La vertu, d'ailleurs, elle s'en était toujours ri et défiée.

(Fin de la dictée seniors.)

This final text is little more than an artificial combination of some of the most recondite rules, difficulties and exceptions standard written

French has to offer. (In this respect, it is relevant to note that the Larousse *Dictionnaire des difficultés de la langue française* runs to 435 pages.) The result is that, as often as not, no one, not even the winner, gets full marks. When this happens it is a cause of considerable satisfaction. 'Pas de sans faute dans la dictée de Pivot!' crow the newspaper headlines. It shows that the French language is exceptionally difficult, which is in turn regarded as proof that the French themselves are exceptional.

It would be interesting to analyse more fully the vocabulary used to describe mistakes made in the *dictée*. The word *faute*, ('fault', 'mistake'), for example, has strong moral overtones and forms part of an interpretative repertoire of terms used in French educational institutions which are systematically ambiguous. They include *discipline, autorité, règle, correction*, all of which have meanings which seem to refer to an external, objective reality but which at the same time refer to the ways those realities are imposed as social norms. For example, *discipline*, as in English, refers both to subjects such as history or mathematics and to the social empowerment of the teacher to enforce approved patterns of behaviour. In the first case, it refers to the way in which society organizes and distributes knowledge, so we are clearly in the field of the sociology of knowledge: in the second, though, we are talking about an aspect of a communicative event (a 'history class'), and we are dealing with an aspect of the ethnography of communication. Similarly, *correction* can mean both 'accuracy' and 'chastisement', and *règle* can refer either to a rule of grammar or to school rules. In the *dictée*, the normative and reproductive functions of school could hardly be clearer: the pupil is expected to produce a text which shows no individual variation whatsoever. Indeed, such traces are sanctioned as *fautes*. Lastly, I should add that this is by no means a recent phenomenon; *dictée* competitions have been organized regularly since the Revolution, and they have been exported, too: there are fascinating accounts of the Russian royal family doing dictations with French teachers and visiting scholars or writers.

In imperial and colonial settings, educational policies were sometimes adopted which were consciously based on a programme of identity engineering through linguistic and cultural conditioning. India was probably the best example, because of the length and scale of the operation, and its undeniable effectiveness, but also because it was the subject of a highly explicit memorandum drawn up by the Whig historian and Indian administrator Thomas Babington Macaulay. In his *Minute on Education* (1835), this blissfully ethnocentric optimist argued:

It is pointless for us, with our limited means, to attempt to educate the body of the people. We must at present do our best to form a class who may be interpreters between us and the millions whom we govern; a clan of persons, Indians in blood and colour but English in taste, in opinions, in morals and in intellect. (1957, p. 723)

His policy was very much a case of adapting the ideological practices of Victorian education discussed earlier (Section 3.5) to local conditions, though it also had to be rooted in a deep contempt for Indian culture.

5.3.2 Scaffolding

The term scaffolding is a metaphor which facilitates understanding of notions such as Vygotsky's Zone of Proximal Development and the view that learning is a socially mediated activity. Donato (1994) says:

... in social interaction a knowledgeable participant can create, by means of speech, supportive conditions in which the novice can participate, and can extend skills and knowledge to higher levels of competence. (1994, p. 40)

Summarizing the results of his own detailed observations, he concludes:

The micro-genetic analysis of collective activity has revealed that in the process of peer scaffolding, learners can expand their own L2 knowledge and extend the linguistic development of their peers ... the current theoretical position supporting group work in L2 classrooms will be expanded beyond the simple opportunities to exchange linguistic artifacts to that of the collective acquisition of the second language. (*ibid.*, p. 53)

Donato lists the following six characteristic functions of scaffolding:

1) Recruiting interest in the task;
2) Simplifying the task;
3) Maintaining pursuit of the goal;
4) Marking critical features and discrepancies between what has been produced and the ideal solution;
5) Controlling frustration during problem solving;
6) Demonstrating an idealized version of the act to be performed.

In a fascinating and richly-illustrated look at the nitty-gritty of autonomous classroom practice, Hanne Thomsen (2002) analyses the discourse of a rich array of classroom activities on the basis of Donato's list. In this example, the learners, Danish thirteen-year-olds in their fourth year of English, are preparing a sketch for their classmates.

At the very beginning, Katrine – as the mother of two daughters in the role-play – sums up what they have planned so far to simplify and to clarify the task:

> L1: You are at a concert, or what? No, you ask me to go to the concert. I'll sit here. I am at home and I'll drink coffee.
> L2: … and we come
> L1: You are … come home after school of course. And then you ask me …
> L2: OK, Err. Can we go to the concert – with Michael Jackson?

Later on she doesn't want to lose time:

> L1: I have to look it up in the dictionary. Just keep on talking.

And in order not to forget what they have worked out so far:

> L3: I think we should write this down … all we have made
> L1, L2: Yes, yes, you are right.
> L1: Tomorrow we can't remember. I know that.

Once the learners are a bit stuck in the process:

> L1: What should happen next? It has to be something so that the audience don't think it's boring.
> L3: Something funny.

Once the outline of the play has been made, Janne takes the role of insisting on rehearsing:

> L2: Let's go through it again.
> L3: Let's do that.
> L1: OK, you are …

And then again Katrine is the one who maintains pursuit of the goal:

> L1: We have to do the scene where I have to yell at you – again.

In order not to lose track and stay focused, Katia remarks:

> L3: Well, let's not go into that! (p. 36)

Thomsen comments

> … not just one learner took up the role of being the more capable peer. All three did, though one learner could be characterized as a more insisting capable peer when it had to do with the above mentioned scaffolds. (*ibid.*, p. 39)

Certainly, this extract shows learners using language as an instrument for reflecting and learning. She summarizes her position as follows:

> This research shows that the development of communicative

proficiency in a second/foreign language depends directly on sustained involvement in genuine communicative behaviour (and) the development of autonomy in language learning is inseparable from the development of autonomy in language use. (*ibid.*, p. 30)

She also points out, however, that:

Even in would-be communicative approaches, target language use is all too often constrained by predominantly frontal teaching methods. (*ibid.*, p. 30)

It is the interaction between learners, engaged as individuals, expressing themselves (the three girls may be role-playing, but it is *their* text) and providing mutual scaffolding which is a necessary condition for the acquisition of both language and autonomy. What we are witnessing here is the detailed operation of the social knowledge system, with the children successively and fleetingly occupying discursive positions according to personal knowledge. They are competent learners because they know what needs to be done to realize the functions identified by Donato. As they do so, they both extend and refine the categories of acts and roles they can perform, the discursive positions they are capable of occupying and they access, share and learn knowledge. They do so autonomously – by *themselves* – actively constructing their own and one another's identities.

Notes

1 The question of perceived discrepancy between self and ethos has two dimensions, depending on whether it is the individual who is dissatisfied with the impression he or she makes on others ('I'm not really like that', 'I don't give the best of myself', 'People don't understand me' and so on) or whether others have made a negative judgement about the authenticity of the individual's ethos. The first case can lead to (at least) three lines of behaviour:

1) increased embarrassment and low self-image. A useful general introduction to the theory and management of embarrassment is Markway *et al.* (1992).

2) a decision to change the image given out: very often, this will express itself through the purchase and display of consumer articles, fashionable clothes and accessories. It might also result in a decision to change one's behaviour, communicative style, etc. and this is where the vast self-improvement literature comes in, as well as self-assertion training, personal coaches, etc.

3) the individual might decide to persuade him- or herself that in fact the situation is satisfactory, or that the opinions of others can be ignored. This

is the 'Méthode Coué': 'Every day, in every way, I'm getting better and better' (or one of its many imitators in the self-confidence market).

The second case is a major point of disagreement amongst the classical rhetoricians as to whether or not speakers should actually *be* of good character (Cicero's 'Vir bonus dicendi peritus') or whether a positive ethos could be faked. It is also relevant to note that Cicero was the first to use the word 'individual'. This debate will not be pursued here, though the author has met one or two pretty convincing liars in his time. And again, 'There's honour amongst thieves'.

2 Including Hervé Adami, Virginie André, Sophie Bailly, Séverine Behra, Elena Désirée Castillo, Florence Garcia, Françoise Karshenas and the author.

3 A point which has been observed but not yet investigated concerns the notoriously slippery referential functions of the pronoun *on*. Since it can be used as a substitute for *any* other personal pronoun, it provides fertile grounds for misunderstanding, in particular as regards the inclusion/exclusion of speaker and/or addressee, with consequences for the attribution of agency or responsibility.

4 I regret being unable to provide further details of this tragicomedy, but understandably the management required confidentiality.

6 Conclusion

I recently had the immense good fortune to spend a term working in New Zealand and at Easter I went touring with my wife and younger daughter. One of our excursions was to a Maori village just outside Rotorua, where we went for a concert and for a delicious *hangi*, a traditional meal cooked on hot stones in a hole in the ground.

We travelled to the village by coach. There were about thirty passengers: half were New Zealanders, who all sat together in the back of the coach, and the rest consisted of a mixed bunch of foreigners, who sat together in the front, including a Swiss, a Frenchman, a Briton (me), a Canadian, and so on.

After the concert and the meal – and, it has to be admitted, generous amounts of New Zealand wine – we all piled back into the coach in cheerful mood.

I have to confess that my cheerfulness evaporated suddenly when the driver announced over the microphone that foreign visitors were now expected to sing a national song. This was greeted with enormous enthusiasm by the New Zealanders in the back, but the whole idea just made me cringe and I went into a state of something like panic. What on earth could I sing? An *a capella* version of 'Land of Hope and Glory'? Or 'On Ilkley Moor Bah t'At' with a phoney Yorkshire accent?

It was little consolation to find that the other foreigners were in similar dismay and disarray. The Swiss seemed completely unable to think of a 'Swiss national song' '– and anyway, what language would it be in?' The Frenchman said in a resigned tone 'I suppose it will 'ave to be "Frère Jacques"'. The Canadian stared gloomily out of the window.

But, to cut a long story short, all our anxiety turned out to be quite unnecessary. Because when the driver called out the name of a country it was the New Zealanders who, to a man, burst into spontaneous song.

'Switzerland,' calls out the driver. The Swiss doesn't even have time to get to his feet.

'Edelweiss, E-del-weiss …' sings the crowd in the back of the bus.

'Canada,' says the driver.

'I'm a lumberjack and that's OK' is performed with accompanying virile gestures.

'France next.' The French man just has time to start. 'Frère ...' but he is hit by a wall of sound:

'NON, rien de rien, NON, je ne regrette RIEN!'

The moment I've been dreading, 'The UK' says the driver.

The massed choir doesn't hesitate for a second. 'I've got a luvverly bunch of coconuts!'

Even such a trivial event as this can tell us a lot about the ways in which identities are constructed. Indeed, it is precisely because the incident was trivial that it reveals aspects of a process that are largely out-of-consciousness yet everyday, an essential part of social reality.

The first thing to note is, of course, that the New Zealanders were on home ground, as well as being in the majority. Whether you explain their behaviour in terms of passports or power, they clearly felt that they could decide on the nature of others' (non-New Zealanders') identities in terms of their own knowledge about Switzerland, France, and so on. In other words, all other identities were to be constructed with reference and in opposition to their own. Clearly, some of the 'foreign identities' the New Zealanders expressed were quite unrecognizable to the individuals concerned. I myself was quite perplexed as to why 'I've got a luvverly bunch of coconuts' should be considered as some kind of archetypical anthem, and the Canadian was very uneasy with 'I'm a lumberjack and that's OK'. But this is entirely the point: identities are largely constructed by others in their own image and likeness.

A second point concerns the role of language in this process. Discourse backed by power can be used to impose identities. This is exactly what the New Zealanders did: they monopolized the discourse – they quite literally 'called the tune' – putting their words in our mouths. Like ventriloquists, they expressed our selves and our own voices were stilled or unheard. Their discourse provided the coordinates for our identities, fixing their subjects in positions in social space – *their* social space.

This incident brought home and summarized for me all the major points about the relationships between language, culture and identity I have been examining in this book. Just as history tells us who we are, identity is made of the stories we tell ourselves.

References

Adami, H., André, V., Bailly, S. *et al.* (Grefsoc) (2003) 'L'Etranger compétent: Un nouvel objectif pour la didactique des langues étrangères', in D. Groux and H. Holec (eds) *Une identité Plurielle: Mélanges offerts à Louis Porcher.* Paris: L'Harmattan, pp. 535–50.

Adebajo, A. (2006) 'Worse than the rest', review of P. Maylam *The Cult of Rhodes: Remembering an Imperialist in Africa.* (London: David Philip) in *The Times Literary Supplement,* 28 July 2006.

Alexander, J. and Alexander, P. (1987) 'Striking a bargain in Javanese markets', *Man,* 22(1), pp. 42–68.

Allen, N. J. (1985) 'The category of the person: a reading of Mauss' last essay', in M. Carrithers, S. Collins and S. Lukes (eds) *The Category of the Person.* Cambridge: Cambridge University Press, pp. 26–45.

Althusser, L. (1971) 'Ideology and ideological state apparatuses', in *Lenin and Philosophy and Other Essays,* translated from French by Ben Brewster. New York: Monthly Review Press.

Alvarez-Pereyre, F. (ed.) (1981) *Théories et méthodes en ethnolinguistique.* Paris: Editions SELAF.

Amossy, R. (ed.) (1999) *Images de soi dans le discours: La construction sociale de l'ethos.* Lausanne: Delachaux et Niestlé.

Andersen, E. S. (1990) *Speaking With Style: The Sociolinguistic Skills of Children.* London: Routledge.

Anderson, B. (1983, revised 1991) *Imagined Communities: Reflections on the Origin and Spread of Nationalism.* London and New York: Verso.

André, V. (2003) ' "BRASMA" Communicative virtues and service encounters in France'. Paper presented at the conference *The Consequences of Mobility: Linguistic and cultural contact zones.* University of Roskilde, Denmark.

Ariès, P. (1962) *Centuries of Childhood: A Social History of Family Life.* New York: Vintage Books.

Arnold, M. (1869) *Culture and Anarchy: An Essay in Political and Social Criticism.* London: John Murray.

Aston, G. (1988) *Negotiating Service.* Bologna: CLUEB.

Austin, J. (1962) *How to Do Things with Words,* (the William James Lectures 1955). Oxford: Clarendon Press.

Bailey, B. (2000) 'Language and negotiation of ethnic/racial identity among Dominican Americans', *Language in Society,* 29, pp. 555–82.

Bakhtin, M. (1981) 'Discourse in the novel', in M. Holquist, (ed.) *The Dialogical*

Imagination: Four Essays by M. Bakhtin, translated by Caryl Emerson and Michal Holquist. Austin, TX: University of Texas, pp. 259–422.

Barth, F. (1969) *Ethnic Groups and Boundaries*. Boston: Little, Brown.

Basso, K. (1972) ' "To give up on words": silence in Western Apache culture', in P. Giglioli (ed.) *Language and Social Context*. Harmondsworth: Penguin, pp. 67–86.

Benson, D. and Hughes, J. A. (1983) *The Perspective of Ethnomethodology*. London: Longman.

Benveniste, E. (1974) *Problèmes de linguistique général*. Paris: Minuit.

Berger, P. and Luckmann, T. (1966) *The Social Construction of Reality: A Treatise on the Sociology of Knowledge*. Harmondsworth: Peregine.

Berger, T. (1970), in Curtis and Petras.

Berlin, I. (1976) *Vico and Herder: Two Studies in the History of Ideas*. London: Hogarth Press.

Berrendonner, A. (ed.) (1977) *Stratégies discursives*. Lyon: Presses Universitaires de Lyon.

Bialystock, E. (2001) *Bilingualism in Development: Language, Literacy and Cognition*. Cambridge: Cambridge University Press.

Billig, M. (1981) *L'Internationale raciste*. Paris: Petite Collection Maspero.

Blom, J.-P. and Gumperz, J. (1972) 'Social meaning in linguistic structures: code-switching in Norway', in J. Gumperz and D. Hymes (eds). *Directions in Sociolinguistics: The Ethnography of Communication*. Oxford: Basil Blackwell, pp. 407–34.

Bloomfield, L. (1933) *Language*. London: Allen and Unwin.

Boas, F. (1912) 'Changes in the bodily form of descendants of immigrants', *American Anthropologist*, 14, 3.

Boas, F. (1942) *Race, Language and Culture*. London: Macmillan.

Borzeix, A. (2001) 'L'information des voyageurs en gare du Nord', in A. Borzeix and B. Fraenkel *Langage et travail: Communication, cognition, action*. Paris: CNRS.

Borzeix, A., Girin, J., Lacoste, M. and Grosjean M. (1992) *'EDF-GDF Bonjour': l'interaction agent–client à l'accueil*. Paris: Ecole Polytechnique.

Boutet, J. (2001) 'Le travail devient-il intellectuel?', *Travailler. Revue internationale de psychopathologie et de psychodynamique du travail*, 6: 55–70.

Briggs, A. (2000) *Victorian Things* (3rd edn). Stroud: Sutton.

Brown, G., Malmkjaer, K. and Williams, J. (eds) (1996) *Performance and Competence in Second Language Acquisition*. Cambridge: Cambridge University Press.

Brown, P. and Levinson, S. (1987) *Politeness: Some Universals in Language Usage*. Cambridge: Cambridge University Press.

Brown, R. and Gilman, A. (1960) 'The pronouns of power and solidarity', in T. A. Sebeok *Style in Language*. Cambridge, MA: MIT, pp. 253–76, also in P. Giglioli, (ed.) *Language and Social Context*. Harmondsworth: Penguin.

Bruner, J. (1999) 'Culture, self and other'. Paper presented at the Inaugural Symposium of the Saussure Institute, Geneva, June 2003.

Burke, E. (1790/1864) *Reflections on the Revolution in France*, in *Works Vol. II*. London: Henry Bone.

Burkitt, I. (1991) *Social Selves: Theories of the Social Formation of Personality*. London: Sage.

Byram, M. (1997) *Teaching and Learning Intercultural Communicative Competence*. Clevedon: Multilingual Matters.

Byram, M. (1998) *Language Learning in Intercultural Perspective*. Cambridge: Cambridge University Press.

Byram, M. (ed.) (2000) *Routledge Encyclopedia of Language Teaching and Learning*. London: Routledge.

Byram, M., Barro, A., Jordan, S., Street, B. and Roberts, C. (1997) *Language Learners as Ethnographers*. Clevedon: Multilingual Matters.

Cabrol Bastos, L. (2002) 'Identity in service interactions: the situated affiliation to social groups', in A. Duszak (ed.) *Us and Others*. Amsterdam: John Benjamins, pp. 429–46.

Calame-Griaule, G. (1965) *Ethnologie et langage: la parole chez les Dogon*. Paris: Gallimard.

Cameron, D. (1995) *Verbal Hygiene*. London: Routledge.

Cameron, D. (2001) *Good to Talk?* London: Sage.

Carrithers, M., Collins, S. and Lukes, S. (1985) *The Category of the Person*. Cambridge: Cambridge University Press.

Castells, M. (1997) *The Power of Identity*. Vol. II *of The Information Age: Economy, Society and Culture*. Oxford: Blackwell.

Castoriadis, C. (1986) *Le polis grecque et la création de la démocracie*. Paris: Seuil.

Cellini, B. (1728) *Autobiography*, translated by George Bull (1956). Harmondsworth: Penguin.

Cerri-Long, E. L. (ed.) (1999) *Anthropological Theory in North America*. Westport, CT: Bergin and Garvey.

Chô Ly (2004) 'Variation sociolinguistique. Etude comparative de l'influence du français et de l'anglais sur le hmong des Hmong de la diaspora à travers le phénomène de l'emprunt'. Thèse de doctorat (Ph.D.) sous la direction de M. L. Kashema, Université de Strasbourg.

Cicourel, A. (1973) *Cognitive Sociology*. Harmondsworth: Penguin.

Clausewitz, C. von, (1832, English translation 1908) *On War*. edited and with an introduction by Anatol Rapoport (1965). Harmondsworth: Penguin.

Colley, L. (2005) *Britons: Forging the Nation 1707–1831* (2nd edn).Newhaven and London: Yale University Press.

Cooley, C. H. (1902/1964) *Human Nature and the Social Order*. New York: Schocken.

Corder, P. (1980) *Error Analysis and Interlanguage*. Oxford: Oxford University Press.

Cortese, G. and Riley, P. (2002) *Domain-specific English: Textual Practices across Communities and Classrooms*. Bern: Peter Lang.

Coser, L. A. (1970) *Men of Ideas: A Sociologist's View*. New York: Collier-Macmillan.

Coser, L. A. (1971) *Masters of Sociological Thought: Ideas in Historical and Social Context*. New York: Harcourt, Brace, Jovanovich.

Coste, D., Moore, D. and Zarate, G. (1997a) *Sociocultural Competence in Language Teaching and Learning*. Strasbourg: Council of Europe.

Coste, D., Moore, D. and Zarate, G. (1997b) *Plurilingual and Pluricultural Competence*. Strasbourg: Council of Europe.

Coulthard, M. (1977/1985) *An Introduction to Discourse Analysis*. Harlow: Longman.

Council of Europe (2001) *Cadre européen commun de reference pour les langues. Apprendre, enseigner, évaluer*. Conseil de l'Europe: Les Editions Didier.

Cowan, G. M. (1948) 'Mazateco whistled speech', *Language*, 24, pp. 280–6.

Crystal, D. (1997) *The Cambridge Encyclopedia of Language*. Cambridge: Cambridge University Press.

Cuche, D. (1996, 3rd edn 2004) *La Notion de culture dans les sciences sociales*. Paris: La Découverte.

Curtis, J. E. and Petras, J. W. (1970) *The Sociology of Knowledge: A Reader*. London: Duckworth.

Davidson, D. (1990) *Inquiries into Truth and Interpretation*. Oxford: Clarendon Press.

Davies, B. and Harré, R. (1990) 'Positioning: the discursive production of selves', *Journal for the Theory of Social Behaviour*, 20.1, pp. 43–63.

de Chavannes, A. (1787) *Anthropologie ou science générale de l'homme*. Lyon: Mugin-Rusand.

De Graaf, W. (1994) 'Identity as moral narrative'. Paper read at the Social Practices and Symbolic Mediation Congress. Neuchâtel, Switzerland, 16–19 March 1994.

Deloach, J. and Gottlieb, A. (2000) *A World of Babies: Imagined Child Care Guides for Seven Societies*. Cambridge: Cambridge University Press.

de Staël, A.-L. (1813) *De l'Allemagne*. Paris: Flammarion.

Destutt de Tracy (1804/2005) *Eléments d'idéologie*. Paris: L'Harmattan.

Dilthey, W. (1883) *Introduction to the Human Sciences: An Attempt to Lay a Foundation for the Study of Society and History*, translated by Ramon J. Betanzos (1988). Detroit: Wayne State University.

Donato, R. (1994) 'Collective scaffolding in second language learning', in J. Lantolf and G. Appel (eds) *Vygotskyian Approaches to Second Language Learning*. Norwood, NJ: Ablex, pp. 33–56.

Downes, W. (1998) *Language and Society* (2nd edn). Cambridge: Cambridge University Press.

Ducrot, O. (1985) *Dire et le dit*. Paris: Minuit.

Duda, R. and Riley, P. (eds) (1990) *Learning Styles*. Nancy: Presses Universitaires de Nancy.

Dupuy, M. (1959) *La Philosophie de Max Scheler*. Paris: Aubier.

Duranti, A. (1997) *Linguistic Anthropology*. Cambridge: Cambridge University Press.

Durkheim, E. (1893/1967) *De la division du travail social*. Paris: Presses Universitaires de France.

248

Durkheim, E. (1897/2004) *Le Suicide.* Paris: Presses Universitaires de France.

Durkheim, E. (1912/1954) *The Elementary Forms of the Religious Life*, translated by J. W. Swain. New York: Free Press.

Duszak, A. (ed.) (2002) *Us and Others: Social Identities across Languages, Discourses and Cultures.* Amsterdam: John Benjamins.

Eagleton, T. (2000) *The Idea of Culture.* Oxford: Blackwell.

Edwards, J. (1985) *Language, Society and Identity.* Oxford: Blackwell.

Elias, N. (1939) *The Civilising Process*, translated by Edmund Jephcott. Oxford: Blackwell.

Evans-Pritchard, E. E. (1940) *The Nuer.* Oxford: Oxford University Press. Cited in Kuper 1973, p. 113.

Faerch, C. and Kasper, C. (1983) *Strategies in Interlanguage Communication.* London: Longman.

Fairclough, N. (1992) *Discourse and Social Change.* Cambridge: Polity Press.

Farb, P. (1974/new edition 1993) *Word Play: What Happens When People Talk.* New York: Random House.

Fasold, R. (1984) *The Sociolinguistics of Society.* Oxford: Blackwell.

Ferguson, C. A. (1959) 'Diglossia', *Word*, 15, 325–40. Also in P. Giglioli; (ed.) (1972) *Language and Social Context.* Oxford: Blackwell, pp. 232–52.

Ferguson, N. (2003) *Empire. How Britain Made the Modern World.* London: Penguin.

Ferréol, G. and Jacquois, G. (2003) *Dictionnaire de l'altérité et des relations interculturelles.* Paris: Armand Colin.

Feuer, L. S. (1953) 'Sociological aspects of the relation between language and philosophy', *Philosophy of Science*, 20, 85.

Feuer, L. (ed.), (1959) *Marx and Engel's Basic Writings on Politics and Philosophy.* New York: Anchor Books.

Fishman, J. (1980) 'Bilingualism and biculturalism as individual and societal phenomena', *Journal of Multilingual and Multicultural Development*, 1, 3–17.

Fishman, J. (2001) *Handbook of Language and Ethnic Identity* (2nd edn). Oxford: Oxford University Press.

Foley, W. A. (1997) *Anthropological Linguistics: An Introduction* (Language in Society 24). Oxford: Blackwell.

Foucault, M. (1966) *Les Mots et les choses: Une archéologie des Sciences Humaines.* Paris: Gallimard.

Frisby, D. (1992) *The Alienated Mind: The Sociology of Knowledge in Germany 1918–1933.* London: Routledge.

Gardener, R. (1966) 'Symmetric respect and memorate knowledge', *Southwestern Journal of Anthropology*, 22, pp. 389–415. Cited in Loveday 1982b.

Gardner-Chloros, P. (1991) *Language Selection and Switching in Strasbourg* (Oxford Studies in Language Contact). Oxford: Clarendon.

Gardner-Chloros, P. (1995) 'Code-switching in community, regional and national repertoires: the myth of the discreteness of linguistic systems', in L. Milroy and P. Muysken (eds) *One Speaker, Two Languages. Cross-*

disciplinary Perspectives on Code-switching. Cambridge: Cambridge University Press, pp. 68–89.

Garfinkel, H. (1967, 2nd edn 1985) *Studies in Ethnomethodology*. New York: Polity Press.

Geertz, C. (1983) *Local Knowledge: Further Essays in Interpretative Anthropology*. New York: Basic Books.

Gellner, E. (1986) *Culture, Identity and Politics*. Cambridge: Cambridge University Press.

Gibbon, E. (1796/1970) *Autobiography,* edited by E. M. Reese. London: Routledge and Kegan Paul.

Gibbs, R. W. (1994) *The Poetics of Mind: Figurative Thought, Language and Understanding*. Cambridge: Cambridge University Press.

Giddens, A. (1991) *Modernity and Self-identity: Self and Society in the Late Modern Age*. Palo Alto: Stanford University Press.

Giles, H. (ed.) (1977) *Language, Ethnicity and Intergroup Relations*. London: Academic Press.

Giles, H. and Sinclair, R. (eds) (1979) *Language and Social Psychology* Oxford: Blackwell.

Goffman, E. (1959) *The Presentation of Self in Everyday Life*. Harmondsworth: Penguin.

Goffman, E. (1967) *Interaction Ritual*. New York: Doubleday.

Goffman, E. (1972) *Relations in Public*. Harmondsworth: Penguin Press

Golding, W. (1954) *The Lord of the Flies*. Harmondsworth: Penguin.

Goodenough, W. (1957) 'Cultural anthropology and linguistics', in D. Hymes (ed.) 1964, pp. 36–9.

Gottlieb, B. (1993) *The Family in the Western World: From the Black Death to the Industrial Age*. Oxford: Oxford University Press.

Granger, C. A. (2004) *Silence in Second Language Learning: A Psychoanalytic Reading*. Clevedon: Multilingual Matters.

Gremmo, M.-J., Holec, H. and Riley P. (1976) 'Interactional structure: the role of role', *Melanges Pédagogiques*, pp. 42–56.

Grice, H. P. (1975) 'Logic and conversation', in P. Cole and J. Morgan (eds) *Syntax and Semantics Vol. 3: Speech Acts*. New York: Academic Press, pp. 41–58.

Gumperz, J. (ed.) (1983) *Language and Social Identity*. Cambridge: Cambridge University Press.

Gumperz, J. J. and Hymes, D. (eds) (1972) *Directions in Sociolinguistics: The Ethnography of Communication*. New York: Holt, Rinehart and Winston.

Gunnarsson, B.-L. (1994) 'The writing process from a sociolinguistic point of view', in E. Ventola and A. Mauranen (eds) 1996b.

Haarman, H. (1986) *Language in Ethnicity: A View of Basic Ecological Relations*. Amsterdam: Mouton.

Habermas, J. (1981) *The Theory of Communicative Action. Vol. I: Reason and the Rationalization of Society*, translated by Thomas McCarthy (1984). Boston: Beacon Press.

Hamers, J. F. and Blanc, M. H. (1989) *Bilinguality and Bilingualism*. Cambridge: Cambridge University Press.

Hanks, W. (1996) *Language and Communicative Practices*. Boulder, CO: Westfield Press.

Harding-Esch, E. and Riley, P. (2003) *The Bilingual Family: A Handbook for Parents* (2nd edn). Cambridge: Cambridge University Press.

Harman, L. D. (1988) *The Modern Stranger*. Amsterdam: Mouton de Gruyter.

Hegel, G. W. F. (1807) *Phänomenologie des Geistes*, translated by J. B. Baillie, *The Phenomenology of Mind* (1910). New York: Dover Publications.

Heller, M. (ed.) (1988) *Code-switching: Anthropological and Sociological Perspectives*. Berlin: Mouton de Gruyter.

Henty, G. A. (1894) *Through the Sikh War: A Tale of the Conquest of the Punjab*. Online: Preston Speed Publications.

Herder J. G. von (1772/1986) *Abhandlung über den Ursprung der Sprache*. Ditzingen: Reklam.

Herrnstein, R. J. and Murray, C. (1994) *The Bell Curve: Intelligence and Class Structure in American Life*. New York: Free Press.

Hobsbawm, E. (1990) *Nations and Nationalism since 1780*. Cambridge: Cambridge University Press.

Holzner, B. and Marx, J. H. (1979) *Knowledge Application: The Knowledge System in Society*. Boston: Allyn and Bacon.

Howell, S. (1988) 'From child to human: Chewong concepts of self', in Jahoda and Lewis 1988, pp. 147–168.

Hudson, R. A. (1996) *Sociolinguistics*. Cambridge: Cambridge University Press.

Hughes, E. C. (1949) 'Social change and status protest: an essay on the marginal man', *Phylon*, 10, 1, pp. 58–65. Cited in Harman, 1988, p. 26.

Hughes, T. (1857) *Tom Brown's Schooldays*. Harmondsworth: Penguin.

Hume, D. (1739/2000) *Treatise of Human Nature*, edited D. F. Norton and M. J. Norton. Oxford: Oxford University Press.

Hutchby, I. and Woofit, R. (2002) *Conversation Analysis*. Cambridge: Polity.

Hymes, D. (ed.) (1964) *Language in Culture and Society: A Reader for Linguistics and Anthropology*. New York: Harper and Row.

Hymes, D. (1970) 'On communicative competence', in J. Gumperz and D. Hymes (eds) *Directions in Sociolinguistics*. New York: Holt, Rinehart and Winston.

Jackson, J. (1974) 'Language identity of the Vaupés Indians', in R. Bauman, R. and J. Sherzer (eds) *Explorations in the Ethnography of Speaking*. Cambridge: Cambridge University Press, pp. 50–64.

Jahoda, G. and Lewis, I. M. (eds) (1988) *Acquiring Culture: Cross-cultural Studies in Child Development*. London: Croom Helm.

Jodelet, D. (ed.) (1992) *Les representations sociales*. Paris: Presses Universitaires de France.

Joseph, J. E. (2004) *Language and Identity: National, Ethnic, Religious*. Basingstoke: Palgrave Macmillan.

Kaufman, J.-C. (2001) *Ego: Pour une sociologie de l'individu*. Paris: Nathan

Kaufman, J.-C. (2004) *L'Invention de soi: Une théorie de l'identité*. Paris: Armand Colin.

Kernan, K. T. (1977) 'Speech and social prestige in the Belizian speech community', in B. G. Blount and M. Sanches, (eds) *Sociocultural Dimensions of Language Change*. New York: Academic Press, pp. 35–50.

Kipling, R. (1901) *Kim*. Oxford: Oxford University Press.

Kitzan, L. (2001) *Victorian Writers and the Image of Empire*. Westport, CT: Greenwood.

Kluckhohn, C. and Murray, H. A. (1961) *Personality in Nature, Society, and Culture* (2nd edn). New York: Alfred A. Knopf.

Kristeva, J. (1988) *Etrangers à nous-mêmes*. Paris: Gallimard.

Kroeber, A. and Kluckhohn, C. (1952) *Culture: A Critical Review of Concept and Definitions*. New York: Meridian.

Kropotkin, P. (1899) *Memoirs of a Revolutionist*, translated and edited by J. A. Rogers (1962). London: Grasset.

Kuhn, T. (1970) *The Structure of Scientific Revolutions* (2nd edn). Chicago: University of Chicago Press.

Kunihiro, M. (1975) 'Indigenous barriers to communication', *Japan Interpreter*, 8, 96–108.

Kuper, A. (1973) *Anthropologists and Anthropology: The British School, 1922–1971*. Harmondsworth: Penguin.

Kuper, A. (1999) *Culture: The Anthropologist's Account*. Cambridge, MA: Harvard University Press.

Labov, W. (1972) *Sociolinguistic Patterns*. Philadelphia: University of Philadelphia Press.

La Fontaine, J. S. (1985) 'Person and individual: Some anthropological reflections', in M. Carrithers, S. Collins and S. Lukas (eds) *The Category of the Person: Anthropology, Philosophy, History*. Cambridge: Cambridge University Press, pp. 123–141.

Lehtonen, J. and Sajavaara, K. (1985) 'The silent Finn', in D. Tannen and M. Saville. Troike (eds) *Perspectives on Silence*. Norwood, NJ: Ablex, pp. 193–201.

Leiter, K. (1980) *A Primer on Ethnomethodology*. New York: Oxford University Press.

Levine, G. (ed.) (1992) *Constructions of the Self*. New Brunswick: Rutgers University Press.

Lévi-Strauss, C. (1977) *L'Identité*. Paris: Presses Universitaires de France.

Littlewood, W. T. (1983) 'Contrastive pragmatics and the foreign language learner's personality', *Applied Linguistics*, 4. pp. 200–6.

Loveday, L. (1982a) 'Communicative interference: a framework for contrastively studying L2 communicative competence', *Intercultural Review of Applied Linguistics*, XX, 1, pp. 1–16.

Loveday, L. (1982b) *The Sociolinguistics of Learning and Using a Non-native Language*. Oxford: Pergamon.

Lunt, P. K. and Livingstone, S. M. (1992) *Mass Consumption and Personal Identity in Everyday Economic Experience*. Buckingham: Open University Press.

Macaulay, T. B. (1835) 'Minute of 2 February 1835 on Indian Education', in G. M. Young (ed.) (1957) *Macaulay, Prose and Poetry*. Cambridge, MA: Harvard University Press, pp. 721–9.

Mackey, W. F. (1976) *Bilinguisme et contact des langues*. Paris: Klincksieck.

Maisonneuve, J. (1988) *Les conduites rituelles*. Paris: Presses Universitaires de France.

Malik, K. (1996) *The Meaning of Race*. London: Macmillan.

Malinowski, B. (1922) *Coral Islands and Their Magic*. Muncie: Indiana University Press.

Mannheim, K. (1936) *Ideology and Utopia*, translated by Edward Shils. London: Routledge and Kegan Paul.

Markway, B., Pollard, A. and Flynn, T. (1992) *Dying of Embarrassment: Help for Social Anxiety and Phobia*. Oakland, CA: New Harbinger Publications.

Marsh, D. and Langé G. (eds) (1999) *Implementing Content and Language Integrated Learning*. Jyväskylä: University of Jyväskylä.

Marui, I., Nishijima, Y., Noro, K., Reinelt, R. and Yamashita, H. (1996) 'Concepts of communicative virtues (CCV) in Japanese and German', in M. Hellinger and U. Ammon (eds) *Contrastive Sociolinguistics*. Berlin: Mouton de Gruyter, pp. 385–409.

Marx, K. (1845/1998) *The German Ideology*. New York: Prometheus.

Marx, K. (1867/2000) *Das Kapital*. Washington DC: Regnery.

Marx, K. and Engels, F. (1968/1848) 'Manifesto of the Communist Party', in *Selected Works*. Moscow: Progress Publishers.

Mauss, M. (1938) 'Une catégorie de l'esprit humain: La notion de personne, celle de "Moi"', *Journal of the Royal Anthropological Institute*, 68. Also in M. Carrithers, S. Collins and S. Lukes (eds) (1985) *The Category of the Person*. Cambridge: Cambridge University Press, pp. 1–25, translated by W. D. Halls ('A category of the human mind: the notion of person; the notion of self').

Mead, G. H. (1934) *Mind, Self and Society*. Chicago: Chicago University Press.

Merton, R. K. (1938) 'Social structure and anomie', *American Sociological Review*, 3, 672–82.

Mitchell, S. (1996) *Daily Life in Victorian England*. London: Greenwood.

Mühlhäusler, P. and Harré, R. (1990) *Pronouns and People: The Linguistic Construction of Social and Personal Identity*. Oxford: Blackwell.

Murphy-Lejeune, E. (2002) *Student Mobility and Narrative in Europe: The New Strangers*. London: Routledge.

Murray, C. and Herrnstein, R. (1994) *The Bell Curve: Intelligence and Class Structure in American Life*. New York: Free Press.

Noonan, H. W. (1989) *Personal Identity*. London: Routledge.

Öberg, K. (1960) 'Culture shock', *Practical Anthropology*, 7: 177–82.

Ochs, E. and Schieffelin, B. (1983) *Acquiring Conversational Competence*. Boston: Routledge and Kegan Paul.

Ochs, E. and Schieffelin, B. (1984) 'Language acquisition and socialisation: three developmental stories and their implications', in R. Shweder and R. Levine (eds) *Culture Theory: Essays on Mind, Self and Emotion*. Cambridge: Cambridge University Press, pp. 276–320.

253

Ochs, E. and Schieffelin, B. (eds) (1986) *Language Socialisation Across Cultures.* Cambridge: Cambridge University Press.

Outhwaite, W. (1975) *Understanding Social Life: The Method Called Verstehen.* London: Allen and Unwin.

Overing, J. (1988) 'Personal autonomy and the domestication of the self in Piroa society' in Jahoda and Lewis 1988, pp. 169–192.

Paine, T. (1791) *The Rights of Man.* London: Everyman.

Park, R. E. (1928) 'Human migration and the marginal man', *American Journal of Sociology*, 33, 8, pp. 881–93.

Petit, J. (1993) 'L'Alsace à la conquête de son bilinguisme', *Nouveaux Cahiers d'Allemand*, 93, 4, 1–86.

Pichon, A. (1936) *Le Développement psychique de l'enfant et de l'adolescent.* Paris: Masson.

Pope, A. (1732/1869) *Poetical Works*, (edited by Sir Adolphus William Ward.) London: Macmillan.

Porter, R. (2003) *Flesh in the Age of Reason. How the Enlightenment Transformed the Way We See Our Bodies and Souls.* London: Penguin.

Potter, J. and Wetherell, M. (1995) 'Discourse analysis', in J. Smith, R. Harre, and L. van Langenhove (eds) *Rethinking Methods in Psychology.* London: Sage, pp. 80–92.

Pride, J. B. and Holmes, J. (1972) *Sociolinguistics; Selected Readings.* Harmondsworth: Penguin.

Raphael, F. (1986) ' "L'Etranger" de Georg Simmel', in Watier 1986, pp. 257–76.

Rapoport, A. (1986) 'Introduction' to Clausewitz 1832.

Renan, E. (1887) 'Qu'est-ce qu'une nation?', in *Discours et conférences.* Calmann-Lévy: Paris.

Ricoeur, P. (1990) *Soi-même comme un autre.* Paris: Editions du Seuil.

Riley P. (1985) 'Strategy: Conflict or collaboration', *Mélanges Pédagogiques du CRAPEL*, pp. 91–116.

Riley, P. (1988a) 'The ethnography of autonomy', in A. Brookes and P. Grundy (eds) *Individualisation and Autonomy in Language Learning.* London: The British Council with Modern English Publications, ELT Documents 131, pp. 12–34.

Riley, P. (1988b) 'Who do you think you're talking to? Perception, categorisation and negotiation processes in exolinguistic interaction', in V. Bickley (ed.) *Languages in Education in a Bilingual or Multilingual Setting.* Hong Kong: Institute for Language in Education, pp. 118–33.

Riley, P. (1989) 'Keeping secrets: ESP/LSP and the sociology of knowledge', *European Journal of Teacher Education,* 12, 2 pp. 69–80.

Riley, P. (1992) 'Pulling your self together: the culture and identity of the bilingual child', in C. Brumfit, J. Moon and R. Tongue (eds) *Teaching English to Young Learners.* London: Collins, pp. 275–88.

Riley, P. (1996) 'Developmental sociolinguistics and the competence/performance distinction', in G. Brown, K. Malmkjaer and J. Williams *Performance and Competence in Second Language Acquisition.* Cambridge: Cambridge University Press, pp. 114–135.

Riley, P. (1999) 'Enjeux identitaires en Pays nordiques', in M. Auchet (ed.) *Le dialogue entre les cultures*. Nancy: Presses Universitaires de Nancy.

Riley, P. (2000) '"Je vous ai compris": aspects ethographiques de la compréhension', in J. Pécheur (ed.) *Une didactique des langues pour demain*, No. spécial, *Le Français dans le Monde*. Paris: CLE International, pp. 79–95.

Riley, P. (2002) 'Epistemic communities. The social knowledge system, discourse and identity'. In Cortese and Riley 2002, pp. 41–64.

Riley, P. (2004) 'Multilingual identities: "Non, je ne regrette rien"' *The European English Messenger*. XIII.1. pp. 11–17. Inaugural Lecture, University of Cambridge 'Day of Multilingualism and Multiculturalism', 18 June 2001.

Romaine, S. (1995) *Bilingualism* (2nd edn). Oxford: Blackwell.

Roosevelt, T. (1899) Speech to the Hamilton Club, Chicago, 10 April, in *Works*, Memorial edition (1925), vol. 15, p. 267.

Roosevelt, T. (1904) Speech in New York, 11 November 1902, in *Addresses and Speeches, 1902–1904*.

Roosevelt, T. (1915) Speech in New York, 12 October, in *Works*, Memorial edition (1925), vol. 20, p. 457.

Rose, P. (1967) 'Strangers in their midst: small-town Jews and their neighbours', in P. Rose, (ed.) *The Study of Society: An Integrated Anthology*. New York: Random House, pp. 463–79.

Rousseau, J.-J. (1782–1789/2000) *Confessions*, translated by Angela Scholar, edited with notes by Patrick Colemen. Oxford: Oxford University Press.

Ruskin, J. (1865) *Sesame and Lilies: Lecture II. Lilies: Of Queen's Gardens*. Great Literature on line www.ruskin.classic/authors.net/sesameAndlilies/SesameAndLilies6.html.

Ryan, E. B. and G. Howard (eds) (1982) *Attitudes Towards Language Variation: Social and Applied Contexts*. London: Edward Arnold.

Sacks, H. (1992) *Lectures on Conversation*. Oxford: Blackwell.

Sainsaulieu, R. (1988) *L'Identité au travail: les effets culturels de l'organisation*. Paris: Presses de la Fondation nationale des sciences politiques.

Salisbury, R. F. (1962) 'Notes on bilingualism and linguistic change in New Guinea', *Anthropological Linguistics*, 4, 7, 1–13. (Partly reprinted in Pride and Holmes, 1972)

Sapir, E. (1921) *Language: An Introduction to the Study of Speech*. New York: Harcourt Brace and World.

Sartre, J.-P. (1943) *L'Etre et le néant*. Paris: Hatier.

Saville-Troike, M. (2002) *The Ethnography of Communication: An Introduction* (3rd edn). Oxford: Blackwell.

Schama, S. (2002) *A History of Britain, Vol. 3 The Fate of Empire 1776–2000*. London: BBC Worldwide.

Scheler, M. (1926) *Wissensformen. (The Forms of Knowledge and Society)*. *Collected Works Vol. 8*. Bonn: Bouvier Verlag.

Scheler, M. (1958/1970) *The Nature of Sympathy*, translated by Peter Heath. New York: Archon.

Schottman, W. (1995) 'The daily ritual of greeting among the Baatombu of Benin', *Anthropological Linguistics*, 37, 4, pp. 487–523.

Schütz, A. (1944) 'The Stranger: An essay in social psychology', *The American Journal of Sociology*, 29/6 pp. 499–507. Also included in collected papers, edited by A. Brodersen (1964). The Hague: Martinus Nijnoff, Vol. II. pp. 91–105.

Schütz, A. (1964) *Studies in Social Theory*, collected papers, edited by A. Brodersen (1964). The Hague: Martinus Nijnoff.

Scollon, R. and Scollon, S.-W. (1981) *Narrative, Literacy and Face in Interethnic Communication*. Norwood, NJ: Ablex.

Scollon, R. and Scollon, S.-W. (1992) 'Individualism and binarism: a critique of American intercultural analysis', Research Report 22, Hong Kong: Department of English, City Polytechnic of Hong Kong.

Scollon, R. and Scollon, S.-W. (1995) *Intercultural Communication: A Discourse Approach* (Language in Society 21). Oxford: Blackwell.

Searle, J. (1969) *Speech Acts*. Cambridge: Cambridge University Press.

Secord, J. A. (2000) *Victorian Sensation: The Extraordinary Publication, Reception and Secret Authorship of 'Vestiges of the Natural History of Creation'*. Chicago: University of Chicago Press.

Sharpe, T. (1973) *Indecent Exposure*. London: Pan Books.

Shotter, J. (1984) *Social Accountability and Selfhood*. Oxford: Blackwell.

Shweder, R. and Levine, R. (eds) (1984) *Culture Theory: Essays on Mind, Self and Emotion*. Cambridge: Cambridge University Press.

Simmel, G. (1908/1950) 'The Stranger', in *The Sociology of Georg Simmel*, translated and edited and with an introduction by Kurt H. Wolff. London: Free Press, pp. 402–8.

Simmel, G. (1950) 'Digression sur le problème: comment la société est-elle possible?'. In Watier 1986, pp. 21–45.

Simmel, G. (1957) *Vom Wesen des historischen Verstehens*. Stuttgart: Koehler. Cited and translated by Outhwaite 1975, p. 68.

Simonds, A. P. (1978) *Karl Mannheim's Sociology of Knowledge*. Oxford: Oxford University Press.

Sirhan, J.-L. (1993) 'Rhetoric, tradition and communication: the dialectics of meaning in proverb use', *Man*, 28, 2, 225–42.

Siu, P. (1952) 'The sojourner', *The American Journal of Sociology*, 58, 1, pp. 34–44.

Smiles, S. (1882) *Self-Help*. London: John Murray.

Snow, C. E. (1977) 'The development of conversation between mothers and babies', *Journal of Child Language*, 4, 1, 1–22.

Sontag, S. (2003) 'The World As India', *Times Literary Supplement*, 13 June 2003.

Sorensen, A. P. (1967) 'Multilingualism in the Northwest Amazon', *American Anthropologist*, 69, 670–84. (A revised version is included in Pride and Holmes, pp. 41–56.

Sperber, D. (1985) *On Anthropological Knowledge* (Cambridge Studies in Social Anthropology, 54). Cambridge: Cambridge University Press.

Stark, W. (1958) *The Sociology of Knowledge. An Essay in Aid of a Deeper Understanding of the History of Ideas.* Glencoe, IL: Free Press.

Stonequist, E. V. (1937) *The Marginal Man: A Study in Personality and Culture Conflict.* New York: Russell and Russell.

Straude, J. R. (1967) *Max Scheler: An Intellectual Portrait.* New York: Free Press.

Stross, B. (1974) 'Speaking of Speaking: Tenejapa Tzeltal Metalinguistics', in R. Bauman and J. Sherzer (eds) *Explorations in the Ethnography of Speaking.* Cambridge: Cambridge University Press, pp. 213–39.

Tajfel, H. (ed.) (1982) *Social Identity and Intergroup Relations.* Cambridge: Cambridge University Press.

Tallis, R. (1997) *Enemies of Hope: A Critique of Contemporary Pessimism.* London: Macmillan.

Tandefeldt, M. (1990) 'Vad är talarens modersmål?' Paper read at the Research Seminar on Sociolinguistics, University of Helsinki Language Centre.

Tandefeldt, M. (1996) 'Några ord om språkets identitetsskapande roll.' Föredrag vid ett Erasmusseminarium for skandinavister, Helsingfors Universitet, 16–21/9/1996.

Tandefeldt, M. (1997) 'De ha blivi mycke nog svårare att tala svenska', in *Språkliga Studier tillägnade Bengt Nordberg på 60-årsdagen.* Uppsala Universitet: Institutionen för nordiska språk, pp. 426–37.

Tarone, E. (1980) 'Communication strategies, foreigner talk and repair in interlanguage', *Language Learning,* 30, pp. 417–31.

Tawney, R. H. (1926) *Religion and the Rise of Capitalism.* New York: Harcourt, Brace and World.

Taylor, A. J. P. (1941, revised edition 1948). *The Habsburg Monarchy 1809–1918.* Chicago: University of Chicago Press.

Taylor, C. (1989) *Sources of the Self.* Cambridge, MA: Harvard University Press.

Taylor, C. (1992) *Multiculturalism and the Politics of Recognition.* Princeton, NJ: Princeton University Press.

ten Have, P. (1999) *Doing Conversation Analysis.* London: Sage.

Thomas, J. (1983) 'Cross-cultural pragmatic failure', *Applied Linguistics,* 4, 1, pp. 91–112.

Thomsen, H. (2002) 'Scaffolding target language use'. in Little, D., Ridley, J. and Ushioda, E. *Learner Autonomy in the Foreign Language Classroom: Teacher, Learner, curriculum and assessment.* Dublin: Authentik, pp. 29–46.

Todorov, T. (1989) *Nous et les autres.* Paris: Seuil.

Tönnies, F. (1887) *Community and Society: Gemeinschaft und Gesellschaft,* translated and edited by Charles P. Loomis, 1957. Michigan: Michigan State University Press.

Trevarthen, C. (1988) 'Universal co-operative motives. How children begin to know the culture and language of their parents'. In Jahoda and Lewis, pp. 37–90.

Trudgill, P. (1974) *The Social Differentiation of English in Norwich.* Cambridge: Cambridge University Press.

Trudgill, P. (1995) 'Sociolinguistic studies in Norway 1970–1991: A critical review', *International Journal of the Sociology of Language*, 115 *(Sociolinguistics in Norway)*, 7–23.

Tylor, Sir E. B. (1871) *Primitive Culture*. New York: Brentano's.

Van Gennep, A. (1909) *The Rites of Passage*, translated by M. B. Vizedom and G. L. Caffee (1960). London: Routledge and Kegan Paul.

Ventola, E. and Mauranen, A. (eds) (1996a) *Academic Writing: Intercultural and Textual Issues*. Amsterdam: John Benjamins.

Ventola, E. and Mauranen, A. (eds) (1996b) *Academic Writing Today and Tomorrow*. Helsinki: Helsinki University Press.

Vinsonneau, G. (2002) *L'identité culturelle*. Paris: Armand Colin.

Vygotsky, L. S. (1978) *Mind in Society*. Harvard : Harvard University Press.

Walzer, M. (1997) 'Communauté, citoyenneté et jouissance des droits', *Esprit*, 3–4, pp. 122–31. Cited in Ferréol and Jacquois 2003.

Warner, M. (2002) *Fantastic Metamorphoses, Other Worlds: Ways of Telling the Self*. Oxford: Oxford University Press.

Watier, P. (ed.) (1986) *Georg Simmel: la sociologie et l'expérience du monde moderne*. Paris: Méridiens Klincksieck.

Weber, M. (1904/1920) *The Protestant Ethic and the Spirit of Capitalism*. New York: Scribners.

Weller, J. (ed.) (1998) 'Les Relations de service', No. thématique, *Education Permanente*, 137.

Wenger, E. (1998) *Communities of Practice, Learning, Meaning and Identity*. Cambridge: Cambridge University Press.

Whorf, B.L. (1956) *Language, Thought and Reality*, edited and with an introduction by John B. Carroll. Cambridge, MA: MIT.

Wiggen, G. (1997) 'Nynorsk – Bokmål', in *Contact Linguistics: An International Handbook of Contemporary Research*, Vol. 2, 948. Berlin: de Gruyter.

Wilson, A. (1968) *The Bomb and the Computer*. London: Barrie and Rockliff.

Wolff, K. H. (1950) *The Sociology of Georg Simmel*. New York: Free Press.

Wood, M. M. (1934) *The Stranger: A Study in Social Relationships*. New York: Columbia University Press.

Zarate, G. (1994) *Représentations de l'étranger et didactique de langues*. Paris: Crédif-Didier.

Zonabend, F. (1977) 'Pourquoi nommer?'. In C. Lévi-Strauss (ed.) 1977. pp. 257–79.

Index

Page numbers in *italics* refer to figures, *n*/*ns* indicate note(s).

Chomsky, N. 11, 34, 52–3, 134
Christian perspectives on identity 74,
  79, 95–6, 236
citizenship 176–80, 211*n*
'civilization' and culture 22–3, 24–5,
  66*n*
Clausewitz, C. von 200–1
Closer, 176–7
code-switching 61–5, 66, 117–18
codification, standardization of languages 234–5
cognitive categories, social knowledge
  system 38
cognitive learning/development 33–4,
  38–9, 40, 137–8
collaborative compensation strategies
  208, 210–11
collaborative discourse 110–11
Colombia, Vaupés Indians of 58
colonialist perspectives 29–30, 238–9
colour and race 28–9
commodification of identity 197, 211*n*
commonsense knowledge 5, 108–9
communicative competence 11, 53
communicative practices 8, 32–3, 92–
  9
  intersubjectivity 17–18, 33–4, 36, *37*,
    40, 133
  questionnaire 97–9
  roles and acts 99–113
communicative strategies 207–8
communicative virtues 215–19
  see also ethos
community
  notion of 180–2
  and societal bilingualism 57–8
'community of practice' 91
compensation strategies 200–11
competence
  communicative 11, 53
  cultural 44
  knowledge, identity and 52–66, 122
'conditions of communication' 128
'conditions of sameness' 70–1
confessional literature 75–6
contestation, membershipping strategy 124
Cooley, C.H. 16, 82
Coulthard, M. 198
Council of Europe 53, 65
creation/production, social knowledge system 31
credibility of speaker/writer 213
Crystal, David 54–5

Cuche, Denys 22–3, 27
cultural acquisition *see* acquisition,
  social knowledge system; social
  learning process
cultural competence 44
cultural markers 41–4, 91–2
culture
  concept of 21–30
  as knowledge 39–52, 188
culture- vs language-specific rules
  and norms 191

Danish 63–4, 195, 239–41
Deloache, J. and Gottleib, A. 133, 136
democracy *see* citizenship
Dickens, Charles 74–5
dictation 236–8
diglossia 58–9
Dilthey, W. 9, 16, 20*n*, 24
discourse
  approaches to 6–7
  bargaining 111–13, 158*n*
  collaborative 110–11
  domain-specific and 'specialized'
    107–8, 113, 115–16, 224–5
  exolinguistic 221
  rights and privileges 100–1, 104–7
distribution, social knowledge system
  31, 46–52
DNA and race 27–8
Dogon of Mali 199
domain-specific and 'specialized'
  discourse 107–8, 113, 115–16, 224–5
Donato, R. 239
Durkheim, Emile 90–1, 174, 181
dyads
  distribution of knowledge 48
  intersubjective 17, 18, 33, 36

ecology of language 187–8, 211*n*
education
  dictation 236–8
  French vs English systems 143, 145–
    51
  India 238–9
  language teaching 101–5, 162, 205–
    6, 239–41
  service encounters, intercultural
    219–33 *passim*
eidos ('world view'), social knowledge
  system 39, 66*n*
Elias, Norbert 4, 5, 23, 25
England